DATE DUE

The Green Marketing Manifesto

The Green Marketing Manifesto

John Grant

John Wiley & Sons, Ltd

Other Wiley Editorial Offices

John Wiley & Sons Inc., 111 River Street, Hoboken, NJ 07030, USA

Jossey-Bass, 989 Market Street, San Francisco, CA 94103-1741, USA

Wiley-VCH Verlag GmbH, Boschstr. 12, D-69469 Weinheim, Germany

John Wiley & Sons Australia Ltd, 42 McDougall Street, Milton, Queensland 4064, Australia

John Wiley & Sons (Asia) Pte Ltd, 2 Clementi Loop #02-01, Jin Xing Distripark, Singapore 129809

John Wiley & Sons Canada Ltd, 6045 Freemont Blvd, Mississauga, ONT, L5R 4J3, Canada

Wiley also publishes its books in a variety of electronic formats. Some content that appears in print may not be available in electronic books.

Anniversary Logo Design: Richard J. Pacifico

British Library Cataloguing in Publication Data

A catalogue record for this book is available from the British Library

ISBN 978-0-470-72324-1 (HB)

Typeset in 11/15pt Goudy by SNP Best-set Typesetter Ltd., Hong Kong
Printed and bound in Great Britain by TJ International Ltd, Padstow, Cornwall, UK
This book is printed on acid-free paper responsibly manufactured from sustainable forestry in which at least two trees are planted for each one used for paper production.

Contents

Section II   THE GREEN MARKETING GRID   57

Foreword

Now that everybody under the sun seems to have gone 'green' in one way or another, and now that there's no longer any serious debate about the need to reduce the environmental impact of our consumption-driven lifestyles, the big question that underpins the whole of this splendidly vibrant and entertaining Manifesto is just about as big a question as they come: cut or switch?

> *Cut* as in consume less, downshift, live lives of elegant simplicity, share more, buy (for the most part) primarily what you need only from those who you know are doing good in the world.

> *Switch* as in renounce today's cretinously carefree consumerism, and instead buy smart, ethical, low-carbon stuff, take the worthiness out of 'sustainability' by getting funky, glamorous, up-market and aspirational.

John describes this as a 'really interesting fork in the green marketing road', either working with or against consumerism as we know it today. And the fact that John is just a little conflicted himself is what makes this such a fascinating journey! For there is indeed something compelling in today's exuberant, profligate, devil-may-care consumerism that it's difficult to ignore, and there will be few reading this book who haven't been entranced and seduced by its lures. We've just got very good at putting consumption at the heart of our lives.

'Our enormously productive economy demands that we make consumption our way of life, that we convert the buying and use of goods into rituals, that we seek our spiritual satisfaction, our ego satisfaction, in consumption. We need things consumed, burned up, worn out, replaced, and discarded at an ever increasing rate.'

These are the words (from 1948!) of Victor Lebow, an astute American retail analyst who precisely read the zeitgeist of the post-war period in the United States and Europe. I still find them shocking, knowing as we now do the appalling consequences of having built a model of economic progress on such a prescription. But I know too that these words would have been seen *then* as both visionary and progressive, re-interpreting the American Dream essentially to liberate people from domestic drudgery, post-war scarcity and shrunken small-town horizons.

Little wonder that much of the Environment Movement's work since then has been dedicated to pointing out the mind-boggling folly of such an approach, with the inevitable consequence that most environmentalists remain deeply suspicious of the vast advertising and marketing machines that have turned these perverse, consumerist aspirations into reality.

One extreme manifestation of this can be seen in the contemporary campaigning in the United States of the Reverend Billy and his supporting choir of the Church of Stop Shopping. Using theatre, non-violent direct action, and protests of every kind, Bill Talen (the real name of the Reverend Billy) has become a cult figure of various video-clip websites for his constant disruption of Starbucks stores and other star performers on the global high street. Behind the fun and games, there are some extremely serious messages inviting US citizens (and particularly social conservatives) to wake up to the appalling personal and social costs entailed in converting America into one unending shopping mall.

I rather suspect that John might not approve of Bill Talen! Indeed, there are some pretty tough words of advice in here for the Green Movement ('We can't leave "green" to the old greens anymore'), urging this particular 'style tribe' to leave behind the exclusivity and party-pooping Puritanism that has alienated so many over the years. He quotes with approval from Bruce Sterling's Viridian Manifesto: 'What is required is not a natural Green, or a spiritual Green, or a primitivist Green, or a blood-and-soil romantic Green. These flavours of Green have been tried, and have been proven to have insufficient appeal.'

That may be so, but if sacrificial restraint is not the answer, nor is the kind of scammy greenwash that we still see far too much of today. What John points to instead is an astonishing up-welling of new green businesses and green brands that are doing it differently, talking to us directly, making 'green stuff' seem normal rather than making normal stuff seem green. That means he's got no time for the mainstream green consumer bandwagon, and celebrates the only-half-visible potential of today's green innovators entirely to subvert mainstream business models. He believes much of the innovation will come through digital 'first-hand brands' and 'empathy brands', with the open-source connectivity and immediacy of the web providing the platforms for sustainable consumption of a completely different kind. The key measure for future transformation is defined as 'ethical velocity', the direction and speed of change with which young people in particular start to take more control of their lives as consumers in such a troubled world.

This is not really the territory that I feel most at home in (IT and marketing, that is), although I'm delighted to think that a series of rather confused discussions with John some years ago (as Forum for the Future was trying to get its head around the whole notion of sustainable marketing) may have had some small influence in stimulating this splendidly provocative and incredibly timely book – for there is indeed a compelling imperative to start reshaping today's cultural norms and aspirations.

And *timeliness* is a theme that beats away here. To feel really enthusiastic about green marketing, as John himself acknowledges, you have to believe that it really is possible simultaneously to learn to live sustainably on Earth *and* for economies and companies to remain both profitable and competitive. On climate change, for instance, Nick Stern's report on 'The Economics of Climate Change' makes it quite clear, for the time being at least, that 'the world does not need to choose between averting climate change and promoting growth and development'. But for how much longer?

Sixty years on from Victor Lebow's all too prescient words, we clearly need a rewrite: our enormously destructive economy demands that we make sustainable consumption our way of life, that we transform the buying and use of goods into rituals for a better world, that we seek our spiritual satisfaction, our aspirational status, in ethical, low-carbon, ever smarter consumption. We need things conserved, shared, reused, recycled, slowed down and treasured at an ever deeper level.

And that's what this manifesto is all about!

Jonathon Porritt

Acknowledgements

This book originates in a conversation with numerous people in business and/or sustainability: Jonathon Porritt, Anthony Kleanthous, Jules Peck, Jeremy Smith, Harry Ram, Tyler Moorehead, Naresh Ramchandani, James Parr, Benny Hermansson, Jamie Mitchell, Dan Germain, Judith Clegg, many of my former colleagues at St Luke's, Paul Feldwick, Russell Lack, Russell Davies, Greg Nugent, Luke Nicholsen, Tamara Giltsoff, MT Rainey, Geoff Mulgan, Paul Miller, Tony Manwaring, Chris Orlandi and Mauricio Mota. Many of the best ideas in this book originated in these conversations. (Where I have forgotten to credit them for the ideas that were theirs, I hope they will forgive me). As a writing project it was the result of a single conversation with Diana Verde Nieto – where we came to the conclusion 'wouldn't it be great if there was a roadmap for green marketing?' I started out to write a short paper. And then just kept going. Thank you Diana! The other stream of help, encouragement and ideas has come from my blog. Numerous people have taken the time to read the draft (or parts of it) and make very helpful comments, sometimes resulting in quite drastic changes in argument and content. Special thanks are due to John

Dodds, Charles Frith, Freya Williams, Fran Van Dijk, Karen Fraser and Gareth Kay, who between them seemed to do more work on the book than I did. And thanks to all the others who chipped in both on the book draft, the naming issue and general green marketing discussions on both my blogs over the last year or so. Thanks to Luke Nicholsen, Tom Williams and the team at More Associates for help with the book design (and also for understanding this book-sized distraction right in the middle of when we are supposed to be launching the future of energy efficient lifestyles together!). Thanks to Claire Plimmer, Jo Golesworthy, Nick Mannion and the whole team at John Wiley for all their enthusiasm, help, ideas and support. Thanks too to Narda Shirley, my ever-brilliant PR guru friend for help with the launch of yet another book.

And finally, as always, a heartfelt thank you to Yong Yong and Cosmo for putting up with the brunt of the four months of distracted, tired, weekend-and-evening working slog. And for being the people in my life who make the world more than worth saving.

About the Author

John Grant co-founded St Luke's the innovative and socially aware London ad agency. Working with clients such as the Body Shop as well as mainstream brands, St Luke's pioneered the view of a company's "Total Role in Society" and operated as an employee shareholder democracy. Since leaving in 1999 he has worked as an independent consultant. John's recent clients include IKEA, innocent, LEGO, O2 and SVT (the Swedish broadcaster). Over the years he has been involved with green brands (the Ecologist), sustainability (IKEA's global ethical and environmental reporting), start ups (ONZO, a home energy monitor manufacturer), social ventures (The Young Foundation), sustainable marketing agencies (Clownfish), committees (Forum for the Future) and reports (WWF). John's previous books which all deal with 'what's new?' have earned widespread praise, popularity and critical acclaim. *The New Marketing Manifesto* was named one of the ten best business books of 1999 by Amazon. *After Image* (2002) was included in a list of 'the most popular business books in the world' on Wikipedia. *Brand Innovation Manifesto* (2006) was described as: ". . . a great addition to brand consumer communication methodology . . . "

(Brand Strategy) ". . . read it . . . " (Admap) ". . . revolutionary . . . " (The Marketer). John was voted the most in-demand event speaker in London in an RAB poll. John is also a prolific blogger and writer of articles and reports. His current thoughts on green marketing can be found at http://greenormal.blogspot.com and he is also the official blogger for the Green Awards at http://www.greenawards.co.uk/

Introduction: Sustainability, New Marketing and The Beautiful Coincidence

	A. Green	B. Greener	C. Greenest
1. Public Company & Markets	Set an Example	Develop the Market	New Business Concepts
2. Social Brands & Belonging	Credible Partners	Tribal Brands	Trojan Horse Ideas
3. Personal Products & Habits	Market a Benefit	Change Usage	Challenge Consuming
	Set new Standards Communicate	Share responsibility Collaborate	Support Innovation Culture Reshaped

Figure 1 The green marketing grid

Green issues and marketing can work against each other. One wants you to consume less, the other more. One rejects consumerism, the other fuels it. But they aren't always opposed. Marketing can help 'sell' new lifestyle ideas. It's a much-needed function today, when we all need to act fast to mitigate the effects of climate change.

Sustainability is the idea that environmental (and ethical) objectives are not incompatible with ongoing economic prosperity. It's a step closer to marketing. Any drastic change is a spur to innovation and opportunity in some quarters; for every loser there are potential winners in need of insightful marketing.

New Marketing is the post-advertising model I have been writing about for the last ten years. It avoids the dangers of greenwashing and offers more authentic approaches compatible with green companies, brands and products. For instance, a core tenet is companies co-operating with customers. It's a step closer to sustainability.

Hence the *Beautiful Coincidences* covered in this book; marketing and innovation examples where what is right for the environment is also good for a business. This is a very fast-moving area. New examples and lessons are appearing every week. This book is a snapshot, consisting of examples up to May 2007. If you would like to follow some of the latest developments since, and how my thinking has developed as a result, do come to my blog http://greenormal. blogspot.com.

A few years ago, my onetime boss Paul Feldwick took an MSc in Sustainable Development at Bath University. He told me that his key realisation, and what was most different from our work as brand strategists, came from what is known as *Action Inquiry*. What this means is that you can't get to grips with sustainability by standing outside it and treating it as an abstract system. You have to get involved as a whole person, step into it and use your experiences, feelings and judgement to develop your view from that very implicated position. My apologies to Paul (and his course professor) if I haven't entirely done this concept justice. But I have been very aware while writing this book how true that insight is. You have to work out what your personal *position* is. I am going to start with mine. And then offer a structure for you, the reader, to think about yours too. In the process, I also hope to make it clear what I think the main point of this book is.

There are many tributaries from my past working life, which have led to this book and retrospectively fit together as a pattern. In the mid 1990s I joined an ad agency (later relaunched as St Luke's) that conducted a farsighted study into the ethics of branding. This concluded that in future, brands would be differentiated by the values and actions of the company behind them – by their *Total Role in Society* as we then called it. Most of our clients at the time were rather nonplussed by this. But it brought us a new client: Anita Roddick (and The Body Shop). She pushed us to put our own house in order, and so we commissioned a pioneering review from John Elkington's *SustainAbility*, the first they had done, which looked at the social aspects of how a business runs and its environmental impacts in a simultaneous and integrated way. Since leaving St Luke's in 1999 I have had a varied career as a consultant, which has included a number of green projects; like consulting on IKEA's sustainability programme (2002). I then tried to establish a mini-agency called *The Generative Company* aiming to turn corporate CSR commitments into funding for documentaries and other creative content (2003). Another tributary was helping *The Ecologist* magazine with ideas on how to broaden its appeal (2004). I also set up a project with Glasshouse, the leading entrepreneurs' network in London, around the theme of 'Real Innovation' – i.e. directing that community to consider more world-changing problems. Together with an academic and a green designer, I then attempted to launch a high street ethical label scheme called 'Not Bad' (2005). Last year (2006) I worked with the Co-operative Bank on what ethical meant for their brand and also for product innovation. I also became an advisor to a creative sustainable marketing agency called Clownfish. By then the green marketing scene was taking off. But my conclusion from most of these earlier projects was that it was 'too early'. At last, in 2007, it seems like the tide has turned. As advisor to Clownfish, one key role seems to be looking out for good hires. (If anyone reading with relevant agency and/or CSR experience is interested, it is a lovely company; ask for Diana and do tell her I sent you!)

Over the last six years, I've also sat on a number of committees, written articles and contributed to reports and projects looking at what sustainability means for marketing, with the Forum for the Future, WWF and Design Council – and also on what sustainability means overall, as part of a BT-funded project called 'Just Values'.

Most of my green projects, especially the early ones, didn't amount to much. For instance, my mini-agency folded after a year; there was a lot of interest, but companies weren't ready to commit budgets, nor clear on whether this was 'marketing' or 'CSR'. And with the IKEA project we actually concluded there should be no communication to a broad external audience, lest it become an exercise in 'greenwashing'. Rather, we focused on the reporting and internal audience programme. I was only working away in tiny pockets, but my general sense is that for most of this time the marketing world (with notable exceptions) wasn't ready to engage with the green world and vice versa.

Now the two have collided, like two great tectonic plates. And we are in the midst of deciding whether this will become an ocean trench (two agendas pushing each other down) or a mountain range (pushing each other up). I'd argue this is up to us. We can create a thrilling new green marketing movement – or pull it down with conflicting agendas and ideas about where to take it, with mutual suspicion and accusation.

One moment in the history of my personal green and marketing work stands out from the others: like many recent developments in green business, you could quite reasonably claim that this book was Jonathon Porritt's idea. I met Jonathon in 2001 and he was very frustrated with the marketing world. His view of the stony ground for sustainable marketing was this: marketers simply *didn't get it!* He had read one of my books and decided he could see a way forward. The old marketing paradigm was antithetical to green agendas. Green did not fit into this old worldview; it didn't have the right 'image' or message. But *the New Marketing*, which I described in my books – of participation, word of mouth, communities, education, events, digital and so on – was not at all incompatible with sustainability. And that, in a nutshell, is what this book is about; the application of New Marketing to the sustainability agenda. What has happened since that time is web 2.0, which greatly enlarges the possibilities of both sustainable new business models (like service systems) and New Marketing engagement.

This thought, which Jonathon planted as a seed five or so years ago, can be developed into two related ideas; one rejecting the old marketing ways and one embracing the new ways.

The old marketing approach could be described as 'imagewashing'. I put it this way to make it clear what the relationship is to 'greenwashing'. Brands were constructed for ugly industrialised manufacturing businesses (including farming, unfortunately) by adding attractive cultural images, personalities and descriptions. A factory-made fruit pie would become a Mr Kipling traditional *home-baked-style* fruit pie. This was a process of communication; an advertising message delivered through mass media. The audience was the passive receiver of this. I say 'was' because many, including myself, have been arguing for over a decade that (except in selected 'image category' preserves such as the perfume market) this model is all but dead. The main reason is growing consumer literacy, marketing resistance and cynicism. People don't trust image ads and they don't trust many companies. Put the two together and you can guess the result.

The New Marketing approach is one of active customer engagement. You work together to create ideas, communities, events and lifestyles. It's not a patronising 'the customer is king' view; it's a new openness, porosity and creative dialogue that can impact product development, retailing experiences and the service – for instance reader reviews on amazon.com – quite apart from activities which actively engage and enthuse people – like Nike's *Run London*. This is far from being the whole marketing story incidentally; there have been big developments in CRM and direct marketing, multichannel retailing, business models and so on. I am really talking about the evolution of *brand* marketing.

With New Marketing, there is an implicit strategic 'brand contract' with customers; for instance, *TopShop brings the high fashion experience to the high street.* And then – as described in my last book, *The Brand Innovation Manifesto* – a molecule of diverse and continuous innovation and ideas bring this to life, including some that make money (TopShop personal style consultancy or their *Kate Moss* range) and some that simply enrich the brand and relationship (*London Fashion Week* and their AIDS celebrity charity auction).

My suggestion is that many (but by no means all) of the ideas in the brand molecule of many companies from now on will be green ideas – but not as we have known them. I will argue that these ideas need to transcend the old 'green' stereotypes. Think of those as similar to the nerdy, 'homebrew' stage of the IT market. Whereas future green brands will be more like the new IT stars, like Apple or Amazon, in being great first and green second (just as those examples are great first and IT second). That's going to call on marketing creativity; it is our skills in building great brands, products, services and experiences that will help green things find mainstream acceptance.

As with my previous books, in place of one type of traditional marketing – selling people 'a green image' (whatever that actually means) – I will describe many possible types of green marketing. That's because the current marketing scene is diverse, we have so many new ways of connecting with people. But it's also because marketing has to do different tasks for different sorts of clients. And the 'one size fits all' old branding approach was always a problem; it worked for chocolate bars but was never that much help to banks.

I'm approaching this as a creative marketer who has long been interested in sustainability and new media, too. How about you, the reader? I think you need to work out your position. 'Are you coming at this from a marketing role or from a green role?' would be my first question. I have tried to write the book to help both sides come to an understanding, but I am a marketer, so that side of the book is necessarily dominant. There will be a difference, for instance, if you work for a values-led little green company or a big company that's trying to be greener.

A deeper question is how far along this picture (Figure 2) you find yourself today. Are you still taking sides or have you reached the point where it is all the same – a blank space – where it's about working together, not fighting over past conflicts? That's where some of the leaders of big business and the sustainability movement have got to. I have been party to a new report by *Tomorrow's Company*, authored by leaders both of companies like McKinsey, Unisys, BP and Anglo-American and also leaders of NGOs, which talks about global businesses expanding their space and having to accept greater responsibility, working with regulators and NGOs to press ahead. As one put it, if things continue as they are, there *will not be any markets*! It's time for a broad view (beyond short-term shareholder returns) as well as a long view. It's all about creating alternatives.

The conflict is a fierce one; people get angry about these issues on the green side, and defensive on the business side. It's so easy to criticise, cast blame and scapegoat others. We all blame the car companies for their fuel efficiency crimes (the 4×4s) but what about the drivers? Even those who have taken on the policing role and

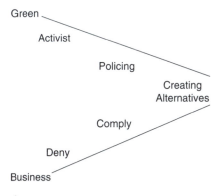

Figure 2 Creating alternatives

engage with businesses can come across as quite angry and hector-
ing. The thing is, psychologically as well as politically, if you don't
overcome a cultural conflict then you tend to act it out. The conflict
drives your thinking rather than the other way around. Yet we do
seriously need to think about these issues, passion is not enough – we
need solutions.

On the business side, those distant from the green position can
exhibit denial, indifference, cynicism or condescension, picturing
the green position as naïve. Those with a greater exposure to green
issues, particularly those facing green challenges and questions from
the media and NGOs – after they get through the 'pretend it's not
happening and it might go away' stage – are also prone to operate
cynically, paying lip service to the issues to defend their share price
with well-crafted PR, while spending the minimum on actually
tackling the issue. That's perhaps yesterday's position, and the hope
is that many companies are now genuinely committed. Without
actions based upon ownership of the problem, without a value set
that says it's the right thing to do (so that it will continue regardless
of whether it always makes the most money), it is all just hot air.

This is a book for those on all sides who have reached the realisation that we need to work together to create alternatives. Instead
of seeing a rotten and hopeless status quo, it's about seeing the challenge and even opportunity of what Thomas Homer-Dixon called
The Ingenuity Gap.[1] The book is intended to provide a basic framework for people looking for marketing and innovation ideas, solutions and ways forward. It has an analytical framework but will only
really be much help to those who are inventing parts of our future.
In personal terms, these people will often be starting or leading a
green business or organisation or having a leading role addressing
these issues in an existing big organisation or developing ideas for
clients of these sorts. Note that when I say 'ideas', I don't mean art
direction, I mean strategic ideas or concepts.

There are marketing policing/curbing/responsibility issues too.
What needs to be done (as well as finding alternatives) is making

marketing *less irresponsible*, aligning it with CSR agendas, which include not only climate change and other green issues but also social issues, including quality of life, health, learning, inclusion and development. What is needed here is voluntary action, and indeed regulation, to outlaw those tendencies in marketing which lead to unsustainable consumption; banning the active marketing of the bottom quartile products (the 4×4s) in any market, looking at codes of lifestyle 'aspiration' and representation. We should also be looking at pricing and promoting responsibly, like 2-for-1 offers on perishable goods; at squeezing suppliers or competitors who are small and vulnerable; at 'cheap' flights and other false economies. Similarly, you need to look at the footprint of your marketing schedule itself. HSBC was criticised recently in the USA for sending out a 'green pack' using paper and packaging intensive direct mail through national postage as the channel. It just didn't look very considered. A corporate responsibility team would be well placed to identify those marketing practices in any particular sector which need to be outlawed, redirected or curbed.

All I want to say in this book is that the issue is there, and needs to be tackled. But my place is to encourage the marketing community to see the opportunity to create alternatives. In my view we should see green marketing as the next revolution (after the internet). There are a number of good books on corporate social responsibility and the implications of green issues for business strategy. There aren't many on creative green marketing just yet, although I am sure there will be quite a few in the near future. My secondary concern is that some other authors (perhaps from advertising and PR) will be advocating greenwash. Why read this book instead? Because *it will help you come up with marketing ideas which are good for the business and good for the world.*

There is every commercial reason to tackle green issues. For a start, if we don't, there may be no markets, and hence no marketing, in 30–50 years' time! People talk about what's ahead as 'a global Somalia'. James Lovelock predicted that 80% of the population wouldn't make it to the end of this century if things continue as they are. As Al Gore would say, it's not just the business case you need to focus on; it's the moral case.

But global gloom isn't helpful. In fact, the problem with pessimism is it has a nasty habit of becoming a self-fulfilling prophecy. Instead of focusing on the problem – which can seem hopeless at times – we need to see the *opportunity* in creating alternatives. There is every reason to be optimistic for a simple reason: the world is so crap from a green point of view there is ample room for quite accessible improvement. The world is so badly organised at the moment – there are so many unnecessary and inefficient and wasteful and harmful processes and products in everyday life – that it should be possible to make drastic impacts. And it's decadent the way we live in the West, needlessly wasteful and supplying 'luxuries' that hardly satisfy. It is possible that we will meet people's actual needs and aspirations better – and even that life will be happier as a result.

But with drastic changes to everyday life there is a big marketing challenge, one that's analogous to the work that's been done in IT to turn us from a population of technophobes to happy surfers. *We need to make green alternatives seem normal and acceptable (as opposed to greenwash, the process of making normal stuff seem green).*

This book is about green marketing as a creative opportunity, to innovate in ways that make a difference and at the same time achieve business success. I don't see these twin objectives as necessarily contradictory.

There are also plenty of not-for profit opportunities and these are also developing quickly. But that's a different subject; it is marketing green (not green marketing). With green marketing, a business pays for the marketing and should expect to see a return. Legally, if it's a public company, it actually *has to* invest in activities expected to make a reasonable return. And from a green point of view, commercial marketing offers an opportunity to get much closer to everyday life and the habits of consumer behaviour (than cause campaigns alone can). I am, hence, *defining* green marketing as being both commercial *and* environmental; a win:win. You can just about argue the Kiva.org example in, because it is a commercial lending bank. And it's worth having here anyway, because it is such a shining example of the best of sustainability, web 2.0 and New Marketing tactics. But most examples in this book will be drawn from for-profit commercial products or services, or at least those which could make a profit or monetise the business in some way, even if they choose not to.

The dual objectives thing is already a well-accepted approach within New Marketing. If you set out only to make money, you tend to focus on very short-term measures like cost-cutting and promotions. In many businesses, profit is the by-product of pursuing a bigger vision, aiming at making the world a better place. These visions don't have to be 'virtuous' in the charity sense. Nike has a view that more people should experience the benefits to your whole life that come from doing sport. Over the years, quite apart from marketing cool shoes, they have done lots to promote sport. Recently, they created the *Run London* event to (as the title of the event says) persuade more of us in the capital to run. The year before the Nike company even began, co-founder Bill Bowerman had a national bestseller and started an exercise craze with the hit book *Jogging*. This craze created a new market for their cushioned-sole running shoes, which they couldn't have dreamed of. But it wasn't a marketing ploy; it was born out of enthusiasm. You can always reduce entrepreneurial business success to financial success. But it is rare to create it that way.

My last book – *The Brand Innovation Manifesto* – was about the recognition that today, it is essential to engage audiences in these broader, cultural ways. The old 'selling an image' model has hit a brick wall of marketing resistance, literacy and cynicism.

To get into the detail of green marketing, it is necessary to recognise that 'green objectives' come in two sorts: you can change what people do and you can change the way they see the world. The second, tackling the culture of consumption, lifestyles and so on, is broader ranging. If you get someone to recycle, that doesn't necessarily translate into other activities. But if, perhaps, you get them to put themselves on a carbon diet, then this can manifest itself in numerous behaviours. Further, you can build new service concepts, new types of market which meet people's needs in greener ways, like city car clubs or power tool libraries. What these often require is *Trojan horse* cultural ideas, i.e. ways to make them seem normal and intuitive.

Based on these green objectives plus the commercial ones, I am going to divide green marketing into three sorts of activity:

A. *Green – setting new standards – communicate*: having commercial objectives only (where the product, brand or company is greener than alternatives, but the marketing is straightforward about establishing this difference).
B. *Greener – sharing responsibility – collaborate*: having green objectives as well as commercial objectives (the marketing itself achieves green objectives, for instance changing the way people use the product).
C. *Greenest – supporting innovation – cultural reshaping*: having cultural objectives as well (making new ways of life and new business models normal and acceptable).

These three categories form the columns of our green marketing strategy grid. The green/-er/-est refers to the extent to which the marketing *per se* contributes. Does it just sell the product/company or does it do more? It may be that an exceptionally green product or sustainable company has a huge impact and 'just selling it' is very helpful too.

The three headings refer to marketing objectives, not the net impact. An important indicator being what you would use to measure success. For instance, the first might be a conventional marketing launch for a car with good fuel economy; you'd talk about the green benefits but measure results in cars sold. The second might be a campaign to encourage owners to use their car more responsibly, for instance, highlighting the huge carbon, money and fuel savings if everyone stuck to the speed limits. You'd measure results in changes in behaviour, and if the campaign was for a car brand, measures like goodwill, affinity and customer relationship. The third might be the launch of a scheme to enable people like me who have a green car that they don't use that much, to rent or lend or share it or co-own it with others. You'd measure results by looking at the commercial and cultural success of this scheme.

One difficulty is that the projects with the most ambitious objectives tend to be those with the least means, for instance because they are start-ups. However, with web 2.0, word of mouth and community there is a much more level playing field for good ideas.

There is also a hierarchy in marketing (and in culture in general) of different levels:

Public: companies, markets, political and cultural values.
Social: identity, meaning and branding.
Personal: products and practical benefits.

This second scale deals with the 'what?' (vs the first, which dealt with the 'why?') Taken together you get a 3×3 grid (Figure 3). These distinctions are only approximate. In real-life examples, you are often working at several levels or boxes at once. Nonetheless, the grid gives us a way of analysing pure brand ideas. How these are combined into a real-life marketing programme is another question altogether. If you are reading this for the first time, it won't necessarily be obvious what each of these nine boxes mean (just as if you looked at the Boston grid and saw 'cash cow' for the first time it might have you scratching your head). But it gives a first indication of the spread of types of idea we'll be exploring.

	A. Green	B. Greener	C. Greenest
1. Public Company & Markets	*Set an Example*	*Develop the Market*	*New Business Concepts*
2. Social Brands & Belonging	*Credible Partners*	*Tribal Brands*	*Trojan Horse Ideas*
3. Personal Products & Habits	*Market a Benefit*	*Change Usage*	*Challenge Consuming*
	Set new Standards Communicate	Share responsibility Collaborate	Support Innovation Culture Reshaped

Figure 3 Green marketing grid

The strategies in the grid were born out of the blending of three agendas: sustainability, web 2.0 and New Marketing. New Marketing, which I have been writing about for the last decade, is a creative renaissance in brand building through alternative means (alternative means to traditional advertising). All three of these trends are based on similar tendencies: the feeling of wanting to change things, social and ethical values, community, a fascination with the future, a belief in the power of the individual and in adhocracy, advocacy and people power. Above all, each is about enthusiasm; they are not top-down but they get their energy from innovative ideas that involve people.

Kiva.org is a fine example of all three agendas meeting in one social venture.

> Kiva.org allows individuals to make $25 loans to low-income entrepreneurs in the developing world (microfinance). By doing so, individuals like you provide affordable working capital for the poor (money to buy a sewing machine, livestock, etc.), empowering them to earn their way out of poverty. (www.kiva.org)

This is a brilliant innovation from social venturing; the microlending model. It's brought to your browser by using a simple, well-designed website. Once you have donated, email bulletins keep you apprised of progress. The credit card system is used not only to accept loan payments, but also to repay them. Like many break-through web 2.0 ideas, it markets itself primarily by word of mouth and PR. But it is also supported through brand partnership; a massive donated banner campaign on YouTube (40 million page impressions a month, supplying 13% of its donations). YouTube gives away the banner space next to any videos with doubtful copyright to non-profits like Kiva, for legal reasons. People are also encouraged on the Kiva site to email friends about the site.

It is such a great idea. Kiva is about ordinary people wanting to change things and the internet enabling them to do that. It is a place for hope in the future, community, values and yet is quite humble and normal; you have to visit to see what I mean. It is access to people's stories which makes it so involving. It also educates people like us about real life in the developing world. Plus, it isn't even going to cost you $25, since nearly every loan repays and you are just donating some bank account interest.

When sustainability, web 2.0 and New Marketing mix, the result is powerful new ideas that we simply would not have thought of ten years ago. The Kiva example also flags something I wanted to say at the outset: when I say 'green' in the title of this book, while I do mean mainly climate change (it's the single biggest challenge, responsibility and potential crisis we face as a generation), I also mean other environmental and social issues too. You can't tackle the environment unless social and economic development are assured; and vice versa. When I call it 'green marketing', I certainly don't mean a return to the 'green consumer bandwagon' thinking of the late 1980s. My reason for not calling this the sustainable or responsible marketing manifesto is that it sounds too tame – like a sort of political correctness – and this book is all about big oppor-tunity (with a careful eye on any unintended secondary issues and effects), not restraint. We need to be *really bold* to get anywhere near the 70% reduction in carbon footprints needed. In the book name discussion on my blog and with my publisher, most felt that 'the sustainable marketing manifesto' was less grabbing, and that words like 'responsible' felt too restraining rather than being about win:win (commercial:sustainable) opportunity. So we're stuck with 'green'. It will have to do. I can't help noticing that 'The Green Awards' (many examples from which are quoted in this book) must have had the same dilemma. They do cover sustainability in its full sense, but to grab marketers and journalists, 'The Green Awards' is stronger. Most consumers would describe what's in this book as 'green issues' too. We do need to be careful though not to repeat the mistakes of the last green marketing boom in the late 1980s. I'll address the lessons of that previous cycle of hype and disappointment in a while. First I need to set the scene.

SECTION I

Background

Setting the Scene

Before we get into the details of the grid, I need to do some scene-setting. In particular, I want to challenge the stereotyped notion of green marketing; that is to do with communicating clichéd green images, green claims and (hippy) green lifestyles.

A good example of what I envisage as the new green marketing was Eric Prydz's 2006 hit single based on a sample from the Pink Floyd song *Another brick in the wall*. The promo video for this song showed a group of apparently delinquent youths, carrying bricks, playing truant from school and breaking into people's homes on a run-down council estate. The twist comes when we discover that they are making energy efficiency improvements; the bricks they are carrying are left in fridges (as heat sinks), in cisterns (to reduce water used per flush) and they also replace light bulbs with energy efficient CFLs. It's a very good pop video and has helped make the song an international hit.

This pop video makes many of the points this book will be making:

- most people are quite 'nice' and not antisocial or apathetic;
- being green is not just for middle class, liberal, educated people – it's everyone's issue;

- the challenge is to make doing green stuff part of normal life;
- it's not all up to governments, corporations and NGOs – we all share the responsibility;
- green marketing can be funky, edgy, intriguing, playful, impactful and creative;
- . . . it doesn't even have to look 'green' (worthy, hippy, natural, etc.).

The video is an example of grid B1. By educating people about what they can do, and by connecting with the green concerns of a young audience, the video creates a very different sort of public standing from other dance acts. Hopefully it also inspires young people to do exactly what the video suggests, at least in their own homes. Of course it's just a pop song, was not making any green innovations (e.g. download only) and perhaps was just tapping into a 'trend'. But tonally it feels right to set the scene; it's not worthy, middle class, hippy-ish or indeed nihilistic. It is playful, surprising and . . . normal.

A Tipping Point – and Then What?

Many have been saying recently that we have reached a 'tipping point' in awareness, concern and potential for change in relation to green issues and to climate change in particular. It is the mass coverage that is usually cited – the *Sun* newspaper's green tips, Al Gore's hit documentary, the Stern report, the Oscars night when stars rolled up in green limos. This summer, *Live Earth* has added jumbo rock concerts to the list. Even Arnie is a green action hero these days. It's clearly something that's caught the public imagination. We'll see research evidence shortly that it is much more than a media fad too; that green concerns, thinking and behaviour have rapidly gained mainstream acceptance. And it's not just about entertainment, celebrities and events getting in on the act; regular news about floods and other catastrophes – plus the atypical weather – offer a reminder that all is not right with the world.

Green marketing is being touted as a part of the potential solution. From the green side, marketing offers a creative way to engage people, to promote greener lifestyles. From the business side, marketing offers a way to engage people for the firms and brands that are doing more than most with corporate responsibility. This message has certainly been well received in the advertising community. A report in the FT found that all the major agencies interviewed were predicting a 'wave of eco marketing' (*Financial Times*, 12/2/07).

However, for all the hype, *what green marketing actually is* is perhaps less clear. It's in real danger of being one of those things everyone agrees is a good idea, but no one quite knows how to do. This could lead to an emperor's new clothes moment when well-meaning but unstrategic attempts to get sustainability into every marketing channel are found lacking. The knowledge levels in the typical ad agency and marketing department can be fairly low, especially in the creative departments, which makes the potential for risky CSR gaffs and blunders (which trigger criticism) greater too.

You get the feeling that any opportunity to add green to the 'shop front' of a business is being seized. And on the whole that's a good thing. Every little does help, both with individual green gains and also with the general cultural momentum. One example is those companies with delivery fleets who are trialling electric vehicles; for instance, Domino's Pizza in Las Vegas. On the one hand this brand is never exactly going to be the poster child for sustainability (health and the pay, safety and conditions of casual labour are sustainability issues too). But it does make total sense, because people who eat pizzas will appreciate better air quality, less noise in late night deliveries and the company is very clear that this is a way to save money with higher petrol prices. You don't need to be perfect to do some good. And as a pizza company would argue, there is a market for their product and a place for less healthy (but very tasty) options in a balanced life; I have to admit I enjoy the occasional Friday night pizza, as does my son.

It has to make sense for the business and the cause. Levi's in the USA decided, for little apparent reason, to have a '501 day'. On May 1st (5.01), customers were encouraged to volunteer. A bit of Googling this 'event' didn't turn up much. There were activities planned in San Francisco, and an ad on Craigslist said they were looking for a DJ to play in a Los Angeles store to 'celebrate giving back to the community'. The reason it came to my attention was that PSFK, the online trend spotters, commented negatively: it 'seems to be very much jumping on the ethical bandwagon . . . This all might sound quite worthy but it comes across as patronizing and cheap.'[2]

It may be a problem of execution, but I have to agree that it feels tokenistic. There is the date 5.01. This has nothing to do with the actual '501' name of the jeans. It seems arbitrary, there is no substance or strategic rationale behind it; which then translates into it having no reference or relevance. Why is Levi's telling me to volunteer? Why on the 1st May? Why in a shop window? What this example highlights is that the construction of ethical brand campaigns has to be intelligent; the question 'why are they telling me this?' is ever present. With branded entertainment you can pretty much do what you want, if it is vaguely relevant. But not so with ethical campaigns. It confuses people, because they want to read your motives. That's human nature, like the 'why are they suddenly being so nice to me?' syndrome. You can't just decide 'ethical is in' and treat it like a fashion.

That's one reason I decided to write this book. If there isn't a road map then people will try green marketing because it is 'in'. And lacking a strategic rationale, plenty of such attempts will fail. It's just like in 1996 when every brand wanted 'a website'. We need to help them figure out *what for*. With sustainability there's a triple danger, not only wasting money plus losing brand credibility, but also being accused of greenwashing.

The alliance of marketing and green is never going to be an easy one, the agendas superficially conflict on so many levels (ideological, cultural, economic, practical). This conflict sets the stage for some breakthrough alternatives – it's when challenges seem impossible in current terms that truly new ideas get considered. But we need to proceed a little cautiously, and avoid pitfalls, because another 'green marketing bubble' could set the whole agenda back five years (just as the dotcom bubble set IT back five years).

Marks & Spencer, following on from its award-winning *'Look Behind The Label'* scheme, announced a massive new *Plan A* initiative, including a commitment to become carbon neutral within five years. They used the fanfare to set a challenge to other businesses. It wasn't just M&S being smug. It was about setting new standards. According to Jonathon Porritt, 'This plan sets a new benchmark in the way businesses should be tackling critical sustainability challenges like waste, fair trade and climate change. It raises the bar for everyone else – not just retailers, but businesses in every sector.'[3] You can readily understand, therefore, *'why they are telling me this.'*

Other high profile corporate initiatives include Sky's *The Bigger Picture*, which combines sustainability initiatives with public engagement and education (grid B1); Virgin's announcement of a $3B fund for new energy technologies (C1); O2 encouraging consumers to keep and reuse their old phone charger (B3); HSBC's green cause-related marketing promotions (A2). Each of these is readily understandable. A recent interview with Rupert Murdoch on *why* he is making his whole media empire sustainable was a lesson in clarity:

- he is personally concerned over environmental issues such as the desertification of his native Australia;
- . . . and convinced of the importance of the general problem climate change poses;
- his son James got him into it, saying it's too important an issue to ignore;

- they are looking at every element of their business processes, to go carbon neutral;
- they are in a great position to integrate green content with TV news and drama;
- and that's a smart thing to do, because a major trend in advertising spend will be other corporations looking for the best context for sustainability communications.

All these developments are to be welcomed. It seems business commitment to more sustainable products, transportation and so on has reached critical mass. It is less certain that the green marketing bandwagon will continue to roll. It partly depends on what *we* do next; do we make green marketing sustainable, or do we over-promise, distort and disappoint?

The Green Consumer Bandwagon of 1989

There is room for caution over the green marketing 'tipping point'. We have been here before in 1989 with what was then called the *green consumer bandwagon*.

A 'bandwagon' is a trend or movement that people jump on simply because others have already jumped on and *they don't want to miss out*. The bandwagon effect is a subset of the *herd instinct*. People tend to do things because others are; for instance, success in opinion polls for a politician can lead to further increases (as floating voters decide to jump on the bandwagon). The bandwagon effect can be the accelerant to something with substance; for instance, witness the rapid adoption of web 2.0 applications. But it can also be associated with irrational enthusiasm, where the substance did not justify the hype. A prime example was the billions spent on Y2K compliance. What were we thinking?

Green concerns in the late 1980s were triggered by a string of natural and man-made disasters across the globe. Back then I worked on advertising for the Disasters Emergency Committee and I remember it being a very busy time: floods in Bangladesh, earthquakes in

Armenia, famine in Eritrea and so on. It felt like a momentous time. The Berlin Wall came down. And in the 1989 European elections, the UK Green Party achieved an unprecedented 15% of the vote. *The Green Consumer Guide*[4], published in 1988, attracted a million readers. By the end of the decade many were talking about 'the green consumer bandwagon', with brands falling over each other to declare their green credentials. The Henley Centre predicted that the 1990s would be a 'caring, sharing' decade. Green brands, such as Ecover and The Body Shop, were celebrated examples. Many mainstream companies launched their own green ranges; Boots launched a Body Shop clone – the *Naturals* range, and household cleaner giant Reckitt's launched *Down to Earth*.

Earth Day in 1990 was a seminal event, picking up where the fall of the Berlin Wall left off. It felt like one world again. Many of the features of today's scene were present then; the lists of simple consumer actions, the commitments from soap giants and supermarkets. *The Green Consumer*, the title of a book by Joel Makower, became a recognised phenomenon. But unfortunately, as Makower reported recently, the substance was lacking: 'Many of those early products were outright failures: biodegradable trash bags that degraded a little too quickly; clunky fluorescent bulbs that emitted horrible hues; recycled paper products with the softness of sandpaper; greener cleaners that couldn't do their job. Much of it was expensive and hard to find, to boot.'[5]

At first, household cleaning brands like Ecover, Ark and Frosch thrived. Previously available only in health food stores, they now appeared on most supermarket shelves. Sainsbury's and Safeway produced their own eco-friendly labels. But as public enthusiasm waned, the distribution for the true green brands dwindled and Reckitt's *Down to Earth* was axed. Ecover, who I met in the early 2000s, had to go through a profound rethink; they had invested all their more recent innovation and marketing efforts in product efficacy. They knew they had failed to deliver on the basics, without which their green credentials were not enough. Previously they had communicated their greenness; for instance in 'recycled advertising' (poster collages made from recycled scraps of other brands' posters). Now they concentrated on cleaning efficacy.

Other notable setbacks included UK frozen food retailer Iceland, which moved its entire range to organic products in 2001, only to see sales slump by 5.5%. Its CEO subsequently described the move to 100% organic as a 'bold but misguided policy'.[6]

How do we avoid the boom in green marketing turning to bust this time? How do we get it right? Part of where it went wrong last time was the rush to exploit green agendas for commercial ends. I am not suggesting green marketing is not for profit; rather that if it is *just* for profit it is almost bound to be questioned. In future we need to work with dual agendas – marketing and green – finding coincidences of interest that are authentic on both counts.

Green marketers therefore need to understand green issues. They are complex and systemic in the way that school geography lessons were. There are controversies where the experts simply do not agree. Plus there is a constant stream of new information and revised views on the merits of subjects like bio fuel and carbon offsetting (both of which have fallen dramatically from grace in the last six months). There are many excellent resources in published books and on the internet, which do provide accessible guides (and not so accessible guides, if you want detail). You also need to *believe*, and get your whole organisation to want the activities to work on green grounds, and that's not something you will get from books. As a matter of fact, internal morale and the 'employer brand' are often cited as a secondary justification for green marketing programmes. Employees are people and most people by now are worried and want to 'do their bit'. They will feel proud to work for a company that leads on these issues. And this can have an effect on levels of satisfaction, service quality and so on.

A lot of the green information is very detailed and there is still a need to see the wood for the trees. But there is one thing that any marketer can get their head around. In our jobs we are used to instantly recognising two types of challenge:

1. Incremental: maintenance/improvement/reinforcement.
2. Breakthrough: step change/disruptive innovation/leap.

Small companies tend to pursue one or other approach; they are either evolutionary or revolutionary. Big companies tend to have a portfolio; the famous Boston Grid of *cash cows*, *dogs* and *stars*, although some big companies occasionally decide that they are strategically inclined to favour one or other approach. For instance, P&G in the 1990s committed itself to 'Breakthrough'. Whereas organisations in financial difficulty have often gone 'back to basics', i.e. incremental change (usually cost-cutting).

The first step towards sustainable green marketing is to grasp that *green issues are pointing to the need for step change*, not cosmetic and marginal improvements. Anything else is fiddling while the planet burns. What's needed is big, urgent, impressive improvement. Fortunately, the world we live in is so wasteful that big gains are possible, even in mundane matters like packaging and food miles. And there are breakthrough technologies and service innovations in development, which can transform industries. Many green innovations make better economic sense too, and they can be highly competitive. Here's an opportunity to leave rivals behind, even in commodity and industrial markets.

There is absolutely no excuse for tinkering at the margins, pretending to make progress, making a big fuss about little changes. To make any meaningful contribution, business needs to be bold. M&S announced its plans under the heading of Plan A: 'We're calling it Plan A because we believe it's now the only way to do business. There is no Plan B.'[7] They say they did this partly because customers demand it (a slight stretch; I would say they were slightly ahead of literal customer demands, and seeking to shape those demands through education and better alternatives).

Some will counter that – even if you accept that a business needs CSR policies, at least in line with current NGO demands, public expectations and government regulations – marketing's role is to make money. Green marketing and making money are *not* incompatible though. This is an indication of a conflict between old green ideology and old-style marketing assumptions. It's not always going to be an easy mix. The incremental approach won't work, because it will stumble over exactly this sort of issue. The breakthrough approach is the way forward; truly alternative ideas that are win:win – good business in both senses. If you accept that marketing might, at times, work to such twin agendas (and I don't claim that green marketing in future will be the only marketing), what does this actually mean? What are the key green challenges?

The Green Challenges

The latest reports on evidence for climate change by the IPCC (Intergovernmental Panel on Climate Change), published in February and April 2007, describe the phenomenon of global warming as *unequivocal*, and state that it is *very likely* (i.e. more than 90% certain) that most of the observed increases are due to the increase in man-made greenhouse gases (GHGs). The increases in GHGs are due mainly to the use of fossil fuels, although also to changes in land use. On current trends, the report predicts an average increase in temperature across the century of between 1.8°C and 4.0°C. Even if levels of emissions do not change from their current level, temperature will rise by 0.1% per decade; on current projections, the actual figure will be 0.2%.

In case that sounds like a slight change, the reports point to *very likely* mass extinctions, droughts, famines, spreading diseases, floods, extreme weather leading to significant peril to human life, especially but not exclusively in poorer regions. Reported in dry scientific terms it is still a terrifying prospect. I see it as like a doctor telling a patient about a life-threatening condition. Substantial lifestyle changes are needed in response.

Environmentalists measure climate impact in terms of our 'footprint'. The WWF has long supported the view (most recently in the *Living Planet* report, 2006[8]) that in the UK, we live a 'three planet lifestyle', i.e. that three planets would be needed to support our current lifestyle. And the UK isn't even the worst offender. The WWF says that the USA has a 5.3 planet lifestyle.

Let's just step back for a moment and marvel at the idea of 'the footprint'. It's exactly the sort of clever, intuitive idea that I think we, as marketing people, should be adding to the discussion. Technical objectives are all very well for government scientists, but the rest of us need a simple set of mental tools. My guess is that the invention, the very existence of this term (and the associated interactive measurement tool) will have made a substantial contribution to progress against Kyoto-type carbon emission objectives.

It is helpful to spell out what climate change means for *marketing objectives*:

- individual lifestyles need to change in the developed world, let's assume they need to change at the same rate as other (industrial, farming, etc.) sectors;
- for each person, there needs to be a reduction in harmful use of resources by 66% (UK) or 85% (USA);
- in other words, our lifestyles need to change *beyond recognition*.

The targets for reduction get even higher if you consider we may need to compensate for the very necessary development of poorer regions of the world. China is forecast to overtake the USA this year in carbon emissions. George Monbiot, to quote one authority, recommends a personal carbon reduction in the West of 90%.

What does that mean for an individual? The best way to figure that out is to use yourself as a subject. If you haven't already, at the next available opportunity, put the book down and go online. Go to http://www.myfootprint.org/ and take the test. They will tell you how you compare with the average in your country. Now try making hypothetical changes to your lifestyle to see if you can reduce it. Try picking things you think you really could do. And see if you can get it down by 70%, roughly what every single person in Western economies needs to do on average. It's hard isn't it? I could only get close by doing all the easy stuff *plus* giving up my car (which was already a hybrid) *plus* drastically reducing my air travel by cutting foreign conferences and holidays. I'm working on this.

Why do individuals need to change at the same rate as intergovernmental agreements? Can't we leave it all up to big business and governments? They could take care of things at an infrastructure level. Some people find that a tempting line of argument; make consumers incapable of doing damage by changing the processes behind the products they buy. The problem is that, ultimately, we drive the cars, take the flights, vote for governments and create pressure on industries. Not as individuals but as a mass average. The perception of where the green or ethical consumer is at is a key pressure point. Plus, it is a flawed approach, if fundamental patterns of wasteful and destructive behaviour are to shift. We can't afford to take five trips to Europe a year, buy gas-guzzling cars, throw away mobile phones, eat food from thousands of miles away every meal and so on. Draconian legislation alone will not be politically possible without a positive consumer climate for change. You might get away with banning patio heaters (just) and incandescent light bulbs, but the politician who rations carbon (and hence flying, driving and heating your home) will be in a for a rough ride, unless the public will matches the political one.

That's the real-politick argument. The humanist argument is that, for our own psychological and spiritual wellbeing, it is vitally important that we respond; it is the right thing to do, the only course which has dignity. Burying anxieties and pretending it's 'business as usual' is not the answer. Eric Eriksson wrote a great deal about the choice we all face at some point in our lives between generativity (acting out of a broader 'concern for the species') and stagnation. A feeling of futility haunts the bustling shopping centres. To go on behaving like that in the face of gathering evidence of resulting human misery is to live in a green version of apartheid. That is very bad for you as a human being. It makes you morally stunted. You will feel much happier if you 'do your bit'. Even if the whole attempt fails, the version where we all try our hardest is the better course. We are, after all, genetically disposed to expect life to be a struggle. That, in my view, is why surveys show that people were actually happier during WW2 and in post-war austerity Britain than they are now. It's not just 'affluenza', or information overload. It's the lack of a compelling necessity, a reason why you *have to* get up in the morning. A nice problem to have, some would say, given the terrible struggle of daily life in the poorer regions of the world, especially those suffering war and violent strife. But it is still a problem and just because it is more social and psychological, it doesn't mean it isn't a cause of suffering. My impression as a onetime Samaritans volunteer was that there was plenty of that to go around, not only because of stressful or traumatic life events, but because of a society which says to people (from an early age) that unless you are one of the few high-achieving somebodys, you are *a nobody*. Conversely, the struggle, uniting to achieve something, is also an engine for community, for individual brilliance or heroism, for everyone feeling part of something and valuing their own daily actions and lifetimes, for a sense of meaning. As Al Gore says in *An Inconvenient Truth*, this is a moral issue. Now that *we know*, it would be immoral not to act.

But we can't let climate change lead to a fear-fuelled fatalism. There's a lot we can do to make a difference, especially for creative marketing people – that's the advantage of working in 'the lifestyle influence profession'! (And it makes a welcome change from trade promotions!) In fact – in my view – once you accept the challenge, it's the most exciting thing to happen to our profession – and business in general – since the internet.

The Marketing Challenge

Green marketing is only the tip of the iceberg. It is only ever likely to represent a relatively small direct contribution to tackling climate change and other environmental issues. A lot of the real work happens behind the scenes. Companies like BASF and DuPont are leading the greening of heavy industry and have had the biggest impact over the last decade (although some say these were one-off changes, and further gains will be harder). DuPont has famously said that its objective as a company is to have a 'zero' net environmental impact. (Yes, zero. From an industrial chemical company!)

We may be only the tip of the iceberg, but our job is important because what we do is so visible. We are where all of the developments behind the scenes in business and governments meet people's lives. We are part of the reason *why* big corporates with responsibility built in, *why* product and service inventors, *why* cultural change campaigns and *why* new business (and non-business) models may thrive. We can fan the flames of public enthusiasm. Which is *why* more companies and politicians will rush into this space. Not just because it is the right thing to do. But because it is smart too.

Marketing is understood to be influential in shaping people's lifestyles and attitudes. Despite their reservations about our historical contribution to consumerism, where some of the darkest greens get interested is the potential for us to help in persuading people to shift lifestyles. That's tricky in the precise form they imagine it, because most people don't want to live that way. We need to make it more attractive and normal. Achieve the same green outcomes, but in a very different cultural guise. Take sandals. These used to be an expression of (nearly) barefoot natural living. Nowadays, cities just get so hot in summer and new sandal designs (with trainer or hiking boot soles) are more fashionable; they keep your feet cool in both senses of the word. They have become normal. It's only people of my generation who see 'sandal wearing' pejoratively these days I suspect.

Also, having looked at the magnitude of the task, it's clear that marketing can do much more than just help spread current good practice. It must help innovate; bring thousands of dramatically better substitutes – products/services and habits – that haven't even been thought of yet to mainstream acceptance. These step change innovations will seem outlandish at times, but marketing can help with that too; marketing is great at normalising things which are otherwise too new and different to be readily accepted. That's what marketing did for computing over the last 20 years. The challenge of the next 20 years is to be part of a green wave of innovation.

The Green Consumer? (Or All Consumers?)

My view is that marketing's main potential role is to make more people willing and able to go green. We can do this in a number of ways:

- education: the more people know about this stuff, the more they want to do;
- get green living out of the green lifestyle niche;
- extend green culture and lifestyles beyond the middle classes (to the 60% of the population who see themselves as working class);
- acculturation: make outlandish green choices attractive in cultural terms, and make damaging current practices (like excessive flying) unattractive, ostracised.

But there is another response to any marketing sceptics. There is now a substantial tide in public interest and concern about the environment. An Inconvenient Truth, the Al Gore book, has already topped the New York Times non-fiction bestselling list a number of times.[9] The video is already the third highest grossing cinema documentary ever[10] and following the publicity around its Oscar win, must be set to attract further interest. And the idea of a tipping point has more substance to it than entertainment hits. In a recent Ipsos MORI poll, the proportion of respondents who believed there was 'no such thing as climate change' was only 1%.[11] We can also see rapid historical growth in UK ethical consumer purchasing:

(£Million)	1999	2002	2005
Ethical food	1037	3617	5406
Green home	493	2434	4149
Eco-travel and transport	3	739	1792
Ethical personal products	0	982	1315
Community	2570	3336	5054
Ethical finance	5175	7680	11552
TOTAL	9278	18788	29268

Source: The Co-operative Bank, *Ethical Consumerism Report* (2006)

It is true that ethical products, despite showing rapid growth, only account for 5% of all consumer spending.[12] But this depends on how you count ethical consumerism. Buying Fairtrade bananas would qualify, but deciding to eat more local, seasonal foods would not. Buying a hybrid or electric car would qualify; deciding to buy a smaller car or reduce car usage would not. And if you think about it, doesn't this data reflect supply as much as demand? It's only recently that supermarkets and clothing stores have embraced items such as organic cotton clothing. The key data point we are waiting for is the data for 2006/2007. We will see that the attitude and claimed behaviour has recently gone through a dramatic change. We will have to await the Co-operative Bank's economic data to see how this translated into actual buying behaviour.

In qualitative research for the Co-op Bank a few years ago, I found that only a minority would make major sacrifices; the majority wanted to buy green options 'all other things being equal'. But the mood may have shifted quite dramatically since then. And that's all also a matter of conscious choice. A great deal of non-green consumerism is simply locked in by habits, lack of awareness, information and alternatives. There are markets such as fridges (*A-rated* energy labelling) and baby food (organic) where ethical goods account for 60% of sales. In these markets it becomes the norm; it doesn't seem outlandishly green, it's just normal. If you look beyond shopping, at the data on individual participation in ethical behaviours, you see a very different picture than '5%':

Consumer behaviour trends (% undertaking in last year)	1999	2005
Recycled	73	94
Supported local shops/suppliers	61	80
Recommended a company on basis of company's responsible reputation	52	54
Chose product/service on basis of a company's responsible reputation	51	61
Avoided product/service on basis of a company's responsible reputation	44	55
Felt guilty about unethical purchase	17	44
Actively campaigned on environmental/ social issues	15	22

Source: The Co-operative Bank, *Ethical Consumerism Report* (2006)

If you compare the evident willingness to do what you can, recycling being a simple example, with the 5% share of ethical goods, you have to wonder actually if the problem is indeed one of *supply* (and accessibility, performance, pricing, availability, cultural normalisation . . . , i.e. marketing) rather than demand. The other thing to note is that these data are historical, the last survey was in 2005, and once again the amplifying effects of whole grocery chains making new commitments in the last 6–18 months and all the recent green 'tipping point' hype has not yet been counted.

Everyone says there has been a tipping point. Yet I have had conversations *this year* with people in marketing and retail who have asserted that:

- only a tiny minority actually care about the issues enough to act on them;
- the mainstream consumer will only respond to a self-interested agenda.

I still meet some people in business (I met one yesterday) who think sustainability is some sort of passing 'fad'. I can understand why; if they have low knowledge of or interest in the subject and yet also are exposed to a wall of public hype, they might well think it's a lot of fuss about nothing. But I remember it was just like that with the internet. People said in the mid 1990s that it would never make any money, that it was a lot of fuss about 'glorified mail order', that people would never trust it with their credit card details. And then one day, one by one, they 'got it'. It's like a conversion. A total change of mind. Sometimes too much so. I do meet people who have so 'got religion' they aren't thinking straight. But that's what it's like; new ideas release energy for action, even if (like falling in love) they can also suspend your critical faculties. We do need to be believers; moral questions aside it's an inoculation against exploiting the issue (and the high risk of this being exposed). But as strategists we need to keep our heads. Not everything that is 'green' will work. Far from it. It still needs to be well planned and executed, and not just well intentioned. The stakes are higher because it is so exposed to public interest and scrutiny.

If what the sceptics say (about the selfish, disinterested consumer) were true, the many voluntary phenomena of web 2.0 wouldn't have worked. The big TV telethons wouldn't raise any money. People wouldn't have been so upset by images of the tsunami or floods in

New Orleans. People do care. It's often the people in powerful, cynical media and marketing organisations that see normal people in these terms. The media scare stories about gangs and so on create an image of the poorer sections of society as some sort of 'mob'. But actually it is this segment of the population who give most to charity (relative to income) and who are most likely to be religious. I interviewed a senior police officer recently for a Demos report I am working on, and he told me that even in the 'worst' estates, it is usually just a handful of dysfunctional families and individuals, out of many hundreds, who cause any trouble.

A very similar situation exists with the environment now; who is driving the 4×4s, taking the foreign holidays and eating the imported mange tout? The image of the McDonalds-avoiding middle classes belies their guilt. And, ironically, McDonalds are – you may be surprised to hear (in independent ethical rating terms) – one of the good guys. A key lesson we have to learn as marketers, and potentially will need to teach to customers, is (to borrow the M&S slogan) 'look behind the label'.

A case in point was the furore over innocent agreeing to a trial by McDonalds, where kids smoothies are being offered for sale in their restaurants. innocent debated the idea and decided to do it for three key reasons:

- it is an opportunity to get some fruit into working class family diets;
- innocent don't have policies restricting who sells their products, and why should they?
- one of the innocent founders phoned Greenpeace:

  '. . . who said that over the last five years McDonalds have changed from being their number one enemy to their number one global partner in reducing deforestation in the Amazonian rainforest, and if McD's wanted to sell healthy food we should definitely engage with them. A surprising input, and one which was important for us.'[13]

They discussed this trial on their blog and it provoked a heated response, with some people saying they would never drink innocent again, because they felt betrayed. McDonalds did used to be that 'number one enemy', so it's not surprising that some still have bad feelings about being associated with them. Jamie, the innocent managing director, spent whole days phoning these customers to talk about the issue, and did have a high success rate in turning them around.

When assessing brands ethically, the past is a poor guide (unless you bear grudges) and the only guide is current performance and future policies and commitments. We need to start judging brands in the way CSR people do, not the way (some) journalists and activists do. I have done some digging and I have to say the more you look at McDonalds, the better it gets. Yes, they make fast food. And fast food is fatty and salty. If you eat too much of it, too often, without exercising, it will make you fat and could lead to heart and other serious long term health problems. And they don't pay their workers all that well. But most of the above is true of a Prêt a Manger and their coronation chicken sandwich. In fact, a *Guardian* journo once worked out these were less healthy than a Big Mac on every count (bar salt). Yes, McDonalds (formerly) marketed its fast food in ways that appealed to kids; using a fun clown character and 'happy meal' toys. And yes, its offensive legal strategy in the 1990s (the McLibel case) made it a focus of activism and protest. And yes, they still have some issues, allegedly (I just read on an anti-McDonalds blog), for instance over their toy manufacturing in China.

That's McDonald's starting point, and most of it is its historical legacy, but the question is how does it stack up now and how much progress is it making on sustainable issues?

The key measure for sustainability is *ethical velocity*; direction and speed of change. DuPont, for instance, is great (ask any tree hugger), because it cut emissions by over 60% and toxic pollution by over

90%. And it aims in future to have absolutely zero environmental impact on every measure. It doesn't matter that they 'look dirty', they (and other industrial groups like Acciona) are getting us where we need to go.

Here's a quote from a recent report on the 100 most ethical companies in the world in 2007:

> Some may ask, 'How can McDonald's be on the list?' The answer is that the food service industry is the largest industry in the world – and McDonald's has clearly stood apart in introducing healthier food fare, sustainable packaging, food safety, and ethical purchasing practices.[14]

This independent research by *Ethisphere* magazine looked at more than 5000 companies across 30 separate industries. Companies were measured in an eight-step process and then scored against nine ethical leadership criteria.

Marketing people are victims of their own greatest success; the promotion of a simplistic 'image'. We have to learn to see beyond the clichés of the world as we've portrayed it in adverts. We have to allow for the fact that companies, just like people, can change and also that they can differ in substance from the persona they project. And we have to get beyond the notion that the good ones are all good and the bad ones are all bad. It's useful to make black and white distinctions if you are running an anti-corporate campaign. But otherwise it gets in the way and could even discourage those who are trying their hardest but who are getting lumped in with those who are not.

On the question of believing in mainstream ethical consumerism, I think we have to believe that the majority *is ready if we are*. But that we haven't always got the right products and services, in the right places, with the right marketing ideas yet.

The one thing I lacked whilst researching and drafting this book was evidence; how do we *know* we have reached a tipping point, that the majority is now holding sufficient green concerns and motivations to transform markets and marketing? Fortunately, right at the last minute, market research survey data have finally caught up with what many already felt to be the case. Here are some recent highlights:

Landor Associates, PSB, C&W (May 2007)[15]

As part of their ImagePower survey, three WPP companies conducted an annual survey into green brand issues. In 2006, they found that green thinking was still a minority concern and that few could name 'a green brand'. But in 2007, they recorded a dramatic shift; to almost universal green concerns throughout their UK and US sample (over 1500 consumers in each country). Landor described their findings as marking one of the most *complete and speedy revolutions in consumer attitudes ever seen'*.

The report highlighted the two key consumer demands: for green products, and for companies to have green practices (i.e. the management of the whole supply chain and all other operations). However, it also said that consumers are increasingly knowledgeable and sceptical about any companies who appear to pay 'lip service' only.

Another significant shift for those considering green marketing is that there were definite signs that brands that have invested in communicating substantial news in green products and practices are starting to see some rewards in consumer interest and recognition. I must admit I have tended to believe that those (dark greens) who would buy products *on the grounds of being green* were precisely the (anti-corporate) group least likely to believe any company hype on these issues. But as the group of those willing to buy green has expanded, the belief in mainstream green companies seems to have taken root. As with so much of this book, it's a fast-changing scene and one uncertainty is how long the wall of media hype about going green can last. The dotcom frenzy went on a good 5–7 years, mind you; it's premature to wonder if it's a 2007 phenomenon. But in the long term we actually do need to get beyond this; to making green (much greener ways of life than now) normal rather than exceptional. The long-term challenge is to normalise radical new models. For instance, everything in your home could be rented and reconditioned – and hence made to last hundreds of years – rather than bought and thrown away. Meaning that no new materials would appear for manufacture; a so-called closed loop system. The interest in climate change could be helpful in encouraging both companies and consumers to seriously entertain such ideas. But the marketing challenge is to make it normal, just as clever design ideas (from the likes of Apple) have helped make personal computing intuitive and seen as friendly rather than threatening. After the green wave of hype, the key challenge ahead is confronting our greenophobia, in other words.

Landor's figures on the new green following for products and companies (which I have seen, but which they have not published for general consumption) are confirmed by the data from another recent American large-scale quantitative survey.

Vizu Study (May 2007)[16]

This US study on climate change (rather than all green issues) found that about 74% think global warming is important. The majority thinks it is extremely important.

Q. How important is the issue of global warming?
— Extremely important 51.9%
— Important 22.0%

Asked how much they were doing personally to tackle the issue, there was a range of responses, but with over 60% now taking action:

Q. What do you do personally to offset global warming?
  — Everything I can 18.5%
  — I go a little out of my way 22.1%
  — I do what's convenient 20.7%

The roughly 20% 'everything I can' segment (for instance, changing the type of car they drive, groceries they buy, ways that they travel) is a huge leap for the commercial viability of green products and services. This figure is also supported by a much larger BBC survey in 21 countries, covered later, which found, for instance, that 28% had changed travel plans due to green concerns. I see this 20%+ as probably 'the new 5%', and it means that a product which presents a strong green alternative (for instance, an electric car or low power consumption PC) has a much more substantial opportunity. The Landor research also showed that people expect, and are willing, to pay a little more for green options as they consider them better quality. And there are 60%+ who will welcome a convenient substitute that happens to be green.

80% say it is important that companies they buy from are environmentally friendly. This sends a different message; it is about the companies being *acceptable* suppliers, ones people feel comfortable short-listing, ones they wouldn't exclude. This figure does provide some justification for the wave of companies keen to announce their (often impressive and substantial) progress and commitments. A year ago the data would have said these corporates were largely speaking to themselves. But now they look prescient. There are difficulties and dangers with communicating CSR policies; it is a complex fast-moving target. And perhaps this is only an initial stage, like early in the internet revolution when companies rushed to have a .com site, almost regardless of the business model or need. But with the current race to embrace these moves, many companies are feeling that they would do well not to be left behind.

This is all for further discussion when we get onto the actual green marketing strategies, but for now what I want to point out is the startling shift in green attitudes in only the last year:

> It is now almost the unquestioned norm that we all embrace some shade of green philosophy and behaviour. Yet just a year ago, the green agenda was out on the lunatic fringe for most people. (Landor press release, 2007).

Sustainability – The Backroom Revolution

The move to green, ethical and responsible approaches is not a marketing decision. We don't need to wait for 10% or 20% or 40% or 60% of all grocery to be 'ethical' before it looks like a big enough segment to go for. Many big companies have already long committed to CSR, and at the highest level. There are projects underway in many major corporations to integrate it with every activity, and marketing is no exception. In many cases the answer to the question 'why green marketing?' could be as straightforward as: 'because the board of directors said so!'

Sustainability is more than just an internal reform movement. It has created a bridge between business and green. It is defined on the UK government website as follows:

> Ensuring a better quality of life for everyone, now and for generations to come.
>
> Meeting four objectives at the same time, in the UK and the world as a whole:
> - social progress which recognises the needs of everyone;
> - effective protection of the environment;
> - prudent use of natural resources; and
> - maintenance of high and stable levels of economic growth and employment.[17]

It should be noted that within the sustainability movement there are two opposing points of view. One sees maintenance of high levels of economic growth for all countries as key. This is called the 'green growth' position, as espoused for instance by David Cameron. It says we need to make changes and reforms, but we do not need to make sacrifices, for example flying. The other view says that growth is needed in the developing countries to lift them out of poverty, but in the West we should be looking at consolidation; living more fulfilling lives by making better use of what we have. On this view we need a more rounded measure of economic success than either GDP growth or shareholder return. The portion of GDP which is driven by a merry-go-round of retail, travel and transport spending and maxing out on credit and housing market optimism doesn't look sustainable even in economic terms. Standing the issue on its head, the potential of ecological damage to have a knock-on effect on whole economies and societies is also starkly evident. As Nicholas Stern put it in his authoritative report on the economics of climate change: 'our actions over the coming few decades could create risks of major disruption to economic and social activity, later in this century and in the next, on a scale similar to those associated with the great wars and the economic depression of the first half of the 20th Century'.[18] Most current assessments say the modest cost of action is far outweighed by the potential disastrous cost of inaction. Stern reckons that by foregoing just 1% of the GDP growth by 2050, we can stabilise greenhouse gases at what will hopefully be a safe level. A major uncertainty though is nonlinear feedback mechanisms. Any ecological factor which meant that the worse it gets, the faster it gets worse, would mean that we need to be much tougher on tackling greenhouse gases. But the point stands. The cost of not doing this and creating a global Somalia is still greater than almost any level of constraint we could imagine now.

Sustainability is both a systemic approach to doing the right thing (looking at the first three together and taking a balanced view) and also contains the radical idea that doing the right thing and economic success are not incompatible. Many companies have taken this second message to heart. In their 2004 sustainability report, Procter & Gamble describe their overall view of CSR as 'corporate social opportunity' – an expansion of their classic mission to meet customers' needs at a profit, which acknowledges that issues such as public health and environment represent unmet needs too.[19]

But the conflict hasn't entirely gone away. CSR has created a split in the green movement. Some do have a foot in both camps; for instance, most major NGOs operate a carrot and stick policy with major corporations, praising some and campaigning against others. But the corporate responsibility vs anti-corporate activist debate really is a schism. From the anti-corporate side, CSR is criticised for helping corporations avoid regulation, for helping them *greenwash* through positive PR, for creating an illusion of progress where there is little, for 'selling out'. From the sustainability side, the anti-corporate position is criticised for being isolated, naïve and destructive. In attempting to stay pure, it fails to engage with real opportunities to make a difference, goes the argument. Not a conflict that can be resolved here. But I do have to assume the sustainability hypothesis is true; that it is possible to reduce the damage and still achieve commercial success. Otherwise, green marketing would be an oxymoron.

The idea of companies (and governments) and greens working together is a new one. And the concession which some greens made was to work to dual objectives: reduction of harm *as well as* economic success. There is no serious large company (that I know of) that would question the imperative of making money, if not growing in size, every year. It may not be their primary purpose; most interesting companies have visions and values as well as balance sheets. But if they are public companies, they are legally obligated to try to make shareholders a reasonable return on their investment. (That's the crux of the argument of *The Corporation*, a thought-provoking film and book, which attacks the modern system of market capital-ism). Accepting some economic growth as a concession is vital to attract the sorts of successful company that could really set the pace in green business. GE aims to sell $20 billion in *Ecoimagination* products by 2010.

Sustainability is transforming the way that companies operate. The current trend is about integrating sustainability in all the activities of the company. Formerly, sustainability was a depart-ment, one that gathered information, reported internally and externally and thus policed those activities of the company. Now, sustainability is thought of as a mindset and a set of tough principles, which everyone in the company should use in its daily work. When I worked with IKEA on communicating its sus-tainability programme inside the company, we set ourselves an objective: make IKEA as eco-conscious as cost-conscious. You'd have to know IKEA to know what a telling phrase that is, they really do watch every cent of costs; for instance, in the days of printing documents, it was common practice to calculate and report on the front of each document: 'this report cost 130SEK to produce and circulate'.

One company that has won international recognition for its advanced sustainability practices in financial services is Banco Real in Brazil, part of the ABN AMRO group. Banco Real, founded in 1917, is the fifth largest bank in Brazil, with over 1000 branches. Since 2001 it has been using assessment of social and environmental impacts within its everyday transactions, for instance in appointing a supplier or approving a small business loan. It went on to define methodologies and eligibility criteria for any project the bank under-takes, either its own or with a client, to determine whether it was environmentally sound and sustainable. These have been taken into the heart of all operations, including credit approval, in the same way as its risk management policies are – making sustainability a compliance type issue. The bank is actively pursuing opportunities to invest in any environmentally positive activities or businesses.

And also pursuing reforms such as encouraging better governance in family-run businesses.

What signing up to sustainable business means is *making decisions not just based upon financial factors, but also based upon the social and environmental impact*. It's about win:win solutions – a search for what I call *beautiful coincidences*. Banco Real believes that sustainable businesses are better run and more viable, less of a credit risk too, and that those who lead on environmental practices will often be more dynamic and successful in the long run. The bank chose this path because it simply represents doing the right thing, but it is able to point to its commercial viability too. There is a history of sustainability in Brazilian business anyway; historically, companies in that region have taken on more responsibility for social welfare programmes, for instance. The whole well-known stance of the bank makes it seem trustworthy, and its advertising slogan is very direct in calling it 'The Sustainability Bank'. (An equivalent in the UK would be the Co-operative Bank, known for its ethical investment policies. Here, the proposition is that your money isn't used for things you wouldn't approve of.)

The Green Marketing Challenge

Where the strategies in this book are different from most CSR work is that we are not just minding out for negative consequences, but actively pursuing positive opportunities. A deeper and more complex issue is that consumerism is to blame for at least part of the problem. And individual actions are not enough; we need overall society-wide change. We may take on a few specific green behaviours, such as not keeping TVs on standby, not accepting carrier bags and so on – but this needs to have a knock-on effect on broader questions about how we live. Otherwise, those few ethical goods in our shopping basket will breed a false security, leaving us where we started. That's why, for the greenest marketing, we need to add cultural outcomes as a third criterion:

1. Commercial outcomes.
2. Environmental outcomes.
3. Cultural outcomes.

Achieving all three of these means a radically new approach. Fortunately, the groundwork for this sort of marketing has already been laid, by the emergence of what I have been describing as New Marketing over the last ten years. We have been moving away from slick, consumerised aspirational advertising, and towards authenticity, transparency, customer experts, word of mouth, participation, community and many other helpful developments. Marketing is no longer about seducing people with empty promises; it is about engaging and educating them.

But we do need to think much harder than marketers traditionally had to (it's always been a fun area to work in and it has never exactly been rocket science). Green issues are complicated, especially when you factor in social and ethical questions too. And often what's required – to really make headway against all three objectives – is not just a new green communication strategy, but a new business model, service, value proposition. Of course that also makes the whole subject more interesting, as a proper challenge. But I do worry that some marketers and their agencies may spoil it for the rest of us, through thoughtless hype, spin and nonsense which discredit green marketing, both publicly and also if it leads to a backlash in the business community. We need marketing that *does good*, rather than marketing that just *looks good*.

We have seen that the climate change crisis means that we need drastic change. This implies that the 'green outcomes' should be read as involving dramatic change, not gradual change. And the cultural outcomes too; it is not enough to create pockets of change – we need ideas about new ways to live, not just new packaging, product or service ideas. I will also argue that green marketing should aim for breakthrough business success. It is almost your duty to show it can work, to set a great example. I know there is a place for things that start small. But it is the end result I am talking about, of taking what works to a new scale. My friend Judith made the very good point when we were chatting about this that there isn't yet 'a Green YouTube'; in the sense of a big start-up which everyone points to as a definitive runaway success. Last time round, this 'first mover' was The Body Shop, and it still tops the polls of ethical brands, green brands and so on in the UK. But start-ups, even in a volatile market, will take time.

If sustainability may be about maintaining a good standard of life, rather than GDP growth, why make sustainable marketing about growing a business? Green marketing needs to be successful in business terms for investment to be sustained. But I think it goes beyond that, it is not a matter of business as usual, it is a matter of total innovation in business models, in operations, in marketing too. Total innovation tends to go one of two ways: ignominious failure or dramatic success.

The idea of profiting from (green and culturally) good deeds may sound dubious. But let's be clear, green marketing has to be separated from 'marketing green', which is the work of charities, governments and NGOs. When we look at businesses that have made an impact on both specific green issues and also changing the cultural context (and in some cases even the regulation of their markets), they tend to be super successful in business terms too; The Body Shop (until Anita Roddick left) was a prime example. Yes, there were critics who said it was somehow 'wrong' for the founders to have become wealthy. But I can think of few who made better use of their wealth, influence and power.

A more surprising example to some would be eBay. This is indisputably one of the most successful companies started in the last 20 years. It has created a second-hand market for consumer goods where one (especially in the USA) barely existed, thus extending the lifetime of products otherwise bound for the landfill sites. It has changed the culture too; it is not an aspirational brand nor a lofty corporation, it is run in close co-operation with a community of self-policing members. Yes, it is not perfect (it can involve deliveries over large distances, especially in the USA), but it has had more impact on all three measures than many other examples in this book.

But eBay isn't 'green'. It sells new goods too. It isn't a 'green business' *per se*. And that is the point. We don't need to live in a world that *looks* like a green ideological utopia. We want to live in a better world, one in less imminent danger of self-destruction, misery and ecological catastrophe. A world with a smaller carbon footprint because it is better organised, its people live more modestly (and hopefully happily). We don't have to call our children hippy names, eat lentils or do yoga to belong (it might be very nice – I'm a fan of all three – but it is not necessary). I hope and expect the world will also be teeming with human diversity. I hope it keeps changing and developing new ideas, new scientific discoveries and new types of sweet. It's the climate change 'volume' we need to turn down; we don't have to change our tune in other ways, unless they relate to meeting this target (bling bling and a jet-set lifestyle are definitively not green).

To get there with today's population and geopolitical situation (rapid development in China, India and other parts of the world, accelerating the damage which the Western liberal market capitalism we invented is doing) is, as the Friends of the Earth campaign puts it, a 'BIG ASK'. We won't get there by slowing down a bit and hoping for the best. We will only get there by 100 or 1000 or 100000 breakthroughs the size of eBay.

Like eBay, many of them won't even look 'green'. Some of them will, but it's a matter of choosing the best approach for the business; if eBay had been launched as an ideological green brand promoting charity shop values, would it be the same success? Probably not.

Green Marketing's Five *I*'s

1. Intuitive – Making Better Alternatives Accessible and Easy to Grasp

It's about making breakthrough green stuff seem normal (and not the other way around). For the majority of people (outside the dark green fringes), living, shopping, working, travelling and enjoying life in a sustainable way appears difficult and arduous. Our job as creative marketing people is to make it intuitive, second nature, just common sense. We need more ideas like 'organic', whereas too much is still at the 'chemical-free horticulture' stage.

Organic, recycling, Fairtrade and – the latest member of this set – carbon neutral are examples of how important the choice of a word, a cultural reference, a human sense of things is. We've seen the same thing in fitness (the invention of 'jogging'), in health (watching the calories) and in IT (the graphical interface 'desktop').

2. Integrative – Combining Commerce, Technology, Social Effects and Ecology

This is a shift for the green movement, which was founded on an anti-technology romantic tradition and was incubated more recently by anti-corporate activists, straight out of Marxism and the peace movements.

The breakthrough idea was sustainability, which is an approach to improving quality of life, both now and for future generations, by combining economic development with social and environmental development. Sustainability also allows a balanced view where one evil (e.g. food miles) doesn't get replaced by another (e.g. poor labour rights). It's also a big breakthrough for commercial (as opposed to charity, or cause or government) marketing, which has seldom in the past considered green and social objectives, except as a means to a business end.

3. Innovative – Creating New Products and New Lifestyles

Many are saying that green innovation and entrepreneurship in the next 20 years will be like the IT space over the last 20 years. People have started using the term *g-commerce* (like e-commerce but green). In fact it's not just an analogy; some developments are enabled by the internet – like the ability to collaborate in design, build c ommunities and so on. The system that enabled the building of Linux, Wikipedia and Craigslist is now enabling amazing ideas like Freecycle – a web service with over three million members where people give away goods, which they might otherwise have thrown out, to other local members. It's a great social innovation, but in technological terms it is Yahoo! groups with a purpose. There are also opportunities in service redesign – like city car clubs – and simple lifestyle ideas – like Ariel's 'Turn to 30' campaign.

The internet has been so successful so fast because it has tackled existing inefficiency; for instance, matching buyers and sellers better. The same is true of ways in which our lives and arrangements are needlessly environmentally wasteful. Some of these changes will hurt incumbent brands though; just like Skype hurt BT. Capitalism isn't suddenly going to be all nice to those who fall behind. But green isn't intrinsically anti-brand or anti-revenue. There are more ways of making money than encouraging needless waste and extra consumption of precious resources. And even within a GDP freeze scenario, most of the action in business is competitive, not cumulative. Look, for instance, at Amazon's 'New & Used' service. There are always winners when there is big change.

4. Inviting – A Positive Choice Not a Hair Shirt

Before the current green marketing boom, there was a previous cycle of hype and disappointment. We have to get it right this time. In the late 80s and early 90s, the limited number of products that launched behind *the green consumer bandwagon* often did represent a compromise, in terms of cleaning results or the tendency of recycled bags to rip and spill. This, plus the traditional green agenda (turning back the clock), has created a suspicion of sacrifice, difficulty and awkwardness.

Green now is partly a design challenge. And green products are often better: more efficient, durable, healthy, affordable and so on. But we also need to tackle the culture of green lifestyles, create new myths and codes which are utopian and joyful and fun, rather than seeming like unpleasant medicine to avoid a dystopia.

5. Informed – Lack of Knowledge Is What Most Distorts People's Behaviour

The classical 'brand' is a substitute for having to give matters much thought. A branded wine is a safe choice for those who don't know their viniculture. A branded car or newspaper can be 'what people like us are supposed to be' driving or reading. The green marketing I am proposing has very little to do with brand image – it's about education and participation. There is revolution going on in health, lifelong learning and citizenship due to the new accessibility of information. I've argued before (in *After Image*) that knowledge is already eclipsing image in mainstream marketing. The 'in' brands are Google, Amazon, eBay, Skype – which have currency but almost zero image. Meanwhile, old 'image' leaders like Coca-Cola, Gap and Levi's are in commercial, as well as cultural, difficulty. True green marketing, leading to a more sustainable culture, is antithetical to dumbing down. If you remember that, many of the perils of *greenwashing* go away.

Endnote: Another Revolution

One 'I' that isn't in the above list is 'Image'. The green marketing in this book is about doing green and at most factually announcing green, but seldom about 'looking green'. 'Image' is old school marketing; it is spin, presentation, PR, hype and all that bad stuff. When you consider the traditional way of marketing, its mass media models of branding, communication and strategy and so on, then it looks hopeless. The old marketing is simply never going to be all that green. But if we just look at what green marketing needs to achieve, and approach it fresh, like intelligent and creative human beings, using the latest media and models, it is easier.

We've already been through a marketing revolution, catalysed by changes in business, media and society. And this is going to be more of the same, only more so. We have already moved past image marketing and spin in marketing anyway; modern markets are too literate, too transparent, too cynical, too authenticity-seeking. A market today is like a kind of group mind and the new pervasive approaches – seeding, advocacy, community, utility and so on – are where it's at. When we get onto the practical options within green marketing, you will see it is actually pretty effortless and easy to understand in theory, even if coming up with unique and relevant ideas will never be easy in practice. All you have to do is ditch the old 20th century marketing and hang onto your creative problem-solving instincts. As with digital marketing, the youngest people in the business who never learned our bad habits could be at a distinct advantage.

Green marketing may involve dramatic changes in the fortunes of big brands. One example is that – like many dark greens I know – I have stopped drinking bottled mineral water. I vaguely knew about the issues with food miles and recycling already. But I didn't know (until I read an ethical consumer guide[20]) that in a *Which Health?* test, 33 out of 40 bottled waters failed to meet the same exacting standards as London tap water! The way I look at it now, it isn't tap water I should filter, it's actually bottled water. It would be dumb to continue buying it. If others follow suit, bottled water may be decimated (except in areas where you can't drink the tap water).

That story may sound anti-brand. But you have to take a broader view. Change is opportunity as well as threat. In the case of water, there is a big marketing challenge for tap water. Evian's loss is Thames Water's gain. What a waste to be purifying water that we only wash and flush with. And how better to justify the water supply charges, in a negative context of hosepipe bans and so on? A really populist movement *back to tap* – celebrating possibly the greatest ever human invention, one which more of the world must share – could work wonders for the industry. I recently heard that a gourmet guide to the tap waters of the UK (in the style of a wine guide) is being written. It's a really accessible way to engage people.

What about those who just really like water chilled in a nice bottle? Is everything lost for that whole market? Maybe not. My friends at SDG in Oslo won international design awards in the late 90s for their washable, and hence reusable, glass water bottle for restaurants. It looks really cool (the stopper is spherical). You refill it with filtered tap water that you chill. Everyone feels good about it. It's a great piece of brand design and is welcomed as an eco-alternative. It even saves money yet delivers the same experience. This case illustrates a 'trick' we will see again and again: *if you need to innovate away from an unsustainable product, invent a service instead.* Marketing isn't just about packaging and ads after all. Innovation is our lifeblood and now we just need to be a bit more lateral; finding new ways to meet old needs.

Marketing is competitive. For every loser there is almost always a winner. Working on the side of the greener alternatives doesn't mean going all 'hippy' by any means. To be clear, this book is NOT for people who:

- aren't interested in business, profit, competition;
- aren't interested in making a significant difference in green terms.

If you are not interested in commercial success, you will run the danger of wasting money (from a marketing point of view) on something well meaning but with no bite. If you are in the second camp, you will try to exploit green themes for short-term gain and will likely get found out. Funnily enough, the most powerful ideas in the book work equally well on both counts. They are win:win ideas because they are breakthrough ideas. There is something about commercial desire which makes green marketing bolder, just as there is something about green ethics that makes marketing more authentic. It's a virtuous circle. It's about the hunt for the beautiful coincidence; an idea that unites these agendas. Creativity is the key – *life-changing* ideas.

• If you work in marketing services, you have always had the task of helping client companies to succeed. It's just that now 'success' itself is redefined. It has three components:

1. Commercial success.
2. Green (and/or ethical) success.
3. Cultural success.

The biggest misconception about green marketing is that it is about making companies and brands look green. No wonder we get accused of *greenwashing*. We'll explore this vexed issue in grid section A1. There are exceptions to every rule, but I would argue that for the most part, we need to leave green cultural themes, imagery (and even the colour green) to NGOs and similar. As the first of the five Is says:

Green marketing is mostly about making (breakthrough) green stuff seem normal – and not about making normal stuff seem green.

For those who don't much like grids, but just prefer to explore and create (those of you who dip into the book in a nonlinear fashion and pluck out examples and insights), that's pretty much the only thing you need to hold on to.

SECTION II

The Green Marketing Grid

Overview

Green marketing is 'in'. Everyone says 'it is a good idea'. No one seems to agree quite what it is. The problem right now is that we have a blanket term 'green marketing'. And of course, there is not just one type of green marketing, but many. I am going to explore 18 different types. And that is only an initial survey, one that covers the examples that have emerged so far. Why 18 types? Because they are derived from a structured $3 \times 3 \times 2$ analytic approach to *what green marketing is for*.

There are three broad types of green marketing objectives:

A. (Green). Setting new standards in responsible products, policies and processes.
B. (Greener). Sharing responsibility with customers.
C. (Greenest). Supporting innovation – new habits, services, business models.

The green/-er/-est distinction refers to the marketing objectives; does the marketing itself achieve just commercial outcomes? Or does it also achieve green outcomes? Or culture change too? It's not a value judgement though. It only refers to the objectives of the marketing itself, what you would measure to decide if it succeeded. A green substitute product (like an electric sports car) which sets a new standard in the motor industry but is given a straightforward marketing sell on its individual benefits (e.g. the coolness of sci-fi technology to geeks) could still be the greenest approach in totality. But you'd only measure the actual marketing on cars sold, not changes in driving. The clever thing was deciding to make it just like a supercar; the new Tesla does 0–60 in around four seconds and looks like a Lamborghini on steroids. But the marketing itself will probably be very straightforward – motor shows, pr, ads and so on.

There are also three levels at which any marketing (including green) can operate:

1. Personal (product/benefits/individual).
2. Social (brand meanings/herd instincts/tribes/communities).
3. Public (company as credible source, as cultural leader or partner).

Through this analytical process we arrive at a 3×3 grid (Figure 4), which helps us see the possibilities and the diversity within green marketing.

Just having a framework is immensely helpful in avoiding confusing and conflating different approaches. There is no suggestion that any one of these approaches within the grid is better. 'Better' is only meaningful on a case-by-case basis – the best choice for *this* product, company or brand. It really depends what you are marketing, what sort of company you are. You have to find your own place in this matrix.

I developed this grid through researching (case studies, articles, papers and blogs) to try to develop a comprehensive study. There will always be examples that fall between these strictly classified boxes, but I mainly wanted to point to the variety and the need to discriminate between different sorts of green marketing. Before we

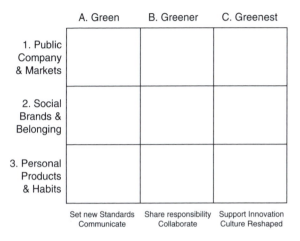

Figure 4 Blank grid

go into those sorts of details on the boxes within the grid, let's step through the three columns and three rows of the grid and ensure that we get our bearings.

A. Green – Setting New Standards for Responsible Products, Services, Brands, Companies

This is classical marketing applied to green(er) products, brands and companies – ones which set new standards. What I mean by green(er) is *greener than the substitutes and competitors* rather than measured against any absolute ideal. The level reached by pioneering brands one year may be absolutely expected of all the next year. Sustainability is a moving target.

In terms of the three green marketing objectives, this activity addresses only the first:

- Commercial outcomes ✓
- Green outcomes
- Cultural outcomes

To be more precise, the second two objectives are 'taken care of' by what is being marketed. A company has got its act together. It has made many reforms to its supply chain, sourcing and so on. If the truth be known, most people don't want to know every detail. But as consumers, they can make the world a greener place by buying their products and not alternatives. These companies can contribute to a culture of green too, for instance if they have grown the market for greener product types, or those under a heading like the 'eco-friendly' label. But mainly it's about 'leave it to us'.

This is marketing as usual. Specifically, the marketing dollars are spent on generating awareness and perceived superiority; it is a selling job, and a communication model. The individual receivers of these messages have little part to play, other than voting with their wallets. These approaches will cause minimal disruption in marketing circles. They know the drill. But of course with less pain may come less gain. Conversely, if you go to your marketing department with your CSR strategy, this is the default option that they or their agencies will likely consider. And in some (but only some) circumstances it is the right way to go. The only question in this approach is whether you really are setting new standards or whether you are just asking your agency to massage and select existing operations; making something normal seem greener. This is called *greenwashing*. It's not a good idea, not only because it is fibbing but also because you will be found out, exposed as a fraud and lose value, trust and pretension to leadership. Conversely, being credible (in a world where people are very cynical about marketing claims) is difficult and much of the interest in the strategies and examples discussed is around how to get people to believe that you are setting new standards for real. The easiest thing being of course to establish such a big lead, with such a bold CSR/innovation programme, that it is obvious. Ford struggles to convince people it is serious about greener cars, but Toyota doesn't.

The key guideline for marketing in this column is keeping it factual. Announce what you are doing, use an eco-label, get people to taste your chocolate; and all these cases leave them free to conclude for themselves that you are better. I don't mean your marketing has to be dull. Just that it has to be rigorously true. Better to be a bit humble than risk stretching the truth (you will get found out). Truth in advertising is very difficult. It is easier to execute these strategies well in other ways, through PR, online and so on.

B. Greener – Sharing Responsibility with Customers

This is a natural approach for those brands and companies which espouse what I have called New Marketing in my previous books. This is collaborative and participative. It embraces such developments as word of mouth, brand experiences and events, education and community. It's what I have been writing about for the past ten years.

In terms of our three objectives, it is tackling the first two explicitly:

- Commercial outcomes ✓
- Green outcomes ✓
- Cultural outcomes

An example is Ariel asking people to wash their clothes at 30 degrees (not higher). This is good for the environment; in their trials they found that it saved around 40% of the energy used. And it is also good brand marketing; it builds relationships and interest in a dull sector, it reinforces the quality perceptions of Ariel (it is so good at getting your clothes clean it barely needs hot water). It is good marketing in every sense. In this column, advertising is often actually okay, because you are not selling your greenness, you are trying to involve people in a public scheme, community or activity. It doesn't often add up to changing behaviour much, beyond your narrow category. People recycle (over 90% do) but this doesn't translate into buying things with less wasteful packaging in the first place. But with decent products and great marketing, there is lots of mileage in this whole collaborative approach – and for many mainstream brands it may feel as far as you can credibly go at this stage.

C. Greenest – Shaping a New Culture of Responsibility Through Innovation

We are on the verge of a green innovation revolution. It's already started in fact. The next ten years will see revolutionary new ideas in smart eco-homes, in travel, in retailing, working patterns and quite possibly in government regulation and taxation too. What all these changes may add up to is a dramatically greener way of life. There is so much waste and inefficiency in the current arrangements. We don't need to travel 1500 miles to have a discussion with some of our colleagues, nor do green beans and fruit out of season need to travel this far to make nourishing and appetising meals.

IT, and web 2.0 in particular, will be a major enabler of these changes. You can scale a local, low-key approach into something (like Craigslist or Freecycle) with colossal efficiency. Network technologies are opening the market to radically new business models. Most are the conversion of products into services that meet the same need (for instance, car pooling vs car owning) and the interplay between nonmoney and money economies; utilities built by volunteers and businesses co-created *with* volunteers (if that sounds too 'hippy' consider Amazon reviews).

The key challenge is the need to combine radical new products, services and daily habits with utterly normal and acceptable cultural codes. It's just the same as the challenge faced by the early dotcoms. It's hard to remember now how much resistance there was in the mid 1990s; people scared to give their credit card details, scared the e-businesses weren't for real, were too 'intangible'. The breakthrough e-businesses knew how to bring in traditional chunks of culture to clothe their digitising of markets; it wasn't a bucket shop it was *lastminute.com*, it wasn't a social network it was *friends reunited*.

This is where the innovators – both the product, service and business designers and also the lifestyle habit pioneers – need our help. Their ideas are often being incubated with an audience of green geeks who will work with this stuff raw. It is our job to help cook it in a way that can become 'the new normal'. It's partly a design challenge and partly a cultural myth-making challenge.

That's why this column of approaches goes the furthest in tackling all three objectives:

- Commercial outcomes ✓
- Green outcomes ✓
- Cultural outcomes ✓

That covers the columns of the grid, what about the rows? The personal–social–public split is basic sociology, for instance Max Weber's analysis of society as operating simultaneously on these three (partially) independent levels.

1. Public – Company Story, Engagement Campaigns, Futures

When the image brand crisis started in the 1990s – with widespread evidence of a turning away from brands and mass marketing, especially in youth markets – a new theory sought to explain why. It was called *postmodern marketing* and concerned the development of brands which were bought for the company behind them; their trustworthy credentials and also their political policies and values. The classic paper on this was by Mary Goodyear, a prominent UK qualitative researcher. Goodyear described a postmodern stage in branding, born out of brand literacy and loss of belief in institutions. She posited two brand roles: brand as company and brand as policy. What this meant in practice was consumers choosing, for instance 'on the basis of political correctness or the absence of e-numbers'.[21]

There is nothing new about the idea of the corporate brand. David Ogilvy, writing forty years ago, pointed to the fact that if advertising could produce a 1% difference in share price for a large company, that would outweigh the effects of any consumer campaign you could imagine. With the way the economy has gone – towards media, services, retail, IT – the number of prominent brands which have the same name as the company behind them has also increased. And often thoughts about the company – their key competencies and so on – are important in these markets; which supermarket has the most buying muscle? (Tesco) Which gadget company has the neatest design skills? (Apple) And so on.

What Goodyear meant though was something different. She meant that *people were seeing through brands* (as selective and flattering and necessarily partial presentations) to the true stories behind them. She was describing something more like what we now know as the ethical consumer movement. The analysis started with consumer literacy; they're 'seeing through' marketing, so that if they are persuaded it is 'only with their knowing acceptance'. Which leads to a different kind of consumerism: 'armed with product knowledge and political convictions, they bring a new framework to the appraisal of brands.'[22] Goodyear saw this as a decline in the power of brands; for instance in her paper *Devolution and the Brand – Is traditional branding an idea past its sell-by date?* (1992). Again, Goodyear argued that brands were losing their mystique because of consumers' growing marketing literacy and cynicism.

Bearing that in mind, we need to approach this notion of brand as company carefully. It is often bandied around these days as a positive opportunity, a new and sophisticated way to brand things. But it is born out of scrutiny and suspicion. Consumers feel that companies seldom have their interests, or indeed any interests except making money, at heart. There are glorious exceptions and these are indeed highly valued. But they are also fragile, both to external disappointments and internal tensions.

2. Social – Identity and Community

The idea of associating a product (or service) with social meanings – for instance, to help reinforce a consumer's identity – is what most people think brand marketing does. But that whole system has been called into question in the last 15 years. The postmodern age of marketing has also meant people don't seem to want to be labelled so easily. They are more marketing literate, and less likely to confuse a cool ad with a cool brand. Levi Strauss jeans have enjoyed some of the best TV ads in the world in the last decade. But their sales declined in nine out of the last ten years. They lost $3.2B (–42%) in value in the eight years to 2005. And the latest results show a 5% decline in sales for Q1–Q3 2006. I am not saying that the advertising was responsible for the decline. Only that it was unable to halt it.

The old image brands seem to be struggling in many markets. Not so much in luxury goods. With these, people do still 'buy the image'. What has been challenged is the 'luxury goods style' advertising for ordinary commodities. It just isn't credible any more. People don't really believe that Stella Artois beer as sold in the UK is 'reassuringly expensive'; it's made in Newport, Wales, not Belgium. People know Stella as a *Chav* (i.e. downmarket, uncouth) drink because that is who, in their experience, drinks the stuff (and popular mythology obviously reinforces this). It hardly matters what the advertising says – if it is different from reality, then it is baffling and wrong. Brand meaning is made by people, not by ads. The watchword for marketing at the social meanings and brand level today is *authenticity*. There is plenty of action at this social level still; it just isn't about advertising an image any more. Strong brands like *The Guardian* or innocent smoothies are associated with a 'tribe'. If you don't have that sort of brand, you can still work in association with something that is that credible and does have a following; for instance the Soil Association or WWF. Or you can build a community. Or similar.

3. Personal – Products and Habits

Marketing is portrayed as mostly brand image marketing. Those examples are so visible. It should be remembered, however, that the overwhelming majority of consumer behaviour happens to be *inconspicuous consumption*; i.e. things we buy which we don't expect others to know about and are based on our own personal needs, tastes, habits and experiences. These products have little to do with status or display. They meet practical needs, are convenient, are part of our routine of daily habits or are 'normal', being 'what everyone buys' (or where everyone shops), they are just what we have got used to.

Large parts of the economy are quite functional anyway, meeting people's practical needs, from financial services to headache remedies. These choices are less visible but can have huge green implications. Many of the 'basic things you can do', such as fitting energy saving bulbs, using public transport, switching energy supplier, fall under this heading. With these decisions the key factor is often habit and inertia, rather than not wanting to let go of life's luxuries. The luxury goods and flashy youth brands and IT gadgets do hog the cultural limelight, and thus tend to be reckoned of inflated size and importance. The strongest brand in the UK in terms of what people actually give their money to though is Tesco.[23] And in case it is objected that Tesco sells other people's brands, do bear in mind that half of its groceries and an even higher proportion of its other goods (from financial services to petrol) are sold under the Tesco brand.

Huge categories of consumer spending are unbranded, like housing (with the exception of estate agent chains and the larger house builders), plumbing, cleaning and childcare services, car maintenance and so on. Statistics on American household spending across the 1990s (from the US Bureau of Labor Statistics) show that the largest single item was housing (33%) and if you add home improvements (14%), nearly half of all consumer spending was accounted for by this item. These grew while spending on clothes, jewellery, audio equipment and eating out – i.e. conspicuous consumption – actually declined across the decade. The other growth areas were health and (children's college) education, reflecting the key financial demands on the baby boomer generation.

Isn't this all a bit remote from green marketing? Not necessarily. One idea I have is a scheme to persuade those in the UK who have made good profits on their houses (prices have tripled in the last ten years) to reinvest a small proportion in energy efficiency, double glazing, loft insulation and so on. Research does show that people are willing to pay more for energy efficient homes. And government regulation next year will mean that people have to have any home (for sale) energy efficiency rated. I'm calling the scheme *Housing Bloom*. I'm planning to present this at a banking conference next month, to see if there are any takers, or perhaps plant the seed for someone else to develop.

In each square of the grid we will explore the typical approach. Figure 5 gives a summary.

	A. Green	B. Greener	C. Greenest
1. Public Company & Markets	*Set an Example*	*Develop the Market*	*New Business Concepts*
2. Social Brands & Belonging	*Credible Partners*	*Tribal Brands*	*Trojan Horse Ideas*
3. Personal Products & Habits	*Market a Benefit*	*Change Usage*	*Challenge Consuming*
	Set new Standards Communicate	Share responsibility Collaborate	Support Innovation Culture Reshaped

Figure 5 Grid with titles

	A. Green	B. Greener	C. Greenest
1. Public Company & Markets	*Framing vs Pointing*	*Educate vs Evangelise*	*Social Production vs Property*
2. Social Brands & Belonging	*Eco-labels vs Cause Related*	*Exclusive vs Inclusive*	*Tradition vs New cool*
3. Personal Products & Habits	*Less vs More*	*Switch vs Cut*	*Treasure vs Share*
	Set new Standards Communicate	Share responsibility Collaborate	Support Innovation Culture Reshaped

Figure 6 Grid with examples

However, these nine strategies are only category headings. Within each box, rather than prescribing one 'answer' (there are no right or wrong answers, the approach taken will depend on your company, brand, industry, etc.) we will explore a key debate, choice or distinction. This is a more enlightening way to get to grips with what it's all about. It's that old student essay twist – 'compare and contrast' – the better to throw light on both headings. So we will end up with 18 candidate green marketing approaches. Hopefully, these will give you at least some starting point ideas for your own business or clients. But as with any creative marketing, the actual end product is endlessly variable.

The examples in Figure 6 will be explained throughout the book. But as a handy reference for when you want to return and look something up, and also by way of summarising what's to follow, here is a box-by-box guide to the green marketing grid.

A1: Set an Example

How do we communicate the values, principles and activities of companies who are trying harder on environmental and ethical issues? While the public has recently become highly receptive to such messages, they are also cynical about corporate spin. You need to be clear *why* you are letting this be known. For instance, GE say they are investing in the innovation itself because the market for their 30 key eco products is growing fast, but that they do the *advertising* ($90m worth) because they want to force the pace of regulation to catch competitors out. Plus, you have to figure they are quite proud of it all, want to attract the best people, boost their investor confidence, etc.

Framing vs Pointing

There are two ways to show people that you are setting new standards as a company; one is to talk about your operations in general and the new principles they are guided by (e.g. going carbon neutral), the other is to talk about specific examples of hero products which you have developed (e.g. the Toyota hybrid cars).

A2: Credible Partners

A neat way to avoid attempting to build a virtuous 'green image' directly (which you don't have to be a Greek tragedian to know is *asking for it!*) is to associate yourself with a credible partner.

Eco-label vs Cause-related

The two most common forms these partnerships take at present are: eco-labels, giving accreditation from the Soil Association, Carbon Trust or similar, and partnering with a charity or NGO. But there are many other types of partnership, e.g. green sponsorships.

A3: Market a Benefit

Green is not actually a benefit on a personal level (unless you include freedom from guilt) – it's for the collective good. Many product companies have found marketing other benefits which are corollaries of green design – be they saving money or eating more healthily – are more persuasive.

Less vs More

Green product benefits tend to divide into economy and luxury brackets.

B1: Develop the Market

Companies with strong credentials relative to competitors, resulting from extensive sustainability programmes and also the resulting differences in what they bring to market (for instance The Body Shop being against animal testing) can benefit from trying to shape the public agenda and move consumer demand in that direction.

Educate vs Evangelise

You can convert people to ethical consumerism either by making them better informed (for instance on ingredients, farming techniques, workers' pay and conditions) or by challenging the status quo through emotive framing of the issues.

B2: Tribal Brands

Many strong – iconic – brands are born out of association with a particular type or tribe of users. The ability to recruit and support such core brand communities has been greatly enhanced by the internet, using word of mouth and social networks.

Exclusive vs Inclusive

There are two distinct kinds of tribal brands; some are associated with aspiration, envy, elite or glamorous 'opinion formers', others are 'nice' – associated with empathy and a grassroots following which is open to all.

B3: Change Usage

Companies can have a much bigger impact on their footprint when they collaborate with customers and change their behaviour in line with the green edict to reduce, reuse and recycle.

Switch vs Cut

Two broad forms of consumer behaviour change are commonly pursued – switching, where there is little difference in the habitual behaviour itself, rather a better substitute or approach is inserted, and cutting, when there is a change in habits.

C1: New Business Concepts

Instead of tackling an existing market, it is possible to effectively create a new one, with a much better green footprint and also a different business model and operation. These are not just new products or services; they are redesigning the life-world or culture. Many of these work on web 2.0 principles, even if they have a substantial offline component.

Social Production vs Property

A fascinating development in the modern economy is the interplay of (amateur, enthusiast) prosumers with commercial ventures. Some business models involve both, e.g. Amazon reviews. Others have a transition, e.g. Linux, YouTube. And some are always voluntary, for instance Wikipedia.

C2: Trojan Horse Ideas

This covers all those examples where a radical green innovation can find acceptance through a cultural 'wrapper'. We've seen a similar approach time and again in the IT market. We need these instantly acceptable concepts to overcome people's *greenophobia*.

Tradition vs New Cool

One class of ideas that can find easy acceptance is the cosy and familiar ideas of traditional culture, updated. Alternatively, something can gain support through being 'what everyone else is getting into' – the fashion or 'cool' model.

C3: Challenging Consuming

The ultimate green marketing strategy is to provide attractive and viable alternatives to the current unsustainable patterns of consumption. It's not a case of hair shirt living, but rather inventing better ways of life. Probably happier ones too.

Treasuring vs Sharing

One key approach is getting people to value products and use them for longer. Another is to get people to own less and share/rent instead.

A: Setting New Standards (Green)

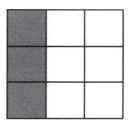

Figure 7 Grid column A

This column is about communicating in a direct way to promote green companies, brand credentials and product benefits. One thing to remember is to keep it as factually true and straightforward as possible. For a company, say what you are actually doing or committing to do. At the brand level, say whose objective external standards you are complying with (e.g. eco-labels) or who you are working with (cause-related). For a product, where possible give people a chance to see, feel, touch the benefits. The other consequence of this is there is no point in doing any marketing of this sort unless you are actually different and better; hence the title 'setting new standards'. The old marketing model of making a brand seem special (when it isn't) simply doesn't work for ethical and environmental issues. It's too important; any overclaim will come back and bite you.

But it's not all about mistrust and restraint. This column of the grid does reflect a newfound public interest in green products and sustainable companies. It was much less certain, even a year ago, that many people would pay more for ethical alternatives (beyond occasional pots of organic yoghurt), or would reject companies (that's probably the right way round to look at it) if their environmental credentials were uncertain. Now that has changed and it's quite hard to read; we are in uncharted territory.

This does mean that if you have a good story, there is a receptive audience. But there are four vitally important issues to cover before we get into the detail of how to use communication to press home an eco-advantage.

GREEN IS A PRINCIPLE, NOT A PROPOSITION

That's why CSR people often use the word 'considered'. It means that all aspects of the products from raw materials, transport, manufacture, other processes, retailing, disposal, the lifetime of the product, the suppliers and so on have to be checked and, where necessary, improved. Those policies are rule based. An example is organic.

Brand strategists will appreciate the difference between communication based upon principles and communication about a proposition. This is *why*, with the company you have to think in terms of 'setting an example' rather than 'selling your green credentials'. It is also why, with products you will often have to find and stress a side effect of the principle (Green & Black's organic Fairtrade chocolate actually tastes really luxuriously good) that is a proposition.

The obvious place to address principles is communicating about the company, not the brand or product. It's the company that sets the rules after all. Many of the high profile recent announcements by M&S, GE, Wal-Mart and others have been statements of principle; the self-imposed rules or policies by which they operate and the overall green objectives which they have set themselves.

But contrary to the impression some ad agencies give – that you can build trust, affinity and loyalty by 'communicating a company's values' in a vague, emotional way – the 'setting new standards' (i.e. tangible, factual) content of these announcements is absolutely vital. It's not what you say you believe in, it's *what you show that you do* which counts. Of course what you do is an enactment of your values. But people simply don't trust either corporations or ads enough to feel that a statement of corporate values in advertising is anything more than empty rhetoric. That's a shame perhaps if you are a trustworthy company, but you are communicating after a long tradition of advertising telling pretty lies to cover up ugly industrial and commercial truths.

If you saw the following statements from two companies, which one would you trust?

- 'The company prides itself on creating healthy, high quality turkeys, maintaining the highest standards of agriculture and bird welfare and meeting all regulations and standards from official bodies.'
- 'We are moving all our fresh turkey, duck and pork to free-range.'

The first one is nicely worded and emotive, but it is just words. Having pride in meeting some 'highest' standards that you set and judge yourself says nothing. The statement only objectively says they work to minimum legal regulations. The second one states a simple accountable policy; meat products will be from free-range farms.

The first statement is from Bernard Matthews, the troubled meat processing company, in the news last year when security footage of two employees playing baseball using live turkeys was leaked to the BBC. And then much more seriously over an avian flu outbreak (the most likely source was thought to be the company importing meat from Hungary) and criticised in a report by government agencies 'for poor hygiene practices at its plant, which may have led to the spread of the disease between holding sheds.'[24] Hardly evidence of 'the highest standards of agriculture and bird welfare' in any objective sense.

The second statement was from the M&S *Plan A* announcement. Only this statement is *setting a new standard*; going further than others in their market, by adopting a specific, objective and accountable policy.

'Green is not a proposition' certainly applies at the product level. It isn't just something an individual will benefit from functionally. It benefits the world as a whole. At the level of product marketing, the best strategy is often to find another benefit, one that reflects the reason why people are buying in the first place. Green & Black's is marketed as a luxury, premium chocolate (which happens to be organic and Fairtrade). It is a moot point whether more people will today buy products on principle, simply because they are looking for ways to act green. But at least to maximise the appeal of green products, this still seems the best approach. There are some products and services, such as eco electricity, which do require people to make the switch on principle, at least as long as it is more expensive than conventional supply. The better way to market these is through a more circuitous approach than selling your benefits to individuals. I signed up with Ecotricity through an *Ecologist* readers' offer, after measuring my carbon footprint, researching the issue on green blogs, talking to several friends and also making the pledge to do so at Pledge Bank. These channels were important because I picked up that Ecotricity and Green Energy are the ones favoured by dark greens, because they are building new supply capacity rather than simply reselling others' renewably sourced energy. Plus, Ecotricity was running a promotion with *The Ecologist*.

Green is not a proposition, but it is even less a viable brand personality or image. Giving something a green image means claiming virtue. Selling and virtue just don't mix. Virtue is something that cannot be claimed, let alone proclaimed. Others can only deduce it from your actions. It's like saying 'trust me'. You can say it, but it is physically impossible to communicate it. Classical image marketing is about giving people impressions of what you are like. It can make your brand look modern or traditional, make it look sexy or sober, brash or refined. These are personality traits. But it cannot easily make you (believed to be) virtuous. That is not yours to claim. And actually claiming piety is often counterproductive. It is seen as a sign that you must have something to hide – inviting suspicion and scrutiny.

Many brands are trying to use green cultural codes – for instance, certain key words or visual images – to suggest their greenness without actually saying it. *Greenwashing* is a term that originated in the anti-corporate movement but there have been examples pointed to by activists in brand consumer marketing too:

- companies describing products as natural, when the products are, in fact, genetically engineered or antibiotic-fed livestock and so on;
- misleading brand names and claims such as the Herbal Essences range, claiming 'a totally organic experience' while being chock full of inorganic chemicals.

I saw an example today – the Fairy Liquid *Naturals* range. They say it's natural because it contains extracts of mint and grapefruit. Unfortunately, the ingredients list on the back reads like a school chemistry lesson. It just has a few natural ingredients added.

Image marketing is selective and tends to exaggerate to make its point; not necessarily lying, but by using all manner of creative devices to make the product or brand seem more special than it actually is. That's what selling means. It is more than just describing. It is motivated by the desire to sell. The use of celebrities, locations, photography, design and other devices conspire to make something like a basic chocolate snack seem like it is part of the lifestyles of the rich and famous. And that is just about okay; it's just a fantasy. And it's often entertaining. But it's *not okay* when it comes to green issues. Just as it is not okay to stretch the truth about medicines or financial risks. When things really matter, we demand good information without spin, hyperbole or exaggeration.

This is just one example of a general point:

GREEN MARKETING MEANS ACTING WITH INTEGRITY

Green issues today also require consumers to think about what they are doing. Many unchallenged habits and assumptions need to be overturned. From an ethical consumer point of view it means thinking about the history and future of what you buy, not just that pleasurable blip as you consume it; where it is from, how it is made and by whom, how it got here, what's in it, what knock-on effects it has, where it will end up and how it will be returned to raw ingredients or reused.

Brand marketers, on the other hand, are very attached to the froth of culture – whims, fashions and appearances. We have good instincts about what we think will *grab* people. But just like the ethical consumer, the ethical marketer must think that bit harder about what he/she is doing. We have to think critically, beyond the surface appearances.

Image branding is showing something from its most flattering aspect. If you'd asked me a year ago where Apple stood in the electronics industry on CSR I'd have guessed – based on their image – they'd have been pretty good. They have a *green-ish* image: Californian, progressive, creative, youthful, cool, anti-establishment, idealist . . . Contrast the image of Apple computers with the fact that in three successive Greenpeace reports they came bottom in the whole electronics industry, over issues like Chinese workers disassembling and salvaging (often toxic) components from their used circuitry and devices. As I write, Apple has made an announcement that it will be implementing much tougher eco policies. It will be severely damaged as a brand if it doesn't soon answer the accusation that behind this idealised brand image façade, it is callous and prepared to let people suffer. It would be a similar shock to when Google (whose motto is 'do no evil') was accused of helping the Chinese authorities to censor websites. The original report in July 2006 by Amnesty was about Google, Yahoo! and Microsoft. But the other two never claimed to be virtuous, so they were soon forgotten. That's an additional peril of image marketing today: a virtuous image of any sort can lead to a crucifixion, should you ever be found less than perfect. You will be judged by the standards that you set.

Such attacks can have very long-term effects on brand value and standing. Nike was once everyone's favourite youth brand. Then it became the brand that *No Logo* activists loved to hate. Now, ten years on it is pretty well reviewed by independent ethical reports. For instance, *The Good Shopping Guide* in 2006 rated Nike positively on 8/10 criteria, and competitors Adidas and Reebok scored worse than Nike. But in the *Ethical Reputation Index* (by the Fraser Consultancy), Nike comes near the bottom of the list as one of the least ethical companies by reputation, along with McDonalds and Shell. Barclays, whose activities in South Africa brought a student boycott 25 years ago, still scores lower than other banks. A good reputation takes ages to build, a moment to lose, and once lost, takes almost forever to rebuild.

Finally, let's consider the arguments by NGOs and similar against greenwashing. It's not just the hypocrisy they are exposing, nor the opportunity to put the screws on big corporates and pressure them for change. They also have some very rational arguments against eco-themed marketing, even if you do have a reasonably clean company and product. They point out that not harming the world ought to be the status quo, a basic requirement of being in business in the 21st century. You don't advertise that your products are free from broken glass. Or that your factory has good basic hygiene. If you are different enough you never need to advertise. If you do have better products and better policies today, then the NGO, the CSR chat room, the ethical consumer guide, the BBC journalist and so on will be the marketing campaign. In today's blogging scene, good green stories get around whether you trumpet your virtue or not.

One of my first forays into big company CSR work was a project on how best to communicate IKEA's environmental and ethical commitments. They had spent twelve years putting their house in order. In many areas they were not only meeting but exceeding any standards in the world; from forestry and transport, to the way they worked with partner factories and influenced their operations. Yet our advice, as far as external communications went, was very simple: 'DON'T!' IKEA decided this was the right advice at the time, and instead we focused on an internal programme. IKEA hardly needed posters to tell people they were a company who could be trusted to do the right thing. Not only could NGOs and other interested parties view all of their information in detail if they wanted, but a number of the NGOs who had worked with IKEA to develop these programmes used it as a case study to show other businesses what could be done.

Lo and behold, in Landor's survey of green brands, IKEA was rated the 7th greenest brand in the US, ahead of GE (at number 9), who spent $90 million on advertising proclaiming their new-found commitment to *Eco Imagination*. And in a recent survey, IKEA was rated the trustworthiest institution in Sweden; 80% said they trusted IKEA, compared to 46% who said they trusted churches and 32% the leading political party.[25] The reason IKEA accepted our advice so readily though, is that it really does have strong company values, one of which is modesty. Its founder once wrote 'glory is in the future'; i.e. being satisfied with present performance is a recipe for complacency.

Companies with good values are usually pretty easy to spot, because these values permeate their operations. They don't need ads. And in fact ads can falsify values; imagine if IKEA did an ad campaign saying 'we're humble'. Boots did for a short while adopt 'Boots cares' as a slogan in its ads (actually it was worse, they said 'who cares?')

The key argument against giving yourself a green image is this: it is the exact opposite of true green marketing. Our challenge is to make radical, challenging green stuff that sets new standards normal (it is not to make normal stuff seem greener).

Enough said about greenwashing. Onto issue three.

YOU MUST BE ABSOLUTELY CERTAIN THAT YOUR BUSINESS CAN AND WILL LIVE UP TO THE STANDARDS YOU SET FOR YOURSELF, IN EVERY FACET OF THE BUSINESS

It's a really important corollary of setting new standards; you are judged by the standards you yourself have declared. BP and Shell get so much flack, not because they are worse than other oil companies (they aren't), but because they suggest they are better. Any exceptions – such as Shell's continued flaring of gas in Nigeria, despite a court order and campaign by Friends of the Earth – cause outcry. Demonstrators at Shell's recent annual general meeting used their advertising green claims as the focus for publicity; FOE even lodged a complaint with advertising standards authorities in some countries.

The biggest blunder in green marketing is to point to one good thing you are doing, as evidence of a general high standard (if this isn't true). Why? Because by setting standards and making such claims, you open yourself up to scrutiny.

The classic example of being hoist by your own green claims was BP. I met Sir John Browne ten years ago when he visited my former agency St Luke's. He impressed us as an inspiring visionary, not at all the sort of 'oil baron' we'd been expecting. And there was his famous speech at Stanford, a moment of inspired leadership; recognising climate change as a major issue facing humanity, on behalf of a major oil corporation.

They had a good story to tell. Most carbon emissions from oil come from the extraction, piping and transporting, not its end use. By simply blocking holes in pipelines, BP was able to make huge strides in the 1990s, beating its targets on reducing carbon emissions. This was a beautiful coincidence because it also saved the company a fortune in lost oil. And as well as drastically cutting emissions, stopping leaks also meant stopping the environmental damage associated with oil spills. According to business authors, Esty and Winston,[26] this 'hunt for carbon' programme, as it was known internally, cost BP $20m and generated shareholder value of $1.5B. BP was also investing heavily (certainly compared to any immediate return) in alternative energy sources. This was a sensible move if it wanted to be in business as an energy company in the long term. Whereas others – notably Exxon – were still fighting to defend the view that climate change wasn't even a problem, funding a network of climate change denying think tanks in a move which was apparently modelled closely on the tactics of the tobacco industry. I am not saying BP is in any way perfect. Activists have a long list of quarrels with BP, and 'being an oil company' is only one of them. But arguably during John Browne's tenure (at least before the disastrous events in Texas which brought it to a close), it had strong claims to be setting standards for the rest of its industry to follow.

But 'Beyond Petroleum', perhaps the most famous example of greenwashing, was still a disaster. It backfired, became a focus of criticism, not support. And the problem was mostly – in my view – taking a complex sustainability programme and *consumerising* it into a branded green message and putting this into advertising. An article by Cait Murphy in *Fortune* interviewed BP's regional president, Bob Malone, who said, 'The oil business has a negative reputation. We are trying to say that there are different kinds of oil companies.' Malone conceded that BP was 'decades away' from *actually* being beyond petroleum. But unfortunately, its simplistic advertising had lost all of this in translation, leading to a claim that the journalist described as like saying *Fortune* was 'beyond words'!

The conclusion couldn't be clearer. The company had a reasonably good story, but blew it by making it a *simplistic green advertising slogan*. Marketing always focuses on the most attractive features of a product or company. But when claiming political virtue, it has to apply to *all* the company's operations, not just those highlighted by marketing. *Greenwashing* became the popular term for this manoeuvre – and BP became the prime example always cited. But it's just common sense. You can't put a lettuce in the window of a butcher's shop and declare that you are now 'turning vegetarian'! And how many big companies are ever *that* clean in every single detail? You have to be incredibly sure, examine yourself from every possible angle.

Accuracy is everything. I am not advocating that companies never talk about their vision. It is fine for Sky and M&S to have told us they are working towards big objectives. You just need to say that. Saying 'we're decades away from really getting beyond petroleum, but *at least we're trying*' would have been fine. It's not a snappy slogan playing with the letters B and P, but then Greenpeace's response was to dub the company *Burning Planet*. I believe the original incarnation of the thought as an internal mantra was *Positive Energy*. Shell's advertising line these days is *Real Energy*, although it has to be noted that Friends of the Earth has submitted official complaints to advertising standards bodies in three countries where these commercials are shown.

There is one additional thing which marketing people need to pay particular attention to: beware your campaign saying one thing but your choice of media saying another. HSBC was recently criticised in the USA for sending out a bulky, packaging and transport intensive 'green pack' by direct mail. The aim was to give customers ways to help the environment. But the use of direct mail for this was a bit of an own goal.

Media schedules are likely to be under increasing scrutiny in future. Some brands, such as Aveda, have long looked at the environmental impact of their printing and so on. A service called Noughtilus has been launched in the UK, allowing marketers to assess their mix of channels and activities from an environmental cost perspective: each activity is entered, along with relevant details about the volume of activity and the resources used (e.g. % recycled content). You can then assess the overall impact, track improvements over time, set Key Performance Indicators and so on.

It will be interesting to see what effect this sort of information has over time. You have to suspect that direct mail will look particularly vulnerable. But decisions over where and how to shoot commercials and so on may come under scrutiny too. It may look odd in future to fly a large film crew to somewhere exotic like Patagonia or Brunei to shoot a commercial about your commitment to protecting the environment. But that's exactly what GE and Shell have done in the last year. We have already seen celebrities committed to the environment (such as Princes Charles) questioned over their flying habits. Why not commercials? Also, I would have guessed that digital media would be greener than any other possible alternative. But it depends how processing and hosting intensive they are. A blogger recently calculated that the average Second Life avatar (i.e. that user's proportional share of the system's 4000 servers) uses electricity at the same rate as the average Brazilian does.[27]

Issue number four addresses the difficulty of the whole subject:

SUSTAINABILITY IS A COMPLEX MOVING TARGET

Sustainability is complex. More precisely it is systemic. The decisions that companies make, if they are genuinely to improve the situation, have to take into account numerous secondary factors and unintended consequences. In 1996, when a picture of a 12-year-old assembling a Nike football in Pakistan appeared in *Life* magazine, it started a chain reaction. Within weeks, protestors were waving this picture on placards outside Nike stores in the USA. But when Nike and Adidas pulled manufacturing of footballs out of Pakistan, reports showed 'the result: tens of thousands of Pakistanis were again unemployed. According to UPI, mean family income in Pakistan fell by more than 20%.'[28] Nike then resumed manufacturing in the region, but set up a monitoring system, a pioneering partnership with civic, factory owning and labour organisations. But in 2007, Nike announced that it is once again to quit the region, as child labour has proved impossible to prevent. Once again, thousands of jobs will go. Many of the women who lost their jobs in sweatshops went into either neighbouring sweatshop factories or prostitution or begging. I am not saying that it is not possible to make improvements, nor that companies should accept sweatshop conditions and pay in their supply chains. There has never been any justification for accepting practices in cheaper factories abroad which would cause outrage (and would be illegal) in your home country. But I am saying it is like an ecosystem in itself, in that simple actions often have complex effects.

What's more, CSR is incredibly detailed. A typical exercise would involve tracing every ingredient through every process. When you get an FSC certificate it doesn't just say the forest was well managed, it looks at every step in transportation, labour, inks and so on. HSBC produces such large volumes of corporate social responsibility information in its report that it is said (if printed) to be too heavy for one person alone to lift!

It's fine to keep the detail for technical experts in NGOs and similar. Obviously what consumers want to know is that things at the end of the day are 'okay'. But it is important that in keeping it simple, marketing people don't falsify what is being done. Ad people are usually looking for the one simple proposition. The truth is rather that, to the best of current knowledge and working within practical and commercial constraints, a company will have made thousands of tiny related changes. When I worked with IKEA's reporting, the issues varied from making sure every factory had a fire extinguisher, to complex rethinking of the logistics – what was made, where and how it was shipped.

If that wasn't complicated enough, it is also a constantly *moving* set of standards, for several reasons:

- We have to progressively reduce the impact. It is not a matter of making a few reforms and sitting back. It is a matter of making new progress every year, starting with the easy stuff, but not stopping there.
- Things get more serious every time we look at them. For instance, comparing the IPCC model predictions with what has actually happened since 1990, we find that the actual changes are at the upper end of those predictions. Also, key indicators like China's total emissions appear to have moved faster than expected. This means that our targets (e.g. Kyoto) are already known to be too low.
- We keep learning and changing our view on what might help. For instance, biofuels and carbon offsetting were both greeted enthusiastically, but are now both controversial, contested and (as far as some NGOs go) frowned upon.
- Once you set a standard, others will catch up. This year's big announcement is next year's common practice. You need to move on to new targets if you want to stay in position as one of the leaders of the industry and hence a trusted choice.

I suspect this is why the Anya Hindmarch *I'm not a plastic bag* got caught out. In the time it took to develop from initial concept to launch, views on organic cotton and Fairtrade had hardened. This is now the sort of thing supermarkets *would* be expected to sell. M&S have sold organic cotton goods for a year now. Putting forward a bag, which claimed virtue but wasn't up with current standards, led to a backlash. The headline on one blog read, 'I'm not an ethical shopping bag'. The national newspapers took up the story and some of the benefit both to Sainsbury's and the cause of promoting an alternative people would carry with pride was undone. I think it's a shame, although I understand the concern; organic cotton helps farmers become self-sufficient as well as reducing the pesticides used, which is a major health issue in the developing world. The bag was arguably only ever a 'poster campaign' and publicity stunt: 20000 bags compared to the 10 billion plastic bags used in the UK every year. Plus, it is still better than the plastic alternatives. We use cotton bags that we have owned for nearly ten years and you can bet those aren't organic. But it stands as an example of the imperative need to ensure every detail is considered if you are going to set new standards publicly.

This volatility is a situation which business knows all too well from working with IT, which is also complex and fast changing in its details and also its strategic implications. As a result, fortune *favours the vague*! Business strategy changes way too far and fast to make five- or ten-year permanent commitments to one particular course (which is what a big corporate brand ad idea tends to do for you). IBM in 1990 was an ailing corporate computing giant. It tried and to a large extent succeeded in conveying a new dynamism across the 1990s. But it also saddled itself with a brand idea: *e-business*. Very clever-sounding (although a tad passé) in 1998. Less clever looking, by late 2001 (the dotcom crash). Then increasingly irrelevant as IBM became a consultancy, buying PwC in 2002 and selling its PC manufacturing business to Lenovo in 2004. By this time, IBM's proposition was that it delivered solutions to business problems.

Brand ideas take three to five years just to fully bed in, and once you establish them, take years to reshape. Volvo has been trying to convince us for over a decade that it is sexy (rather than safe). Business models often change faster; most giant corporations have had to learn to be nimble. The best kind of branding for a dynamic or changing business is a strong identity, yet a bit of blank canvas. Google is simply the leading internet company. It is obviously known for search. But that's nothing against Gmail, or Blogger.com or Google books, or buying YouTube or doing citywide wi-fi in San Francisco, or whatever they think of next. The same with Amazon. It didn't have to be just a leading book etailer, because they kept it broad. The main reason these brands are so flexible is that they aren't defined by any ad idea. Old-fashioned brand marketing defines you. That used to be seen as a strength, but these days that's something you could do without. It's the equivalent of typecasting for actors. It limits your options.

The same is very true for sustainability. Imagine if a parcel delivery company made a big thing about going 100% biofuel. The brand might well be left up a blind alley. Whereas, with Plan A, M&S is committed to a comprehensive plan of measures, of which transport is one part that easily could be modified in the light of new knowledge.

And that brings us on to the other part of that statement; sustainability is a *target*. It's a subtle notion, but when we are choosing a good company to purchase from, we should be looking at it like a shareholder would; based upon its future plans, not just current position. M&S and Sky are telling us they *will* go carbon neutral over the next five years. If we support them, their reductions will have a bigger impact on the overall situation. That's why the Carbon Trust labelling scheme currently being trialled is predicated on awarding those who have good commitments for the next two years. We need to buy their progress, hitching a ride on that for the sake of the overall numbers.

Of course the absolute figures matter too. But if two brands were about the same at the start, it's the reducer who would be the best bet, from a climate change point of view. It's different with ethical issues. Here, it's about an acceptable policy – for instance, factory safety, unionisation, pay and conditions, animal welfare, (anti) child labour – and then not buying anything that doesn't comply. To some extent you could say that climate change innovation is positive, whereas ethical social issues are 'not negative'. Another way to think about it is this:

- Carbon reduction purchasing is like *dieting*. And people do buy diet foods, as well as cutting down how much they eat and habits like no eating between meals.
- Ethical purchasing is more like *Halal*; consuming some things which have best practice built in, as well as avoiding or boycotting certain 'bad' things.

But the branding of Fairtrade does show how you can put a positive interpretation on ethical factors too.

Some of the debate between sustainability and business people could be due to which out of environmental and ethical considerations you see as primary. They are quite different things; for instance, practical vs moral. It's impractical to use a big car for small journeys, and it's just common sense that it is bad for the air quality, global warming and so on. We can't live without using resources, but we need to be more prudent, judge which is essential, prioritise. But wearing a fur coat is seen as immoral; ignoring the cruelty to animals, which are raised for fur. Some cars may come to be seen as like fur coats too, incidentally. Not because they are cruel to sheet metal, but because they are irresponsible nonetheless!

The clean tech movement in business is purely a climate and efficiency thing. CSR people preach carbon reduction too, but my feeling is that many practitioners' hearts are in quality of life and human rights. Just as the greens had a strong cultural mindset (nature = religion) before the global warming data came to light within the last ten years. Politically, these issues are entirely con-nected, for instance, the worst effects of our emissions will be felt in Africa. But in consumer and business terms, they are quite dif-ferent to tackle, you need to do both but they are almost opposites in some ways; one is an attempt to avert a (near) 'end of the world scenario', one is attempting to redress existing injustice and suffering.

Taking all these points together, traditional image marketing and sustainability are a disastrous combination. I can certainly see why many clients are talking to new sustainable marketing specialists, rather than their regular ad agencies, about this sort of brief. What is required anyway is often not 'big ideas' but PR, word of mouth, events, communities, partnerships and so on; ones which are as well considered as the rest of your CSR pro-gramme. You do need to engage people, grab their interest, even spark their enthusiasm. But you can't do that at the expense of getting things right.

That's not to say advertising can't play a role. There is a place for a mix of ways of communicating and getting ideas into circula-tion. Advertising is great for high profile announcements. It's a punchy place to put out key messages, to underline your agenda. It's the image advertising models you need to ditch.

To reiterate:

- green is not a proposition, it's a principle;
- green marketing means acting with integrity;
- you have to check the substance is all there – no exceptions to your new rules;
- sustainability is a complex moving target.

Above all, you need to apply higher standards of truthfulness. If you stick to the truth (including aspects of the truth where you are putting things, that weren't great before, right) then you can't go too far wrong.

A1: Set an Example

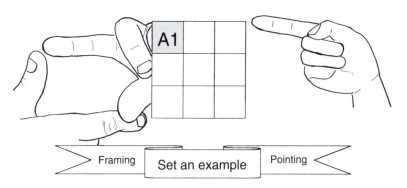

Figure 8 Grid A1

This is a tough one. Should you communicate about your CSR commitments at all? Broadly, there are three views and they align (roughly but convincingly, due to both corporate culture and consumer receptiveness) with distinct country cultures:

- *if you've got it, flaunt it*: (e.g. GE) – America;
- *it's important people see you are doing your bit* (e.g. M&S) – UK;
- *do the work and keep quiet about it* (e.g. IKEA) – Scandinavia.

Many corporations have been rushing to share their plans to go carbon neutral. In America, carbon offsetting has been all the rage, allowing corporations to rush their green credentials and even promotional offers (free offsetting with every PC or flight) to market. In the UK, the emphasis has been on getting solid work done and reporting this. In Sweden, corporations such as Tetrapak have been carbon neutral (at least) since 2003, but don't want to talk about it because there are no agreed external objective standards, and because they see green as being about 'less harm' (and a natural responsible activity) rather than a virtue to make a song and dance about.

I've got a lot of time for the Swedish view. It just seems safer (it doesn't tempt fate with future revelations and events, or invite scrutiny) as well as more authentic. But the scene has changed so fast in the last year, I can well understand the case for not wanting to seem left behind, which is the prevailing opinion in the UK at the moment. I do struggle with the full-on ethical exuberance of the United States.

But let's put our doubts and reservations to one side. What is relevant and required will be specific to your industry situation and what your competitors are up to. The starting point for this section is: assume that some action *is* warranted – how best to do it?

Greg Nugent at Eurostar made an interesting point when I was quizzing him about their carbon reduction marketing initiative. He said the fact that Eurostar was always in the political spotlight was a very good base to build on. They knew they would face questions, just like they do if their track turns out to cost more than expected, or the Queen gets stuck in the tunnel. They were used to checking things from all angles. They treated it like a political policy launch, and as a result did a thorough job, both on the substance of the programme and also the communications (they had Tony Juniper, Jonathon Porritt *and* Stuart Rose all extolling the company's initiative). Nugent told me his CEO had been ruthless about getting every facet green enough before they could communicate their own carbon reduction plan. At the outset they were already ten times greener (in carbon emissions) than flying. But they went out of their way to look at any detail that was less admirable and put it right.

One thing they got right was being 'on message'. Carbon offsetting today is out of favour with NGOs, you have to do some real work. And so what the press release pointed to was setting a new exacting standard in carbon reduction, by going that extra mile to reduce carbon emissions in every way possible, before having recourse to a carbon offset for the rest. They looked at reducing power use in the trains, buying electricity from better sources, making better use of capacity and even little extras like paperless ticketing. This is a good place to start thinking about *why* corporates are all over the newspapers setting standards. It's very nice of them isn't it? Far from it (although Eurostar is a nice company as far as I know, and very proud of what it is doing with carbon emissions). It is also bitingly strategic. Here's the punch line, delivered by one of its advocates:

> Friends of the Earth executive director Tony Juniper said: 'It's great news that Eurostar is leading the way in the travel industry with its initiative to cut passengers' carbon emissions by actually making a real reduction rather than just offsetting. It's easy for travellers to go green by opting for the train instead of taking short-haul flights. If all the passengers who currently fly between London, Paris and Brussels went by train instead of plane, it would cut CO_2 emissions by over 200000 tonnes – more than the annual CO_2 emissions from all homes in Oxford.' (Eurostar press release, 17/4/07)

According to a BBC World/Synnovate[29] survey earlier this year, 28% of those questioned (14220 respondents in 21 countries) said they were changing travel plans due to concerns about climate change. You can bet lots of these are going to be taking the train into Europe in future. This could easily become one of the standard 'ten things you can do'; several such lists already mention reducing flying.

To be fair, Europe also appears to be leading on this issue as far as the flying industries are concerned. By way of contrast, I was incredulous last week when someone told me about a Boeing presentation they went to in Asia, where the airline played down the threat climate change poses to its industry, citing the reliance of the world economy on air freight and so on. Boeing, after all, makes a big play about its fuel-efficient Dreamliner 787s. Branson just bought 15 of these jets and announced Virgin was working with Boeing and GE on a biofuel version. The 787 has been Boeing's most successful aircraft ever, with 444 sold in just the last three years. It ought to be the Toyota of its industry, yet it appears to be taking an Exxon line, playing down climate change as an issue and being one of the few companies who refused to respond to an inquiry by the Carbon Disclosure Project group of investors, who collectively hold assets of $10billion, including 10% of Boeing stock (even Exxon responded to this). It's not the role of this book to criticise backward corporations, but you have to wonder if the aviation industry is inviting the very problems that the car industry has been quite successful in avoiding. I can understand that big proud corporations struggle to accept criticism. But again and again we have seen that it's the proud ones, the ones that refuse to engage or listen, who suffer the most reputation damage. If they simply set out a progressive agenda, the debate would move on. People may fly less in future. On the other hand, the low-cost airlines who destroyed the whole industry's margins will be the first casualty if so. High fuel prices might even be a good thing. As things get expensive, people are less wasteful with them. All we want is companies who share responsibility and offer solutions. It does seem that the US air industry is on a different flight plan to the rest of us. A UK government minister recently described the US aviation industry as 'irresponsible.' A report by Sabre Airline Solutions, an airlines services consultancy, asked the leaders of 197 airlines around the world about their views on a range of issues. Only 3 out of 62 North American airlines surveyed thought environmental concerns were 'a significant challenge' in future. Whereas almost half the executives in Europe, Asia and Africa described it as a top three challenge they already faced this year.[30]

The UK air industry, led by Branson, is to launch a campaign shortly. They are dropping the (contested) 'we're only 3% of emissions' line. Instead, they are accepting that it is a concern and announcing the action that's been taken; like moving to more efficient planes and changing schedules to ensure planes are never empty. According to a spokesman from Virgin Atlantic: 'Where there is a train alternative, customers are taking it. On long haul, customers want to know about offsetting their flights and how we can contribute in other ways.'

Meanwhile, the activists are sharpening their bayonets. Greenpeace has targeted domestic flying wherever there is a rail alternative available between the same two cities. They protested early in 2007 against BA opening a new route between Gatwick and Newquay. Greenpeace took full-page advertisements in the newspapers and sent activists into the airport; offering passengers queuing for the inaugural flight the chance to swap their BA tickets for train tickets. Flying was also made an issue in the UK council elections of April 2007, with fake advertisements for 'Spurt-Aviation.com' featuring a humorously un-pc character Sir Montgomery Cecil asking people to vote Labour as the party who most supported the aviation industry, and the slogan 'Sod It, Let's Fly'!

Eurostar's position in all this is to seize upon what a recent business strategy book (*Green to Gold*, by Esty and Winston) dealing with sustainability issues calls 'eco-advantage'. The airline industry is finally about to respond and set a positive agenda. But you can see what a well-timed announcement Eurostar has made, with the climate change agenda reaching boiling point in early to mid 2007. I also heard from someone working with the UK tourism industry that they are feeling fairly jubilant; presumably they believe the domestic increases will outweigh potential losses in overseas visitors.

Change brings opportunity. If the world decides to eat less saturated fat, butter does worse and olive oil does better, and the companies who sell 'yellow fats' benefit or are devastated as a result, depending on their starting point position but also their agility. Branson's billions to be invested in alternative energy could, apart from anything else, be seen as the biggest hedge by a (travel) brand in history. He is reported to be a personal convert on the issue anyway, but also serves as a shining example of a business strategist who only sees opportunity with change and lumbering competitors.

Branson has always been a 'people's champion'. But some of the recent corporate announcements are just jaw dropping, because they represent the conversion of figures that were far from being seen in this way, to the eco cause. The Murdoch family is a case in point. BSkyB has been trailblazing on this issue and we'll cover its programme later in the book, under educating customers. But now the whole Murdoch empire is following suit and Murdoch senior has declared for the cause:

> 'I've become more enthusiastic day by day. I don't think there's any question of my conviction on this issue – I've come to feel it very strongly. The more I've looked into it, the more I've been able to see what we can do, not just from an operations standpoint but by subtly introducing [the climate issue] into our content.'[31]

What Murdoch is planning (and his stated reasons) are as follows:

- News Corp moving to carbon neutral operations within three years, justified both on grounds of operation efficiency and also morale and attracting talent;
- more eco-content throughout their many media, which will offer advertising opportunities as whole industries (like cars on fuel efficiency) want to proclaim their latest products and initiatives;
- they have already opened a climate channel on MySpace, called *OurPlanet* (which has gained 62 000 friends in the network within two weeks) and plan to seed eco storylines and products into sitcoms and so forth. Fox will become a home to more climate change content (whereas in the past it has provided a home to notable climate change sceptics like Sean Hannity);
- in future, Murdoch will not donate to politicians who oppose action on climate change and now drives a hybrid Lexus;
- he is adamant that George Bush now (at least privately) has seen the light too; if so, it's one of the sad features of sending a book to be published that so many of the more interesting stories this year are probably yet to be written.

It's a significant conversion and has that sort of quasi-religious feel. I think it's also very significant that he gave an interview on *Grist*, a heartland green blog, and was welcomed with open arms.

I've heard of a number of other global media groups who are aiming to be 'the home of green advertising'. Yahoo! has an early lead, starting with its 2006 *18seconds.org* campaign to get America to switch to CFL light bulbs (18 seconds being how long it takes to change a light bulb). In May 2007, they launched the *Yahoo! Green* site that, among other things, features blogging by Amory Lovins (author of *Natural Capitalism*). And it has launched a competition to find the greenest city in the USA based on how many people sign up to about 30 pledges in different locations. The winning city will get a fleet of hybrid taxis and each participant gets a free CFL light bulb. They launched this initiative in Times Square, alongside Global Green and an obligatory Hollywood star (Matt Dillon). The only slight shame was that the hybrid taxis, some of which Yahoo! already donated to the city of New York, are Ford Escape hybrids; lumbering SUVs which claim an average of 34mpg and which an independent report claimed are only 2mpg better than a normal Escape SUV on the freeway. In London, the hybrid taxi company *Green Tomatoes* has used Prius cars – much better on fuel efficiency. The legroom in a US yellow taxi is pretty nonexistent anyway, why move to a car which is halfway to a monster truck and is designed to drive up a mountain? Mine wasn't the only blog to raise an eyebrow about this decision, and it's a shame, because most seemed to think overall it was an exciting move by Yahoo!, which is hardly a major polluter or resource hog in the first place.

The religious right in America are also waking up to the climate change agenda, and I find their take on the spirituality of living less materialistic and more spiritual/natural lives intuitive and quite compelling; it's *Puritanism the Remake*, via Walt Whitman. Politically in the US this is probably the most significant development on the road from superpower in denial, to eco-leadership. Biofuels protests in Brazil aside, you sort of know that when the US decides to go for it, it is going to lead on the innovation ('clean tech') front. It's what they do.

The reformed character (like Murdoch) is a potent cultural myth and this naturally links with testifying; setting an example to others. Many doing corporate communications on this issue would do well to learn from this. In religious movements, penitent sinners or unbelievers who are 'born again' are usually welcome. But how should they behave? They must be penitent indeed:

- having a provisional status, on probation;
- acknowledging that they are a convert (not a lifelong saint);
- talking about how and why they have seen the light;
- being humble and human about it;
- testifying to the truths they now 'get';
- acting as an example to others, to repent their sinful ways.

What this involves is abasing the ego; admitting that you were previously in the dark and now have seen the light. It is submitting to the greater goodness and wisdom of the faith. Penitents might go barefoot, live on the streets, wear ashes or in other ways humble themselves. In return they are welcomed with open arms, not rejected for past misdeeds. Everyone deserves a second chance. Let he who is blameless cast the first stone.

It's almost unfair – the *prodigal son* story – because we seem to love those who come into the fold even more than those who were faithful all along. In a recent book by the current pope, he refers to this parable as the story of *a good father* (we focus on the good son/ bad son, but actually the real learning is through the attitude of the parent). It makes total sense, whether you are tackling sin or climate change, it's sinners repenting who make a much bigger difference, rather than preaching to the converted. Sites like *Grist* are enthusiastic about declarations by GE, Wal-Mart and Murdoch.

So what's the worst thing a penitent could do? Boast about their newfound virtue. Sing loudest in the choir. Wear bright conspicuous

Sunday finest. Hide their past. Keep a proud bearing and pretend they had always been in the right. Sound familiar? The words corporate and pride sit rather too well together. How many corporations will admit that they have been wrong in the past? ('Jesus!!!' says the legal counsel. 'What if they sue?') Actually there are a number of corporations on the CSR circuit that you don't see making such a song and dance of their virtue in the public domain. Eventually it all comes out in their behaviour anyway, and it's perhaps more the European way. I met representatives of Philips at a *Long Now* environmental conference in 2002, talking about extending the life of consumer products. Back then it was quite a brave move and there was a mixed reaction in the crowd of environmentalists, artists and green-leaning designers. But today they are leading the way, calling for regulators in the USA to ban incandescent bulbs and working on better CFLs (less mercury) and also LED technology, which is generally thought to be the best long-term solution. Incandescents account for 95% of Philips global sales now, so it's not a decision they will have taken lightly! But it has endeared them to every green commentator in the world and paves the way for Philips to take a lead in smart/eco home living and hence in electronics overall – it could be the new Sony.

If you find this talk of religious conversion fanciful, you can still take a very important lesson from the successful corporate conversions: *modesty is the best policy*. Yes, talk in very positive, emphatic terms about your actions. But don't paint yourself as a saint. That's where you will get in trouble, sooner (accusations of greenwash) or later (a counter-story which is ten times worse because of the claims to virtue).

The way to communicate on these issues in my view is as follows;

1. Acknowledge the situation is new, explain why and how you are changing.

2. Get the substance right, be very concrete and transparent about how you report it.
3. Make sure all your own people are involved first, enthused, on board.
4. Report humbly on progress (rather than claiming to be instantly perfect).
5. Speak when asked questions, be interviewed, get into dialogues.
6. Set out some ambitious tough standards; ones that are hard for others to follow.
7. Let others (media, NGOs) tell the story.

Two other policy announcements we will look at in some detail in this section are GE and M&S. In some ways they look quite similar; big company makes big carbon emissions and innovation commitments. Both are setting a new standard for others to follow if they can. Both are highly strategic from a commercial point of view. But they are subtly different. One is framing, the other is pointing.

The Framing Approach

There are two key political strategies when it comes to presenting policy which involve framing:

1. Giving a progressive policy a familiar, intuitive and accessible frame (for example, Margaret Thatcher selling monetarism as 'kitchen economics').
2. Giving something you want to oppose an alien, scary and threatening frame (for example, the GM foods protests against 'Frankenstein foods').

The notion of a *frame* in this context comes from my favourite cognitive psychologist (readers of *After Image* will recall) George

Lakoff, linguistics professor at UC Berkeley. In the last couple of years, Lakoff has become a media celebrity in the USA, largely as a result of his bestselling book *Don't Think of an Elephant*[32] and the follow-up DVD *How Democrats and Progressives Can Win: Solutions From George Lakoff*.

'Progressives are constantly put in positions where they are expected to respond to conservative arguments,' Lakoff wrote. 'But because conservatives have commandeered so much of the language, progressives are often put on the defensive with little or nothing to say in response. We understand the world in terms of frames, in terms of conceptual structures and if the facts don't fit the frame, the facts . . . (they) bounce off.' Lakoff advised the framing of liberal arguments using words like *accountability*, *responsibility* and *common sense*. To counter the Republican arguments which would so often be built around concepts like *defence* and *freedom*. 'Once your frame is accepted into the discourse, everything you say is just common sense. Why? Because that's what common sense is: reasoning within a commonplace, accepted frame.'[33]

Just like politicians, businesses that want to galvanise public interest and support need to frame their ideas well. The framing of the M&S Plan A announcement, for instance, was straight out of political rhetoric:

'Plan A: because there is no Plan B.'

Others have talked about commitments, about carbon neutrality, about responsibility. M&S do something different; they talk about a *Plan of Action*. Not a big claim of virtue, nor a pretence that Stuart Rose is the new Anita Roddick. But rather a portrayal of a programme of heroic effort. It's deceptively simple, but brilliant in my view. This programme is also deeply strategic for the company. You have to see this in the context of an overall revival since 2004 under the leadership of Stuart Rose. M&S is once again the retailer that has exactly caught the mood and aspirations of middle England.

Other supermarkets may have some similar items, but M&S is once again that little bit special: 'it's not just food, it's M&S food' and so on. Even so, it's not just about corporate image. M&S setting standards for UK retailing to follow on sustainability grounds seems to have proved very successful in commercial terms. Citibank analysts claimed that *Look Behind the Label* was one of the most successful marketing campaigns in the company's history, and established a six-month lead over the supermarkets on environmental and ethical credentials. Plus, it has brought a lot of product news and interest into the stores.

What you are looking for with a frame is THE STORY: this company is doing X because Y. It should feel like a dramatic outbreak of common sense.

Sky and News Corps's story is that – now they are committed to tackling climate change – as media owners they have the power and creativity to influence and educate viewers (whose footprint according to Rupert Murdoch is '10000 times bigger than ours'). Hence BSkyB's *The Bigger Picture* campaign.

Too many people treat company branding as though it was product branding. Consumers weren't born yesterday and neither was your company. The right framework is a narrative, which takes proper account of the history, has leading actors and a future plan, and which preferably has a deeply stirring archetypal form (of which *penitent sinner* and *prodigal son* are just two examples). I don't mean what consultants call *story telling*. This simply means that you frame your strategy with human examples rather than just numbers. What I mean by stories is dramatic human narrative structures; a coherent pattern in how companies act (as opposed to what they say). It goes back to the stories people used to make sense of the history and identity of their tribe in their oral traditions. Similar archetypal stories animate our feelings about companies. The company whose narcissistic leaders *fly too close to the sun* will probably crash. The company that engages in *scapegoating* will never find peace (it's a cycle, like revenge). The company with *a noble quest* (the vision and mission statement) will tend to inspire more heroic employee efforts. Organisations in their raw bureaucratic, institutional form baffle people as much as the inner workings of their computer. People only intuitively grasp things that are this complex through stories. These stories are vital to company success or failure; they become self-fulfilling. The story which many a company now wants to weave about being a *born again true environmental believer* is a compelling one; a story of redemption.

What's fascinating in times of disruptive change is how dramatically your story can be rewritten. It was the same with the internet. The biggest companies in the world like GE and Microsoft transformed their reputation for agility by addressing the entrepreneurial dynamism of the new economy. Microsoft has been quiet on corporate responsibility; perhaps Gates's pursuit of philanthropy through the *Gates Foundation* has been splitting off the 'doing good' function. But I can't imagine it will leave it at that; the company known within some IT circles as 'the evil empire', the company that struggles with piracy in China and so on, has a lot to gain by setting out a different account of its role in society and the importance of buying the real thing. Also, it is one of the world's biggest companies, and it owes it to us.

The Pointing Approach

GE has a framing idea too; it is all about its flair for ingenuity – the company whose founder Thomas Edison after all invented the light bulb – being applied to the challenge of sustainability. But the substance of its announcement was all about pointing to good examples; 30 key existing *Ecoimagination* products (growing from $6Billion to $20Billion), investing $1.5Billion in new research into clean tech, a 30% greenhouse gas intensity reduction target in the first three years to 2008. The 'intensity' point relates to the fact that they expect their business to grow substantially especially in these areas, so their emissions output needs to be measured relative to their overall throughput.

GE is far from being entirely philanthropic on this issue. It is aiming to put competitors out of contention by forcing the pace of US regulation in its key industrial product sectors, like coal-fired power stations and locomotives. It's also the right thing to do for the good of the planet, to tackle the problems imaginatively, at the fastest pace imaginable. But it plots a path of steep growth for GE as the company that could lead this.

GE *Ecoimagination* is very much a slogan. I'm not personally a big fan. I think it slightly trivialises something that could have been positioned as the biggest clean up since Roman town planning. But politicians do often use similarly clumsy sound bites to nail their policy concepts. I am prepared to admit that UK and American sensibilities are different though. The phrase has had a positive reception in the US media. The BBC journalist who picked up the story on the other hand referred to the new slogan repeatedly as 'Ecomagination (ugh!)'. The substance of the GE announcement is clever in claiming prowess rather than virtue, incidentally. Also it doesn't say 'we've cracked it' it says 'we're working on it'. The TV ads they produced were a bit iffy, if you ask me. But those are part of a package and many party political broadcasts are equally senti-mental and overbearing.

This campaign was reported in a fairly supportive way on the green news sites like Grist and Treehugger. Although they did add a few notes of caution over the fact that somehow nuclear power was never mentioned (whereas elsewhere GE have claimed it is a key sustainable energy source) and nor was the Hudson river (toxic chemical dumping) controversy, which GE still refuses to apologise for. As I write, Jeffrey Immelt, the CEO, is just about to conduct a live online Q&A broadcast, answering questions posted on YouTube on *Ecoimagination* to mark its second anniversary. This reinforces the suggestion that they know all about the power of winning round the green opinion formers, who in turn put pressure on regulators. But they make it crystal clear in their presentations (as opposed to their sentimentalised public TV ads and online films, narrated by Kevin Bacon) that they are doing this for business reasons. CEO Immelt has said in interviews they are doing it 'not because it is trendy or moral but because it will accelerate economic growth.' Greener technologies will grow and the competitors who don't meet tough regulatory standards may well be edged out of markets.

The thing that makes the GE programme compelling is the concrete examples; the products they are making. In *After Image* I looked at the cognitive psychology behind why examples are so powerful. We often do think with concrete examples in mind (if I say 'tree' you will have a picture in your head of a specific type of tree – probably oak if you are English, fir for a Swede). With the GE announcement, we are being given similar mental pictures. The first thing you see when you go on the website is a picture of an eco-efficient jet engine.

Contrast this with BASF and DuPont. If you read the green blogs and comment sites, these are the companies people REALLY get excited about. GE has set a target of reducing future emissions by 1%; this is said to be ambitious because it will very slightly reduce its footprint while growing in sales. DuPont, on the other hand, is aiming to be carbon (and in fact environmental-) neutral and has cut greenhouse gas emissions by 75% since 1990. BASF is working on a further 10% greenhouse gas reduction and 40% pollution reduction by 2012. And it has designed an amazing award-winning near-zero energy house ('*Passivhaus*'), which is 80% more energy efficient; so much so that it actually doesn't need a central heating system, it recycles heat from bulbs, cooking and hot water. Even George Monbiot, one of the stauncher anti-corporate figures, has written enthusiastically about this house.

Because of their hybrid locomotives, their cleaner coal power stations and so on, with GE we feel that we know what they are up to because we have examples in mind.

Outside the heaviest chemical industry, surprising new converts have been joining the 'church of climate change'. Perhaps the most surprising to some was Wal-Mart. Again, they have taken the pointing route, focusing on specific products and actions; with a package of new measures including less packaging and use of fossil fuel, more organic food and green stores, a billion fluorescent light bulbs and even trialling both growing weather-resistant cacti like shrubs and placing solar energy panels on their store roofs.

Compare and Contrast

Pointing and framing come straight from the psychology of human information processing; we think both in broad categories and specific examples. A general quality plus a specific list of unique features is a natural way to report something that is innovative in the public space (it is the unit of school history teaching; the royal dynasties vs the list of events and dates).

For instance, the Cadbury family:

- (framing) built their business on Quaker moral values;
- (pointing) were the first to introduce half-day work on Saturday, factory closure on bank holidays, elected councils representing workers' interests, worker education. Their factories had kitchens, gardens, sporting facilities. They later introduced medical and dental services and an employee pension fund. Cadbury also campaigned on social issues and animal welfare.

Many do a bit of both; it's more a matter of thinking about what your primary message is.

One additional point is that by mixing commerce and doing the right thing, you get positioned in people's minds not as saints, but as 'good enough' companies. That's a more robust and enduring position (less vulnerable to scrutiny and setback). You do need to be rigorous in covering all the bases and ensuring there are no details that let the whole side down. But you aren't saying you are perfect anyway; you are pointing to efforts. Whole Foods is an interesting case study, as it is a values-led corporation with a very explicit commercial edge. The company made $4B in 2004, projected to grow to $10B by 2010. It was originally a simple idea; a whole food shop (selling things people could eat) rather than a health food shop (selling primarily vitamins and supplements). Originally the single store was called Safer Way and was entirely vegetarian. To expand, they found they needed to sell other stuff like meat, coffee and so on. It is not entirely organic, but it is healthier and more humane across the board than most. The founder John Mackay is an unusual green pioneer – a staunch Republican. Mackay points to a misunderstanding that 'people are either doing things for altruistic reasons or they are greedy and selfish, just after profit. That type of dichotomy portrays a false image of business. It certainly is a false image of Whole Foods. The whole idea is to do both.'[34]

Whole Foods is opening its first European store in central London shortly. It is a fascinating company, with policies like offering workers a good living wage and benefits, with no executive making more than 14 times the employee average. Its only Achilles heel could prove to be the buy local movement. Time will tell.

A2: Credible Partners

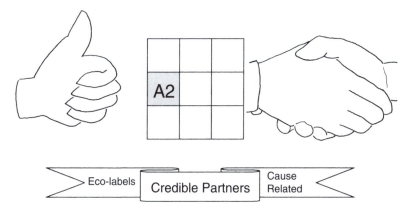

Figure 9 Grid A2

This box is about people not just being sold to, but persuaded in a more subtle emotional way that they want to buy; because they identify with the image, values, identity, personality of what is on offer. That's fine for perfumes and cars. But how could you possibly sell a green branded offer on this kind of emotional and/or social appeal without *greenwashing* – i.e. giving it a green image?

The answer is that you can do this by using *someone else's green brand* (one which is already appealing, credible and widely accepted). This way, you are not claiming green credentials, you are standing next to others who support yours. We've already seen this principle in action in the public space, with corporates making announcements supported by leading figures from NGOs.

This manoeuvre is also in line with a major shift in brand-building in recent years (which in turn comes under a broader trend in marketing – from *saying* to *doing*):

- from *suggestion* – using celebrities in advertising and other such devices to create emotional associations
- to *partnership* – working with partner brands (including celebrities) to create something genuinely new and different.

As an example of the latter, consider the U2 iPod. It wasn't just a band appearing in the ad for a gadget. It was a joint venture. It promoted the U2 special edition iPod, which in turn promoted U2's *Vertigo* album release – available exclusively first on iTunes – and it helped the band's image (showing they are up with the times). Apple got the biggest band in the world in its ads for free. U2 got a free ad campaign for their new album and tour.

Before we enter into this alternative model, let's remind ourselves what social brand identity building is about. The idea of 'brand image' is attributed to David Ogilvy:

> Ogilvy's advertising broke new ground and was talked about. He took the concept of brand image from the academic world and injected it into the lexicon of advertising. In 1955 he told the 4As – the

American Association of Advertising Agencies: 'Every advertisement should be thought of as a contribution to the complex symbol which is the brand image.' (Kenneth Roman, 2004)[35]

The 'complex symbol which is the brand image' remains a key factor in conspicuous – i.e. identity-defining – consumption. That's as true when dark greens buy a brand of mountain bike as when yuppies buy a luxury Porsche 4×4 car. What has changed since Ogilvy's time is the credible means to construct such an image. The modern way to do this (other than partnerships) is to be adopted by a tribe or community. This approach is covered in section B2; it involves participation, co-creating the brand, rather than classical marketing where advertising sends a brand image message. The audience owns the brand in other words.

The partnership route is another modern way to build an image while staying authentic. And just as it gets you off the 'phoney image' hook, it also gets you off the greenwashing hook. It's like assumptions people make about you based on your life partner. It says a lot about you without you actually claiming anything.

The Accreditation Approach

This covers the many varieties of what were originally called *eco-friendly* labels. Consumers of these don't need to be dark green. They just have to be concerned enough to want to put some eco-friendly goods in the trolley. These labels are very much like brands in their own right (they have a name, symbol, associations and form the basis of decisions and emotional preferences), but are split off from individual commercial businesses to provide universal bases of categorisation to enable avoidance of the (non-friendly) alternative. There are a lot of these label schemes. For example, in the UK:

- organic
- carbon neutral
- recycled

- GM-free
- dolphin-friendly
- biodegradable
- energy efficient
- additive-free
- not tested on animals
- Fairtrade
- free range
- sweatshop-free clothing
- vegan
- FSC-certified (forestry)
- European eco label
- UK fuel economy label
- energy star
- confidence in textiles
- Marine Stewardship Council

'Eco-friendly' labels started appearing on personal care products in the 1980s. The main green consumer worry at the time (as I recall) was over the role of CFCs in depletion of the ozone layer. This kind of labelling relies in the long term on trust. The most trustworthy version with many (but not all) the labels on the list is the backing of an independent verifier. Organic goods, for example, are certified by the Soil Association. Organic in itself is a term now enshrined in (EU) law. The Soil Association certifies 80% of organic produce in the UK. Its familiar mark – the website claims – is recognised by consumers as 'the ultimate mark of organic integrity'. The mark now covers not only farmers and their produce, but also retailers, caterers, textile manufacturers, health and beauty products and goods for import and export.

Leaving aside the fact that the labels refer to specific standards and certification, what is going on here in cultural terms? It is the joining of two brands. It is like the Coca-Cola that came with your McDonalds meal, the Goodyear tyres with your car, the Intel

Pentium processor in your PC. Marketing academics call this *com-positioning*. Such partnerships are of growing importance in modern marketing and we increasingly see these sorts of direct partnerships substituting for advertising with its 'entertainment properties for hire'. These tend to be two-way deals rather than the old advertising fees, product placements and sponsorships. They often work as joint ventures. A mobile phone company will do a deal with a film, more for the content rights and point of sale marketing opportunities than the placement in the film.

I know there are questions on the green side about labels and the way they hide complexity. And also if people think that by putting a few eco-friendly labelled packs into their shopping basket they are solving all the world's problems, they are sadly mistaken. Some organic products are shipped great distances, for instance.

One intriguing new possibility is the labelling of products to indicate their carbon footprint. Just such a scheme is being trialled by the Carbon Trust in the UK, working with Walkers' crisps, Boots (on two of its personal care products) and innocent smoothies. The potential being that if you were buying a bag of crisps you could choose one which was not only low in salt, saturated fat, made with organic ingredients and no additives but also less harmful in its carbon footprint. This scheme has been much discussed on blogs (including my own) and I have chatted to innocent about it too. Many point to several question marks:

- the product is attributed a footprint rather than the company – leading to a rather arbitrary choice of what emissions in their total operations to include;
- only the good guys will adopt the (voluntary) label – leaving a situation analogous to one in which only the healthiest foods had disclosed what the ingredients were.

The Carbon Trust has clearly thought this through though. Its approach is to say people can only use this kitemark if the company is committed to significant *further reductions* in the next two years. It's a label for the good guys (like organic) rather than a universal measurement (like calories). What you are doing, therefore, is supporting those who are moving us closer to our overall targets for emissions reduction, both with their relative starting position and their further reductions over time. I am not sure that's an entirely intuitive notion, but it does tally with meeting Kyoto and other targets.

What labels rely on is currency. Carbon is very current. *Carbon neutral* was named 'the word of the year' in 2006 by the *Oxford American English Dictionary*. You read about carbon everywhere these days, even in the *Sun* newspaper. Corporations are tripping over each other to declare that they will go carbon neutral: Sky, M&S, Virgin, HSBC . . . The very first report I saw of the carbon-labelling trial (although it was misreported as a brand decision on the part of Walkers) was in a freesheet newspaper on the London underground.

Rather like diets, what I mean by currency is that they are intuitive and enjoy massive coverage – 'what everyone is getting into' – and they offer a simple solution to a compelling and worrying problem. Let's flesh that comparison out slightly, by comparing the trendy glycaemic index with carbon:

	GI	Carbon footprint
New	The 'in' diet craze	The 'tipping point'
Intuitive	Low = good	Low = good
Coverage	Health press, TV	Al Gore film, press
Simple	Choose foods <55 GI	Low carbon (kg)

We haven't yet reached the point with carbon where people know what 'good' vs 'bad' is for any category, like they do with calories or GI. Figures like the emission bands for various cars are becoming better known (through tax bands). But knowing how to compare different goods and manage your total is in its infancy. The carbon footprint calculators are very crude, just relying on very broad types of behaviour; for instance, they don't tell you which airlines will have lower emissions on the same route. But all of this will undoubtedly come.

This kind of labelling works on a number of levels:

- the very existence of the label and the distinction it draws attention to can put pressure on retailers and manufacturers to improve their practices;
- there is a bandwagon effect (applying mainly to marginal brand decisions in lower interest categories) 'everyone is talking about carbon' and some brands have a label, therefore 'they must be better' than those brands which don't;
- there are instances where labels can get more 'bite', for instance because it is a more cautious category or contentious issue – GM-free and organic baby food;
- finally, these labels also work for the purists who are strict about what they buy – just like those on a low GI diet.

The best thing about labelling is it creates a decision where none previously existed; as they say in business, if you can't measure it you can't manage it.

The less good thing about labelling is (like the image branding it is descended from) it's a substitute for thinking and may distort your view. For instance, if you buy ten 'labelled' products in a basket of 100, you may feel quite virtuous. Whereas the impact of the 90 (or even some of the ten, in the case of organic food with high food miles) is left unexamined.

But it's a start. And is certainly, in marketing terms, an effective way to promote better (greener) products if they happen to conform to any of these standards.

The Cause-related Approach

Cause-related marketing is another common partnership strategy. It's been all the rage for the last five years. I think this is because it reliably creates a feelgood factor for brands, in a time where 'nice ads' are falling short on this. Some people in advertising get CRM (cause-related marketing) confused with CSR (corporate social responsibility). To be clear, the first is a promotional tactic, the second a deep set of reforms. CRM allows you to link your brand with 'doing the right thing', by linking with a charity or similar with a pure purpose (rather than claiming virtue for yourself, support someone else's good deeds). It's an opportunity for your company to do a little good, whilst also renewing its relationship with customers and making employees feel good about who they work for.

Like every example in the 'Green' column, how much good it does for the environment largely depends on whether your background CSR activities make you the better choice anyway. It is hard to fault in cases like innocent, but veers towards *greenwashing* if you are an energy company. I don't think it is right to measure cause-related marketing schemes on their impact on the charity itself; the amounts raised are often much less than the amount spent on advertising the cause-related promotion for instance. They may appear to be major charity campaigns, but boil down to '1% of profits to charity' or similar. This is giving new money and profile to the charity, but not as much as it appears. And that's just the nature of the beast. If you *really* want to tackle an issue, give your whole marketing budget straight to that charity! Many companies have charity foundations to do just that. This, on the other hand, is image marketing.

An example of doing CRM quite well is HSBC's *Green Sale*. For every *Green Sale* product – including mortgages, savings and current accounts – which was sold during January, HSBC contributed £2, shared equally between Earthwatch, Botanic Gardens Conservation International, the Climate Group and Environmental Campaigns. HSBC has extended this promotion across the year for its internet savings account. According to presentations made on the conference circuit, the idea behind the promotion is not only to attract customers to these products, but to do something (without overtly greenwashing) to build 'green' into the brand, connecting with HSBC's much weightier sustainability commitments. Working with environmental charities allows you to look green, without claiming it. HSBC does have a huge CSR programme and has recently been named one of the 100 most ethical companies in the world. But it is wise not to greenwash.

The financial services market is hyper competitive. Cost of acquisition per new customer is often in the £30–£100 range. On the other hand, the profit on a mortgage or pension sold, or even a savings account or credit card can be considerable. If this green charity promotion made any difference to the sales figures – and helped HSBC compete on any basis than having the best rates on the market – it would be a goldmine. From the fact it has extended the promotion to run throughout the year and is advertising it on TV, I rather suspect it has been a commercial hit. Donating £2 per high-ticket product sold to charity is not necessarily going to save the world. But it would have sold a lot of these products anyway. And because of HSBC's scale, it still managed to raise £1million, which isn't bad.

Regardless of the question mark about how much they actually do for the charity, the good schemes are very effective brand and loyalty building tools; cause-related marketing could certainly work against commercial objectives. Where it is weakest is that it only works well when the cause is already popular and accessible – CRM will seldom break new ground. Some have pointed out it is unlikely Amex would have supported AIDS charities in the Reagan years, when the disease was stigmatised. But now the RED brand makes it an easy choice.

How does cause-related marketing work, exactly? A brand, which is unashamedly commercial, aligns itself with a cause, which is unequivocally good. This works in a number of ways:

- sponsoring a charity programme of activity;
- PR or advertising to raise the cause's awareness;

- facilitated giving, including purchase-triggered donations;
- affinity branded products such as charity credit cards.

One of my favourite such schemes is innocent's *Supergran* 'woolly hats' promotion. In selected outlets in the run up to Christmas, innocent smoothies have been sold with little knitted woolly hats on top. The innocent website explains that they decided to do this promotion after news that almost 25000 older people died of cold-related illnesses the previous winter. The woolly hats sat on the top of innocent smoothie bottles in Sainsbury's and EAT cafés and, for each hat-wearing smoothie sold, the company donated 50p to Age Concern. So far the scheme has reached 220000 hats; £110000 to help keep older people warm when it's cold outside.[36]

As well as being able to buy these bottles, complete with their dinky little woolly hats, people were also invited to join special knit-in sessions at EAT and Sainsbury's outlets. And there are instructions on how to knit your own little woolly hats and send them in (humorous instructions; item 1 says 'Tune into Radio 4' which, for those who don't know UK radio, is the BBC's serious news and drama station, associated with older listeners).

This illustrates a core truth of any creative marketing, including green. It's all about the idea. *Supergran* is a great idea; incongruous, counter-cultural and fascinating. They back it up by making a very generous donation (50p per bottle plus the work of putting the hats on must make this promotion a no-profit exercise I'd guess).

Another popular scheme in the UK has been the Tesco *Computers for Schools* initiative. It is the classic example quoted when cause-related marketing is discussed. This is such a clever loyalty-marketing programme. Like the *Supergran* promotion, it gives people plenty of opportunity for involvement; with parents of local school children collecting avidly, people without kids offering vouchers to others in the queue and so on. It fits well with Tesco's *Every Little Helps* slogan. Some anti-Tesco activists do criticise the scheme as 'token-ism'. But the scheme has raised enough to give roughly one computer to every school in the UK (47000 PCs in total). Tesco is also a major charity donor (giving roughly £32 million a year). There is no doubt that the halo effect of the scheme exceeds its cash value, because, like the woolly hats, it's not just a charity promotion, it's a big involving idea. And so it is also presumably very good for business. According to the Charities Aid Foundation, 48% of the public has changed buying behaviour due to a cause-related marketing programme. The average consumer is involved in three such schemes.[37]

Another recent example of cause-related marketing is the Pampers and Unicef immunisation promotion. Pampers as a disposable nappy have a mixed reputation in green circles, but this is about a different sort of issue. In November and December 2006, for every pack sold in the UK and Ireland, Pampers committed to funding one tetanus vaccination for mothers-to-be (and hence protecting babies) in the developing world. This is part of a huge push by Unicef to tackle this issue. At the end of the scheme it was announced that the promotion had resulted in over 7 million additional vaccinations being funded. However, what Pampers are actually saying is they donate 2.5p to Unicef, for every pack of nappies costing around £8. Their 7.4 million vaccinations amount to a charity donation of under £200000 from sales of roughly £60 million. And consider that the TV airtime announcing the scheme would have cost probably more than ten times the amount donated. Meanwhile the Bill Gates Foundation wrote a cheque for Unicef for $26million to fund tetanus immunisations with very little publicity or fuss.

What cause-related marketing does is make a big splash, and a big commercial result, whilst generally doing only a little good for the actual cause or charity. (At least innocent gave 50p from a product costing around £1.75). That's actually still good for most in the charity sector, where it represents additional income for the charities at no extra marketing costs, and can raise the profile of their charity and cause too. But it is a concern if cause-related marketing comes to dominate green marketing and makes people feel that they have done much more than they actually have.

Carbon offsetting is actually a form of cause-related marketing; a small proportion of the purchase price is used to do some good work: like the *Eco-Insurance* I bought from the Co-operative Bank for my car. I really bought it because I wanted to give it my money as it is a nice bank overall, with a strong ethical investment policy. It has also been a client of mine, so I felt I owed it. But I worked out that what this purchase did was donate roughly £3 to carbon balancing. I could have made a much bigger donation to some such cause with the money I would have saved by buying the cheapest insurance instead. Looked at against our three green marketing objectives, cause-related marketing scores roughly as follows:

- Commercial outcomes   7/10: an effective promotional tactic
- Green outcomes   1/10: a few pence to a charity, but it raises the profile
- Cultural outcomes   −3/10: gives impression you are doing more than you are

Nice conservation projects and similar could benefit from such schemes, as the partners could help them afford a marketing media budget and public profile which they could not have otherwise justified. Is there anything wrong with this approach? Not really, unless you count making people feel like ethical consumers (and generous charity donors come to think of it) when the impact is slight compared to the challenges of climate change.

The other danger for cause-related marketing is that there seems to be a bit of a backlash. In response to the (RED)™ initiative, and parodying its partner Gap posters, one activist group has launched an online appeal at www.buylesscrap.org claiming that 'SHOPPING IS NOT A SOLUTION' and inviting people to donate to the (RED)™ campaign's beneficiary The Global Fund, without consuming. There are also questions being asked about what (RED)™ has raised compared to what the brands have spent marketing it – probably ten times as much on advertising alone. But that is always the catch with cause-related schemes: big splash, big sales, but small donation. Also, it's very early to judge the results of this specific scheme; they have been selling brand licences for $10million so they should certainly have raised a lot of money in the longer term. But if such attacks continue, it may be that this 'get out of jail free' approach to building a green image by association with a charity may get worn out, in the same way image advertising did.

Compare and Contrast

Both approaches are basically about linking your brand with another 'brand' to give it mainstream green appeal. You are not claiming virtue for yourself, you are simply partnering with something else that confers some virtue and/or environmental integrity and which people want to engage with through buying your product.

Both have question marks. Both have the danger of overstating the effect that buying a few things may have. They are very visible – because that's what branding does, it puts the spotlight on things and co-branding even more so (it's like spotting a new celebrity couple). But to achieve real change, you need to green your entire grocery shopping list – and even that is only one part of what you spend in total. Buying Walkers' crisps is good (if you were buying crisps anyway). But the average person in the UK churns out 11 tonnes of carbon every year. A 75g emissions packet of crisps, even if it was 100% better than a competitive substitute, only represents a 0.0007% improvement. It's a start; but you could probably achieve more by holding your breath occasionally!

Overall we do have to recognise the incredible effect that things being labelled has on markets; it creates debate, pressure, choice, sets an agenda. Imagine people trying to diet without knowing about calories. And imagine farming policy if organic, free range and so on didn't exist and it was just a case of if it looked 'okay' in the stores.

With cause-related marketing it is harder to be so sure. It looks like a bit of a free ride. If you are a lovely company (innocent) and if your more significant sustainability work is hidden from view, then the argument for any form of traditional effective marketing holds. And yet there are signs that some are starting to question it. It will only take a few prominent attacks on *causewashing* as it might become known.

I have confidence that partnership will remain a viable alternative to image marketing in general and greenwashing in particular. The general principle of partnering rather than imagewashing is a flexible one. It is not restricted to labelling and cause-related marketing. What if, for instance, a consortium of like-minded companies picked a relevant issue to tackle? Marketing is a creative discipline, and if the approaches I outlined wear out, then new ideas will take their place. But do note, I am talking about brilliant creative ideas with strategic relevance, not the sorts of 'partnership marketing' contra deals arranged by a sales promotions agency. It's about 1 + 1 = 3.

A3: Market a Benefit

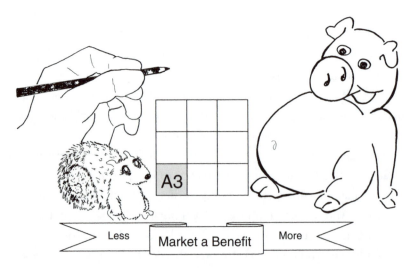

Figure 10 Grid A3

As anyone who watches daytime commercial TV will tell you, most advertising for low-interest consumer goods is based upon announcing 'new improved' formulae and features. Bold washing powder has had 30 product reformulations in 30 years. Detergents overall have been in liquids, tablets, *liquigels* and now (drum roll . . .) *liquigel capsules*! Some of this innovation is eco relevant. Concentrates have positive eco effects (less packaging waste, transport cost and so on) as well as being more convenient. Liquids may allow you to wash with cold water (which may not have dissolved powder). On the negative side these detergents (apart from eco brands such as Ecover and method) contain suspect chemicals, including hypochlorites, 'optical brighteners' and bleaching agents. And there are questions about whether the fixed amounts (in tablets, capsules, etc.) cause people to use more (and hence pollute more) than they actually need per wash.

The selling of products based upon unique and innovative features has been a (perhaps *the*) standard advertising approach for most of the last century. *USP* (*Unique Selling Proposition*) is the central term for this approach; communicating a singular benefit, which encourages people to choose your brand over others. Most ad agency creative briefs still centre on 'what is the proposition?' (or *promise/message/benefit/desired takeout*, etc.) Here is the original statement of the *USP* idea:

> Each advertisement must make a proposition to the consumer. Not just words, not just product puffery, not just show-window advertising. Each advertisement must say to each reader: 'Buy this product and you will get this specific benefit.' The proposition must be one that the competition either cannot, or does not, offer. It must be unique – either a uniqueness of the brand or a claim not otherwise made in that particular field of advertising. The proposition must be so strong that it can move the mass millions; i.e. pull over new customers to your product. (Rosser Reeves, *Reality in Advertising*, 1961)[38]

There's nothing much wrong with this approach when the product actually *is* different and better. Where this style of marketing is questionable is when claims that *sound* better ('Nurofen targets pain where it hurts') are used to sell functionally similar products. And it is an approach which is nearly always used in markets with little true differentiation. In fact, one historical justification of advertising which magnifies 'seeming differences', as one author (Claude Hopkins) called them, for these sorts of basic products is that it resolves *Fredkin's Paradox*: the more similar two choices, the harder it is to choose.

What has happened in most markets as customers have gained better information (on pricing, features, etc.) is polarisation: vacating the middle ground where brands and companies are relatively undifferentiated and hence under severe pressure. The smarter brands have moved into either category killer (ultra low cost) mode or well-defended (high value) niches, where relevance and affinity mean that consumers are not as price sensitive (Figure 11).

The middle ground is increasingly untenable because people have much more access to information and choice. The mainstream travel operators now struggle to compete with independent travel bookings direct to hotel and budget airline via the internet, and the high-end specialist holiday niches like trekking, skiing and ethical safaris.

There are 8000 mortgage products on offer in the UK. You can find the best rates in tables in the newspapers, or on online com-

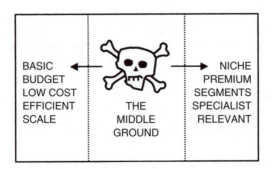

Figure 11 Three market positions

parison sites like Money Supermarket. The biggest players like HSBC can afford to compete selectively on price and also have a huge existing customer base to market to aggressively (with 8000 products, short-listing is the key process to target). Specialist lenders deal with markets such as sub-prime and buying abroad. But for the guys in the middle it is carnage at the moment. Many middling banks and building societies simply cannot compete; a spate of mergers and takeovers is the result.

Where does this leave green products? Actually it is quite helpful, as they are often competitive either by being stripped down and cheap, or niche and premium.

First – just to note – 'green' itself is not actually a functional product benefit. It does nothing for me directly, unless you count saving the planet that I am standing on. There can be social, psychological and political benefits (these are addressed elsewhere in the grid). But a green product does not answer the ultimate USP question: *what's in it for me?* This is not a failing. It just isn't that sort of thing. This was the exact response which early sustainability programmes hit, when they got to the marketing department: 'we can't sell this'; our survey data or hall tests don't indicate that it's a compelling proposition.

But green products often do have secondary benefits; they can be more efficient, durable, affordable or basic (like the budget brands) or they can be healthier, better made or more indulgent (like the premium brands). It is these secondary benefits that can be used to sell green products. In line with the overall polarisation of consumer markets, green product marketing strategies therefore tend to divide into two very different sorts: the less approach and the more approach.

The Less Approach

Environmental design is less wasteful. It uses less extraneous packaging. It may also use refills or pay people for returns. This means less frills and these were not actually adding to the functionality anyway. It is more durable or efficient. One way to sell green products is therefore value for money, convenience and other such basic benefits. Forget selling 'green' virtue (a nice extra); the products are often just better value for money! One advantage to this pitch being you can reach beyond dark greens and appeal to common sense.

Muji is Japanese for 'no brand' (or 'no logo'). It makes simple products at affordable prices from environmentally conscious materials and innovations. There is little packaging, the materials are recycled and undyed – which also makes each of their woollen and card products unique. The thing most readers will know about Muji is that it is also such 'cool design'. The use of basic materials and simple designs leads to a kind of eco-minimalism; warm and craft-like, but stripped bare. It is a bit pricier when exported, but in Japan the products are *staggeringly* cheap. The other fascinating thing about Muji is that because of its *Less* positioning, this is an idea that scales, well beyond its core audience of considered consumers. From a single store in the mid 1980s, it now has 285 stores in Japan, over 40 overseas and is now entering the USA, with a 5000 square foot flagship in the New York Times building opening in late 2007. In the case of Muji, less is arguably also more. But in its home market it appeals primarily to the thrifty, e.g. students.

Less does not just have to mean cheap, stripped bare and funky though. Less can also mean longer-lasting and hence better value for money. Linen and furniture used to be made for a lifetime's service, and quite possibly to be passed on as an heirloom. We have moved to a throwaway culture. We don't design for eternity any more. Libraries used to be recorded on media that were designed to last forever, which is why we have such good records of early religious texts. Compare that with cinema, which has trouble with artefacts less than 100 years old. As for digital, it is always just one crash from oblivion. And the media and software change so fast, how many will be able to read files from now in even 50 years' time (without also storing legacy machines), let alone 5000 years' time?

A really beautiful ingenious design that achieves longevity through growing with your child (and hence long-term investment and value for money) is the *Tripp Trapp* chair. I bought one of these, not originally for environmental reasons, but actually so that our son could eat with us, rather than having a weird airplane style integrated tray of his own. It was expensive, but on the other hand it was nicely designed, made of wood not plastic, and crucially is adjustable to last 7+ years by an ingenious series of grooves which the seat and footrest can fit into. It's actually so sturdy that I use it as a chair too. And it is so well made that when it finally outlives its usefulness, I can well imagine another family taking it on; some day it might even be a retro classic. It's certainly built to last. The *Tripp Trapp* chair, while it is admired in eco circles, could go further; using FSC certified woods and organic cotton fabrics. But it illustrates how great design and great eco design are actually very close to being the same thing.

Joel Makower, the green consumer guru, chastened by the experience of the green bandwagon crashing last time, advocates a low-key approach to environmental brand marketing, where you do your product design for green reasons but then sell it on other benefits. Makower cites Electrolux and Philips as prime examples of this tactic, selling green products to mainstream consumers on the grounds of efficiency and durability (i.e. both about saving money).

The More Approach

Birds Eye worked with Forum for the Future to develop world-leading policies in sustainable farming. If people are buying frozen food, then this range will do much less harm than many others (note that is different from the debate about frozen food *per se*). The trouble is how do you sell this? Frozen foods are bought for convenience by time-stressed working mums, who can't go shopping every day or even every week. Iceland (a frozen food chain in the

UK) had already shown in 2001 with its 'moving to organic' debacle that this is not a heartland 'buy it because it's green' audience.

What Birds Eye has done in its most recent campaign is reframe; it's not about green, nor about convenience or family appeal (its old standard propositions): it's about health and food integrity. It is selling other benefits of frozen foods; that they don't contain preservatives or saturated fats; do retain nutrients, like vitamins, better. They could have said most of that ten years ago, but they could not have persuaded ultra credible food critic Giles Coren to present it; he only agreed when he was convinced that actually this company was totally committed on issues like sustainable cod fishing. Somehow, the streams do mingle here; any frozen food could claim these benefits, but it's only really credible from Birds Eye (and evident in little details, such as fish fingers with no additives in the coating). Overall, Birds Eye is a good example of the avoidance of greenwashing; do the right thing at an industrial level, make great products, make great marketing and the world will be improved by your success. Those things don't have to entirely connect; they just have to work together. But as with the *Less* examples, some *More* approaches do make an explicit link to the environmental credentials, which they translate into other benefits, be they naturalness, taste, health or even luxury.

Green & Black's is a great case study in building a premium quality brand on firm environmental and ethical foundations. Back in 1991, the co-founder, Craig Sams, was then the head of an organic food company called Whole Earth. He had been sent a sample of organic chocolate, which was so much better than anything he had tasted before; intense and unique in flavour. Sams and his wife went into business and launched a 70% cocoa high quality dark chocolate bar – the first commercially available organic chocolate – for hardcore chocolate fans. After a trip to South America, when they discovered the local farmers being penalised by the big buyers, they agreed to pay farmers a fair price, a move that later earned them the UK's first *Fairtrade* mark.

Their marketing has been smart. They decided to move beyond the organic chocolate sector (which they already had 95% share of five years ago) and compete with the mainstream luxury chocolate brands. Rather than hype the image, they have mostly just given samples away with key foodie magazine titles. The insight was that the chocolate itself was the best advertising. The company has been sold to Cadbury's, the founders say to enable it to scale and reach a global audience and help it to expand its organic production. It certainly made our Easter egg decision easier (not something I recall them making pre-Cadbury) and I can testify that the chocolate still tastes great!

The other key feature in the success story is packaging. Green & Black's reinvented chocolate bar packaging to be luxurious rather than cluttered with information. They used rich, deep colours and beautiful traditional typography. If you had never heard of the brand and had to guess what it was for, from the design and name alone, you might have said something like Fortnum & Masons (one of the world's most luxurious food-oriented department stores). The name itself was chosen to represent the eco values (Green) and high cocoa content (Black). But cleverly, it sounds a bit like a Victorian confectioner (since they chose two surnames with these colours). As well as its mainstream grocery distribution, this must be one of the few brands to be stocked both at Harrods and in whole food stores. The brand today has a retail value of £50m, is growing at 50% a year, and after a successful entry to the States, is set to grow even faster. This is an example of what any marketer would recognise as a great brand, built on solid ethical and environmental foundations – which act in marketing terms as a support to the promise of a luxury chocolate which is different and worth paying more for.

Yeo Valley Organic is another big success – about 20% of the UK yoghurt market. The founder, Roger Mead, summarises what they are all about as 'caring'. They care for the cattle in their herds, their hedgerows, their people and their customers. The company's stated objective is to grow the UK organic market, with profit simply an outcome of succeeding in that. The authenticity extends to the name, since the business is a family-owned farming and dairy company based in – you guessed it – a place called Yeo Valley in Somerset. People who have met the company describe them as just unbelievably nice folk, who seem to really care about their cows as well as their people. They also offer 'Fairtrade' style contracts to a farming community under pressure from supermarkets (who often offer 'market prices' which are less than the costs of production for smaller farms). Really deep thought has gone into many elements of the business, for instance the packaging, which is made from the thinnest possible plastic, reinforced by a card cover made from recycled board. When it comes time to recycle, the label is perforated so that you can separate the two materials and recycle both. They already had more than half of the organic dairy market in 2003, when (like Green & Black's) they revamped their packaging and positioning to tackle the premium quality mainstream. At the time of these changes, marketing director Chris Cull commented: 'The "natural" look that many organic companies adopted at the start is now too worthy for the mass market. What the majority of consumers want are additive-free, organic products, which look like those that they normally buy, but that taste better, cleaner and more natural. That's what we are offering.'[39] According to company information, in 2006 Yeo was the number three brand in the £1.2 billion UK yoghurt market (after Danone and Müller). The brand is growing six times faster than the market and faster even than the overall organic market.

The irony may be that Yeo Valley has been so successful in popularising organic dairy products that its main threat may now be from own label versions. As we explored in the last section, eco-labels (such as organic) have become powerful quasi-brands in their own right. At the end of the book we will explore the potential development of a post-branding world based upon new knowledge structures such as standards (organic), transparency (knowing what farm it comes from) and other similar (repersonalised) means such as advocacy, affiliates, affinity and community.

Compare and Contrast

For people in mainstream audiences who are not primarily motivated by green concerns, other propositions are needed. Either stripped-down green products, which are cheaper, more efficient, more durable and so on, or premium products with added value, which are foodier, healthier, more luxurious and so on.

So what's the difference? In creative marketing terms it is the difference between easyJet and Kuoni. Marketing for *Less* propositions is expected to be functional to the point of puritan. There is no personality, beyond perhaps bold use of graphics. It is about appealing to everyone's inner accountant, with perhaps a nod to their inner minimalist or ascetic. Simplicity is a virtue in this approach. Marketing for *More* propositions is about luxury, nuance, a more personal and indulgent vision of brands as part of a certain quality of life. It's more associated with expensive-looking packaging, lush photography, being close up.

In my view, the *More* propositions represent evolution, the *Less* are revolutionary. It's a generalisation, but think about the psychology. In the first case, existing patterns, like pampering yourself with luxurious chocolate, are tapped with greener substitutes. In the second case, you start to get used to a different lifestyle and adjust your standards and expectations. Both represent progress, but the *Less* route runs against the grain of consumerisation. It is frugal.

It is a moot point whether we need to sacrifice all luxury and indulgence, that's perhaps too ascetic. There is another definition of luxury around quality of life; a beautiful view, playing with a child, watching a sunrise . . . the things that make us glow with contentment do not have to cost lots of money. A green world can still be fun; in many ways it should be more fun, with more time for people, relationships, to taste your food.

Others will argue that we need to demonstrate that green living doesn't have to be a sacrifice. But what is the cumulative impact on consumerism, so much of which is decadent and not even that satisfying? Also the basic *Less* products tend to be more mass affordable, whereas niche, premium, exclusive is more limited in market size.

The one thing that is hard to read right now is to what extent simply *being green* will override other considerations, with so much current concern and intention to act. The situation has changed very quickly and it is probably too early to tell. But in areas where the green products find such ready acceptance, they will soon be competing on secondary benefits again. Given a wide choice of organic cotton T-shirts, the questions of style, quality and price will come to the fore again anyway.

B: Sharing Responsibility (Greener)

Figure 12 Column B

I've been writing about *New Marketing* for nearly ten years. In that time it has become the norm. TV advertising used to be thought of as the pinnacle of marketing sophistication and effectiveness. The marketing director of a household name brand recently told me he'd need a special reason to advertise on TV *at all* these days. There are many New Marketing formats, such as virals, branded events, social networks, user-generated content, brand utilities. But really I believe there has been one simple shift: from selling (Figure 13) to sharing enthusiasm (Figure 14).

Figure 13 Selling

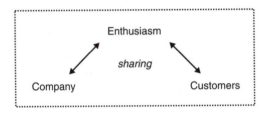

Figure 14 Sharing enthusiasm

This is not to say that shared enthusiasm has replaced selling altogether. On the contrary, the advance of CRM systems means that people are being targeted with ever more effective, timely and relevant offers. What I mean is that brand image marketing is being superseded by this New Marketing model.

What do I mean by sharing enthusiasm? There are three essential features:

1. A bigger enthusiasm, clearly separate from just 'buy my brand'.
2. Ways the audience can contribute and participate.
3. A bigger outcome, the commercial results being a by-product of this.

Below are a few examples.

Amazon

Readers leave reviews of books they have read. These provide a resource to others in deciding what to buy. Amazon also matches up your queries with what others also viewed or bought. This enables much smarter, broader browsing.

1. A bigger enthusiasm, clearly separate from just 'buy my brand'. You could describe the core business as being like a kind of 'book club'. It has word of mouth built in.
2. Ways the audience can contribute and participate. You can write reviews, draw up wish lists, follow your own enquiry/ browsing pathway, and your every move creates pathways for others to follow.
3. A bigger outcome, the commercial results being a by-product of this. Amazon encourages people to find and try a wider range of books. It can't be a coincidence that the global book market had its best ever year in 2006.

Nike's *Run London*

An annual 10000m race in central London. The third biggest run, in numbers taking part, in the UK. There is a year-round training programme, with routes from Google Maps, and an enrollment system. You can recruit friends to run with you. There are practice runs, pledges and digital extras, like a gallery of finishers and getting texted your time as you cross the line.

1. A bigger enthusiasm. A 10K race is a big challenge in the amount of preparation and also the sense of achievement.
2. Ways the audience can contribute and participate. They are the performers/athletes in this event; their pledges are used in public advertising, the 'North vs South' twist, etc.
3. A bigger outcome. About 35000 take part every year – a big boost to fitness/running culture in London (which, compared to US cities, had been quite sedentary). Research showed many bought new trainers and many of these 'felt obliged' to buy Nikes.

As the Nike example shows, this isn't just about the internet. Although it does enable you to do more with offline enthusiasm. What is new is how online businesses integrate everything into one space: Amazon being simultaneously 'a book club' (where people share their thoughts), an amazing browsing resource (recommendations engine); and a very efficient e-commerce site with huge inventory, fast simple navigation and killer prices. Increasingly, offline retailers are also integrating utility and service, knowledge and entertainment. Not just high end (e.g. Apple flagship stores, which run seminars) but high street stores too (e.g. Sainsbury's *Try Something New* campaign uses recipe suggestions made on the web by customers, in store – printed as pamphlets). Soon, multichannel retailing will mean having the same customer records and information resources offline and online; you'll be able to scan a product in-store and retrieve any info you want; like the existing Tesco.com competitor price comparisons, but also with details on origins, ethics, ingredients and so on.

Web 2.0 sites do tend to work with the same three key principles:

1. A bigger enthusiasm, clearly separate from just 'buying'.
2. Ways the audience can contribute and participate.
3. A bigger outcome, the commercial results being a by-product of this.

The enthusiasm point is the key one. Online, people cluster around shared enthusiasms. All the web 2.0 examples either draw upon existing enthusiasms or create new ones. The social networks may look initially like pure meeting places. But consider how Facebook (American campus), MySpace (music), and earlier Friends Reunited (school reunion) used a specific interest as the hook. Most others are identifiable as hobby type activities as well as resources: YouTube, Flickr, Digg, Wikipedia, blogging . . .

With web 2.0 examples, the line between commerce and hobby is being rubbed out. *Second Life* (the massive, multiplayer role playing game) has spawned real world property millionaires, and the currencies in other games such as *World of Warcraft* has provided an

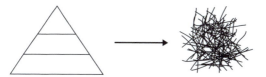

Figure 15 Hierarchy to network

income for 'professional' players in China and elsewhere. YouTube recently announced it is now to reward those who upload videos with a share of ad revenue from the page views generated by that video.

What has changed? It's not just because it's so much easier for people to participate; to post comments, text in, blog, submit their own home shot and edited videos and so on. The configuration of the relationships that make up society has changed. *There is no audience, only actors.*

If you want a simple picture of the historical transition, my sketch would be the one shown in Figure 15.

One implication is that real life (folksy) is the natural idiom of a network where people access each other – a network is grassroots all the way through. And suddenly, classical marketing looks too showy and glossy. Just as the Paris Hilton channel looked out of place on YouTube. Cue reality TV, and agencies making 'home-made style' viral videos.

A key New Marketing rule is that the barriers and distinction between customer and company are reduced. That's great for green marketing. There is so much more that can be done to reduce the footprint of companies if their customers co-operate and use the products differently. A them-and-us attitude to responsibility holds things back.

Sharing responsibility has general significance. It is a key step in the development of a sustainable society. There is a danger that we all stand by and vaguely approve as activists attack corporations on our behalf. But there is hypocrisy in this public position. We drive the cars that Ford, Toyota and others make. We take the flights and throw away the packaging. Expecting companies, governments and charities to sort it out for us is old world thinking. By working together, the companies and customers can do so much more. But also there is the prospect of us all waking up to our collective responsibility.

B1: Develop the Market

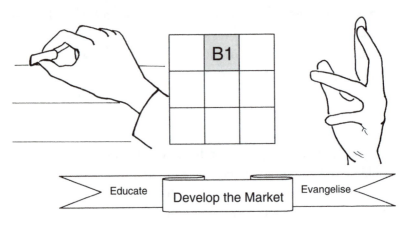

Figure 16 Grid B1

This is about companies developing the market for green and ethical products, i.e. collaborating with customers to create broader/faster mainstream demand for the companies to go green. If you get this right it's a virtuous circle. This can dovetail with marketing agendas as well as green ones. One simple example is M&S, whose commitments were far in advance of prevailing consumer knowledge and demands. This meant they needed to engage with and develop customer appreciation of these moves. Educating customers is a natural way of doing this without running the dangers of greenwash. It's just passing on good information and encouraging informed choices.

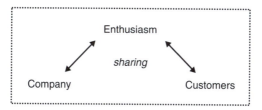

Figure 17 Sharing enthusiasm

Corporates have to escape the trap of being like the Woody Allen character who said 'enough about me, what did you think of my movie?'! And sustainability actually isn't just about them. That's why it comes under sharing responsibility and collaboration. It is marketing enthusiasm, working with a bigger shared issue with your customers (Figure 17).

To recap, there are three essential features of this approach:

1. A bigger enthusiasm, clearly separate from just 'buy my brand'.
2. Ways the audience can contribute and participate.
3. A bigger outcome, the commercial results being a by-product of this.

The word enthusiasm is very important. There are endless opportunities in public media to get depressed about the problems. And it isn't often a company's place to critique society. But there are opportunities to be part of building the solution, to get switched on and to make a difference. Companies are in a unique position to bring the public around to a sustainable outlook and way of life. Companies have the budgets and (in some cases) the trust. They also have a relevant, regular place in people's everyday lives; things that politicians and NGOs lack. A message on a pack gets right to the point of purchase decision and also potentially right to the point where the product is used (responsibly or otherwise). There are two broad approaches to consider under this heading: education and evangelism. The net result of either should be the same, of people moving up the ethical or green consumer ladder:

from INFORMED to REFORMED
from ACTIVE to INFORMED
from INTERESTED to ACTIVE
from DISINTERESTED to INTERESTED

At first glance, this may not look quite right. Surely being active comes after being informed? You can argue it either way. But think about how many people already DO a fair amount. For instance, nearly everyone recycles. And quite a few buy organic or Fairtrade goods. Yet how many are fully informed? And becoming an expert – i.e. not just knowing about stuff, but being able to apply it and teach others about it – is the biggest step, i.e. the one most conducive to change. Could you write an essay on the pros (and cons) of organic farming? Yet you probably buy organic every week.

This ladder climbs towards the *Ethical consumer*. An ethical consumer is one who has a good grasp of the facts and is thus able to make expert judgements of their own, on knotty debates like organic vs local. It is a new take on the old political idea that only an informed person can become an active citizen. The more you know about this stuff, the more you want to change your lifestyle overall. People who work in the sector are also motivated for reasons of professional identity and consistency – whether they are green designers, conservationists or CSR professionals. But there is another class of citizen – experts who come into it via blogging, NIMBY protests about local roads, a schools project, etc. The internet is primarily the home of the amateur expert, the citizen journalist and so on.

In the BBC's *Ethical Man* experiment, Justin Rowlatts, a BBC *Newsnight* reporter, was 'volunteered' to make the biggest reduction possible in his family's carbon footprint for a whole year. As well as featuring a regular strand within *Newsnight* (the most serious and influential of the mainstream UK TV news shows), Rowlatts and family were the subject of a BBC documentary. He interviewed the Archbishop of Canterbury, Al Gore and others, as well as submitting regular reports on what it was like giving up your car (not too bad) and switching to washable nappies (trickier). It formed an innovative and accessible thread for regular ethical and green issues reporting; a bit like the strand in broadcasts of budget news where they say 'what this means for a typical family'. One of Rowlatts' most eye-opening lifestyle decisions was over how his funeral will one day be managed in a sustainable way (he decided to be composted!).

'We're in this together' is a key sentiment for green marketing. There is so much more that can be done to reduce the footprint of companies if their customers co-operate. This is manifestly good for commercial objectives; customer relationship marketing in its richest sense. And it is directly contributing to green objectives too.

The Education Approach

Educational marketing – building programmes on knowledge rather than image – was the subject of my second book, *After Image*. It is most obviously accessible, as a way of engaging people, to broadcasters, portals and other media. The BBC now does mini language courses on its website, a natural extension of travel programming and so on.

BSkyB, the Murdoch UK cable and satellite TV network, carried a week's news reporting on 'Green Britain'; all from a single UK town called Lutterworth. The week's reports looked at the impact of current lifestyles on carbon emissions, at travel habits, renewable energy and so on. Every household in the town was given a free copy of a *Rough Guide to Saving Energy and Reducing your Carbon*

Footprint, produced in association with Sky. This editorial strand was just one part of a companywide initiative, *The Bigger Picture*. In the first two years of this initiative, Sky succeeded in halving its carbon footprint by using motion-sensitive lighting, hybrid taxis and buying only renewable energy. It also voluntarily offset unavoidable emissions. A key issue it needed to work on was making the set-top boxes more efficient. It has just launched the first auto-standby service, to stop set-top boxes consuming energy when not being used.

The other side of the *Bigger Picture* scheme is to take advantage of Sky's presence in so many people's daily lives to educate and inform the public; to help them make simple effective changes to their lifestyles at home.[40] As part of this public education programme, Sky invited viewers to make their own short films to illustrate these simple actions. One such film featured a teenager turning off all the lights in their home – ending with the last light switching the picture to black – while he talked about what he was doing to reduce his footprint. Sky's informative website includes a carbon footprint calculator, energy saving tips, podcasts and so on. The initiative has already won BSkyB a number of awards, including at the Green Awards and the National Energy Efficiency Awards. The need for the educational part of the scheme, over and above the many measures Sky has made to reduce its own footprint, was amply demonstrated by a recent survey quoted on the BSkyB site:

69% feel they are responsible for taking action against climate change;

57% also say they don't have enough information about reducing their impact on climate change;

44% of those surveyed did not know what a carbon footprint was;

83% said that they did not know how to calculate one. (Sky/ YouGov)[41]

The campaign demonstrates Sky's own commitment, but it is much broader in scope than that; it is a public education campaign, to share the responsibility with customers and staff. There are many smaller initiatives within the scheme; like the distributing of free energy saving light bulbs by satellite installers, while they call at people's homes. Each of these bulbs saves enough energy to offset that used by the older set-top boxes (before the energy efficient versions were developed). It's a really thoughtful little touch.

What I like about the Sky initiative is exemplified by a two-page spread the company put into its recent TV listings magazine (sent free to all subscribers) on eating local food. It argues in some detail for this; telling us, for instance, that the apple you buy in the supermarket could be a year old, covered in fungicidal wax and so on. There was no attempt to integrate this with the info on the latest from showbiz. They just took the opportunity to add an ethical consumer education break to their programme advertising!

Sharing the Green Awards with Sky was Marks & Spencer, which won three separate awards for its *Look Behind The Label* campaign. This educational scheme encouraging and enabling customers to find out much more about Marks & Spencer's policies and product sources was launched *before* they announced their sweeping *Plan A* commitments; to become carbon neutral and so on. Why do it first?

The only rational explanation as to why M&S would lead with its education campaign is that it needed to teach its mainstream, middle class customer base *to appreciate* the changes that were taking place and yet to be announced. That's exactly what the 'look behind the label' campaign did. It covered the following education areas, detailing the company's track record to date (not bad) and priorities:

- Fairtrade
- salt

- environment
- fats
- durability
- recycling
- sustainability
- washability
- free range
- non-GM
- animal welfare
- natural cleaning

The net effect of getting into the detail under each heading is a bit like reading the ethical consumer guides. It isn't as independent, but it is closer to the mainstream audience and their daily shopping habits, having an in-store presence. Yes, it is serving a different purpose than reviewing the alternatives available in every outlet; it is a *shop within* rather than *shop around* resource. But there is an interesting psychology to this. M&S is letting customers be ethical consumers, through products they may already have bought; it is therefore a much smaller psychological step to do more. Educators and parents will recognise the power of encouraging and praising existing good behaviour to reinforce it.

The campaign seems to have achieved a lot in only 12 months. It launched with window displays in 420 stores, providing information on ethically traded products, health and quality. Stores began stocking T-shirts and socks made from Fairtrade cotton, followed by vintage style jeans and underwear. They also replaced all tea and coffee ranges with Fairtrade alternatives. It has come at a time when M&S has seen generally revived fortunes. The M&S marketing has been all about re-establishing M&S and its difference from ordinary grocery and clothing retailers – a premium positioning. The environmental, ethical and health commitments have supported that overall effort. It has certainly been noticed by consumers – according to survey data from TNS – ahead of other supermarkets and well ahead of the clothing retailers, who only responded with their own ranges (with organic cotton) some 15 months later.[42]

What M&S has done is involve its customers, educate them and by making them feel good about some very everyday shopping decisions, encourage the view that they are already ethical consumers. It's quite effortless and nonconfrontational. Because it is education, it doesn't seem like greenwashing. The company is doing stuff with customers rather than simply boasting about its efforts to customers. The result is that it is seen as a true leader (leaders don't boast about their exploits, but rather are on a journey, leading people with a destination in mind).

Starbucks recently launched a nice initiative called *Welcome to Evergreen*. This is an educational online game and a plain example of marketing enthusiasm. Starbucks does a lot of good stuff in its cafés, giving causes the chance to communicate to people having their coffee and so on. It has done major tie-ups, for instance with Timebank to encourage more people to volunteer. It is also making a visit to Starbucks more interesting and less anodyne (without all of this, it would be the McDonalds of coffee). *Welcome to Evergreen* is an online game where you can explore, with a Sims-like character walking around a fictitious town, what the impact of different decisions and behaviours is. They produced it in partnership with Global Green, the environmental charity founded by Mikhail Gorbachev. The game's 'take action' section has three elements: calculate your carbon footprint, locate and join in Earth Day activities and the 'Pledge of Allegiance to American Energy Independence', which is an online petition targeting the US Senate; the idea being that by reducing reliance on oil, the US would be less embroiled in Middle East politics. I find that a slightly cynical 'sell' to the US public of the climate change agenda personally (why not just stop contributing 25% of the world's carbon emissions, do we have to evoke fears of terrorism?) but I am prepared to believe it might be an effective slate.

The Evangelising Approach

In the classic paper on company-values led branding from the mid 1990s, Mary Goodyear's two examples of companies that communicated political values are telling in retrospect: The Body Shop and Benetton. It is clear today that these political views were those of leading individuals: Anita Roddick and Olivieri Toscani. Others in the company may have agreed, but only these powerful individuals had the power to direct these campaigns. When things got too difficult – when there was a conflict between the commercial imperatives of the business and the political stance – both individuals were removed.

Anita and Gordon Roddick founded The Body Shop and their political values were integrated into all their activities, starting with products offering *Beauty Without Cruelty*. There is every reason to believe that many customers identified with these values too. It was a coincidence of interests: a true win:win. As Anita Roddick told me (when she was a client of my past agency), their business idea was to 'put the money into the product not the packaging'. Since packaging costs, specifically retooling costs, dominated the economics of the cosmetics industry, The Body Shop's range was able to trade at a killer price point and quality. They also avoided spending money on advertising.

The rift came when the company went public and Roddick found herself increasingly at odds with a board of directors. She was finally ejected after a comment she made in a public lecture that the company had become a 'dysfunctional coffin'.[43] She had wanted all the shops to mount a challenge to the World Trade Organisation (not an atypical action for them, the shops often got involved in petitions and political campaigns). But the campaign was blocked by those now responsible for the company's day-to-day operations – who were accountable to a public company board, to shareholders and the City. It was a moment of modern corporate myth making; Roddick's new target was the boardrooms of major corporations –

like a corporate *St Joan*, she was (apparently) betrayed by those very interests in her own camp.

Toscani joined Benetton in 1982 as advertising director. His vision was to use advertising in a completely different way, to communicate the company's values by tackling controversial political issues. Apart from anything else, this had the commercial merit of creating the most visible and most discussed print ads in the world.

The business had every reason to be pleased with the results. The company had grown to be the fourth largest in Italy. It courted controversy and challenged attitudes to AIDS, religion, sexuality and above all race, cultural understanding and tolerance. It won the top advertising industry awards. Some criticised the campaign for using politics to sell woolly jumpers. Toscani countered that all fashion advertising was political (in projecting an ideal of beauty which he labelled fascistic), it was just that his went against the grain.

The story came to an abrupt end when a campaign featuring death row prisoners caused a backlash in the USA. The campaigners said Benetton was upsetting the families of victims. But it seemed more like Benetton's campaign being seen as an affront to the pro-death penalty right; how dare some Italian fashion company criticise the USA by pointing to the fact that nearly all of those executed happened to be black? The protestors mobilised supporters, who waved placards outside Benetton stores and stockists. Sears cancelled their contract as a result; and Toscani was fired.

Another, less discussed feature of the Benetton and Body Shop cases is whether major companies – as opposed to leading individuals within companies – can even actually be said to have a political value system? Is it authentic to say 'the company believes in . . .'?

Another key thing to note is that when the idea of political evangelising (recruiting people to a progressive point of view) by brands is raised, it is assumed to be about communicating *radical* values. I will suggest that it would be better to learn from mainstream politics: the policies may be radical, but the presentation ultra-normalising and accessible. Otherwise, while it may look and feel 'cool' to be radical (and has some notional relevance to fringe funky fashion brands, as a form of transgression), it is counterproductive in the mainstream. But it depends; are you doing it for effect or to effect change? If the latter, a more toned down version is usually more likely to work.

The outstanding question, which arises from mainstream examples of companies espousing political values, is whether they mean it; whether they will only stick to it when the commercial return on doing so is positive (so that the messaging is actually just an unusual and persuasive form of brand appeal).

You have to wonder in cases like Dove. Are they really a bunch of committed feminists? Were they feminists in the 1950s when all they sold was soap bars? Or was it when they walked into the beauty care market of the 1990s that they were outraged by the prevailing fashion industry norms? If it is a genuine corporate conversion, what of those in their sister companies within Unilever like Axe, which – even an apolitical and impartial view would concede – portrays women as sex objects? The Dove campaign has continued so far, but what if people get bored, if sales wane?

When the business is suffering, who wouldn't change their marketing campaign? Perhaps it is unfair to single out political and social values advertising in this respect. It's just that if you only state your values when it brings increased sales, it is open to questions about how genuine the values were in the first place and to what extent the whole company was really behind them.

What I do believe that we could learn from political campaigning is a version of the green/normal formula:

- it's not about making fairly normal stuff (Benetton jumpers) seem radical;

- it's about making a radical position seem normal . . .
- in order to get mainstream people (e.g. floating voters) involved.

The mainstream is fully capable of getting agitated and pressing for change. But the politics of the mainstream is all about the *rejection* of extremes.

The harder political issues which are surfacing in the current debates about sustainability include: championing the little local farm against the major grocery chains (even including chains such as Whole Foods); and the notable absence of women's voices in sustainability – as workers in factories, as consumers and also as leaders of the debate from business and NGOs. Those could be popular and generally understood issues.

But the true potential of campaigning on public and political issues by companies I believe is in *pressing for change*. Not just winning hearts and minds, but actually signing up a public movement – for instance like The Body Shop's *Against Animal Testing*. By getting people to *do* something, even if it is writing an email or signing a petition, a completely different dynamic is created. One example is celebrity chef Jamie Oliver, who successfully lobbied, through TV documentaries and grassroots schools programmes, to increase government investment in decent state school food. Oliver's *Feed Me Better* campaign attracted 271677 signatures of support. The government responded by making substantial new commitments on the amounts to be spent on school dinners.[44]

Pressing for change takes you off the pulpit. It gets people involved. And paradoxically, it is somehow easier to get people to do political actions than it is to get them to adopt political attitudes. It's why single-issue politics gets so much more traction. The almost ubiquitous 'Make Poverty History' wristbands surely outnumbered the people who were truly immersed in the arguments about development, foreign policy, Fairtrade and business practices?

Compare and Contrast

I am a huge fan of education. People who are well informed make better decisions. So many of the problems of current unsustainable lifestyles are actually unthinking habits of behaviour and lazy, unchallenged assumptions.

There are situations where you do need to develop public support around your initiatives. My view would tend to be that the M&S approach of educating your audience is more inclusive and effective than agitating for a change in political outlook. Although very effective public campaigns for change in industries and government policies have been run in the green space, notably by The Body Shop.

But there is a definite strategic approach for major companies, using the following line of argument:

- we are making changes;
- public pressure can make these changes demanded by regulation;
- competitors who fall behind will therefore suffer;
- and we'll be the leading brand in a newly redefined category;
- hence, doing good through politicised campaigns is entirely justified.

That was the commercial rationale for Against Animal Testing as an industry campaign, which The Body Shop waged and won. And it's been GE's rationale for its amazing conversion to greening heavy industry. It is too simple to say there is only one interpretation of corporate self-interest. Certainly in marketing there is every argument (commercial, ethical and environmental) for involving people and collaborating with them.

Some years ago I set up a company with a friend from broadcasting to make ad-funded documentaries. These would be funded by organisations who were investing philanthropically in an issue (it would help all their efforts work harder). You could produce books, TV programmes and so on. These wouldn't have to be branded. They would be viable media properties in their own right.

Just say you decided to be the one supermarket that sourced all fresh food locally. Local food is a good thing environmentally, provided it is in season (but imported green beans from Kenya are environmentally preferable to growing under glass, with heating in winter, here). There is a Fairtrade argument for supporting farmers in developing countries to some extent, but there are other ways to benefit those communities through charity giving, micro-lending and so on. If launching 'local food only' as a policy, it would make sense to spend on education or evangelising to further this cause. So that as far as possible, the announcement would be 'by popular demand'.

Readers of my first book will know something similar was done in the launch of Playstation 1; they invented a fake 'society against technology', leafleting electronics trade shows and so on, which led up to their launch idea 'society against Playstation', looking as if it was plucked straight from the zeitgeist.

But the preparing-the-way view has been somewhat superseded by the ability in web 2.0 to do *everything* in one place; to be a cause, community, information resource, enthusiast . . . and a retailer. It's the Amazon model, and it's very applicable to new green businesses. Companies have already only started to realise the potential for real time involvement of customers in every aspect of their business. In the age of twitter and blogging, no company needs to be an island. And a major milestone of green brand development is when people see the whole company, its operations and its policies, rather than just the image and façade. I think we'll increasingly see windows into the company; a corporate version of the restaurants where the food is prepared in front of you and you can chat to the chefs.

B2: Social/Tribal Brands

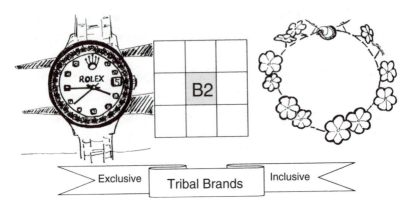

Exclusive   **Tribal Brands**   Inclusive

Figure 18 Grid B2

This type of marketing is about collaborating with customers to create brands. How this works is through the desire to belong to a tribe or community, and to confirm your identity as a member of such groupings. *Tribal* is a key word for such iconic signs of membership. Think, for instance, about gang culture and its colours. The Harley Owners' Group (with one million members, the largest ex-factory club in the world) is modelled on the old cycle gangs, with local 'chapters' and organising 'rides'. The only difference being, members of H.O.G. tend to be law-abiding middle class, midlife bikers (those who can now afford a Hog).

Classic branding was invented for people who knew what was expected of them. Brands reinforced existing social diktats. My father, as a white, middle class manager working in industry (not the professions), knew what to wear, what to drink, what to drive and so on. It wasn't that everyone conformed to these views. It was that the matrix of 'normal' signs and meanings was agreed, whether you conformed or not. A similar set of closed and clearly demarcated meanings used to surround 'green'. Leon, my maths teacher at school, was an ardent green; he was also chair of the local vegetarian society, had a beard and so on; he was also a member of a defined style tribe (frayed jackets with arm patches and roll your own cigarettes . . .) as a schoolteacher in the late 1970s.

Postmodernism, which emerged into the mainstream across the 1980s, scrambled these meanings into a collage; you could pick and mix. It was around this time that Ted Polhemus (an anthropologist studying youth identity groups like mods, punks and so on) says that the *Style Tribes* ended, giving way to much broader, looser groupings, for instance rave and indie culture. It wasn't just a fashion thing though. The world became less certain, the job for life was gone, IT was changing everything, and due to a series of scandals and scares, people lost faith in traditional institutions. The Cold War ended. Since then, we seem to have been rebuilding. Despite predictions of a Babel effect in the internet (when everyone speaks, no one can hear anything), the apparently random network has evolved around clusters, to do with particular interests, tastes, passions, ideologies, professions. Blogging is like medieval Europe, with little central organisation, but rather a network of influence flowing through villages and fiefdoms. The same goes for friends' lists in social networks. And the culture is folksy, going back to the time when stories and other cultural memes were all like urban myths; the good ones spread. The tribes are perhaps re-emerging online, but they are now fluid networks of inclusion, rather than static, exclusive sets.

What this means for brands based upon groupings and belonging is that they have become more important, but also correspondingly more fluid and miscible. It is still possible to be identified as 'a *Guardian* reader' (and also a *Telegraph* or *Sun* reader); but it no longer accurately predicts your profession or voting intentions. William Hague and others on the right write for *The Guardian*. It's a true broad church of people willing to think about issues, as opposed to having a narrow doctrinal view. Social class related to occupation has proved one of the most stubborn features of social structure and meaning. But you no longer know how a *Guardian* reader votes, dresses or speaks. In the 1970s, a *Guardian* reader would be a social worker or teacher; a politicised educated leftie; a child of the post war redbrick university education boom. Now, a *Guardian* reader could be a judge, an environmentalist or an IT worker . . . The commitment to liberal journalism is still there, but *The Guardian* prides itself on the fact that it actually thinks through issues and you cannot predict what it will say. *The Guardian* (through its online *Guardian Unlimited* and *Comment is Free*), has over four million readers in the USA. Its third biggest city after London and Manchester is New York. A *Guardian* reader today is not a stereotype, you couldn't pick them out in an identity parade, but it is still – perhaps even more of – an iconic brand. Why? Because in a less certain world where anything goes, it is a *fixed place*. As diverse as a real place (like a city), but still a community to which you feel you belong. *The Guardian*'s decision not to go tabloid (rather taking on the Berliner format) was a very important one in this context. It is possible that they could have sold more papers in tabloid format. But they'd have lost the physical sense of difference; it would be like getting rid of London's windy streets.

The sign of an iconic brand is that you can add '–er' and get to a meaningful social grouping. 'Google user' doesn't work (it's like saying 'breather') but Blogspot-er does. eBayer does work, but Yahoo-er does not. Interestingly, I would argue that many style brands have largely lost this power to signify; 'Levi's wearer' means next to nothing. Whereas your choice of mobile phone or laptop can and does signify; 'iPod user' for most of its earlier history did feel like it said something about someone.

Why is this identity issue important for green brands? Traditionally, green was exactly such a style tribe, associated with niche identities such as vegan, anti-vivisectionist, conservationist, activist, NGO worker or hippy. If you said someone was 'green', you'd have a fair chance of guessing what their style (of home, clothes, etc.) was.

Part of the problem for green was that the tribe of professional and political dark greens *was* so exclusive. Without any intention to sabotage their own cause, there was an exclusion effect on those outside these ways of speaking, dressing and living. The movement itself has gone to great lengths to tackle its holier than thou image in the last ten years. Sites like Grist have deliberately set out to tackle the subject with a sense of fun and inclusion.

But there is also a potential value – some believe – in iconic green brands being used to create exclusive aspiration and desire around green choices and lifestyles. Many have called for a change in the way green is presented culturally, for instance media theorist Sut Jhally. After his polemical attack in a seminal essay on the consumerism (individual, selfish, greedy) he saw as simply the net effect of advertising, Jhally advocated not an exclusion of the seductive and feisty images of advertising from public life, but rather a redirection of the same sentiments behind a better way of life. According to Jhally, we need to 'make the struggle for social change fun and sexy' – i.e. to 'find a way of thinking about the struggle against poverty, against homelessness, for healthcare and childcare, to protect the environment, in terms of pleasure and fun and happiness'(Jhally, 1998).[45]

Another statement of this agenda is by Bruce Sterling (award-winning sci-fi author, futurist and *Wired* contributor) in his Viridian Manifesto, in which he observes that 'Civil society does not respond at all well to moralistic scolding. However, contemporary civil society can be led anywhere that looks attractive, glamorous and seductive.' According to Sterling, what's needed is 'basically an act of social engineering'. It won't be achieved with the tired old green messages and images. Rather, we need to build a new vision of green: 'a new, unnatural, seductive, mediated, glamorous Green. A Viridian Green, if you will' (Bruce Sterling, 2000).[46]

This 'making green aspirational' message has spread, becoming a new consensus. Arnold Schwarzenegger promoted the same theme recently in a speech at Georgetown University, 'Bodybuilding used to have a very sketchy image . . . but we changed that, we consciously changed that. And then, all of a sudden, everyone wanted to exercise. It became mainstream, it became sexy, attractive. And this is exactly what has to happen with the environmental movement.'[47]

I'm in cautious agreement. An iconic brand is one built by a sense of belonging to a tribe. 'Sexy' is just one approach – one that tends to be associated, as Sterling himself says, with the emotion of envy. The opposed view to 'sexy', 'cool' 'aspirational', etc. is that of building brands on empathy. Which implies a different set of (still attractive – but broadly 'nice') values, a different style of collaboration and organisation. The fundamental question being: is this brand exclusive – does it offer to make you better than others? – or inclusive – does it make you feel at one with other people?

The Envy (Exclusive) Iconic Approach

This is becoming the stock view in modern green circles. And it's certainly a welcome counterpoint to 'worthy'. The idea is to sever the links with a sandal-wearing, self-sacrificing green past by enlisting sexy celebrities (and similar devices) to make green attractive to the mainstream. Allied with this is making green products attractive and superior in design terms as well as their functionality; products which, far from being a compromise, are actually things that people can show off.

There is a cynicism I don't share at the heart of this view. It assumes that the 'masses' are celebrity-obsessed, style and fashion-victim conformists. This strikes me as 'in for a penny in for a pound' thinking; if we are going to embrace consumer culture, says this view (which requires overcoming a certain amount of disgust, for ardent greens), it might as well be a grossly *over-consumerised* version.

It is true that modern consumerist culture – including the cult of celebrity – is laced with envy. John Berger described this in his book on art (based on a populist TV series) called *Ways of Seeing*:

Glamour is a modern invention. In the heyday of oil painting it did not exist. Ideas of grace, elegance, authority amounted to something apparently similar but fundamentally different. Mrs Siddens as seen by Gainsborough is not glamorous because she is not presented as enviable and therefore happy. She may be seen as wealthy, beautiful, talented, lucky. But her qualities are her own and recognized as such. She is not purely the creature of others' envy, which is how Andy Warhol presents Marilyn Monroe.[48]

You have to see each in its social context. In Gainsborough's time the lack of envy partly related to a lack of mobility; people 'knew their place' and 'accepted their lot'. Today, people see Branson or Beckham and think 'I could be you'. Envy is a bitterly negative emotion, the shadow of 'aspiration' ('I want to be you' is an envious thought). And Monroe is an interesting choice of example. In her lifetime she was vilified by the media and Hollywood establishment, yet it is hard to see why looking at the historical record of her films and acting. I love the description of Monroe on screen by Ayn Rand as projecting 'the confidence, the benevolence, and the joyous self-flaunting of a child or a kitten'.[49] Monroe was very aware of the envy herself – and apparently quite damaged by it – she spoke about this in a *Life* interview days before her suicide: 'It stirs up envy, fame does. People you run into feel that, well, who is she – who does she think she is, Marilyn Monroe? They feel fame gives them some kind of privilege to . . . say anything . . . and it won't hurt your feelings – like it's happening to your clothing.'[50]

Most luxury brands are marketed on envy and its counterpart, exclusivity. It's the same feeling – 'if others having it means that I can't, then I want it'. Sterling's idea, in his Viridian Manifesto, was that by creating products adopted by the pampered super-rich and famous, you could create a cult of envy, aspiration and adoption. Brands have long known this about Hollywood stars. Cinema was only a couple of years old as a mass medium when Coca-Cola started featuring stars of the silver screen in its adverts (quaintly they used illustrations, rather than photos). These days, brands try to get their products adopted more naturalistically. Altoids ships free products to any celebrity known to be a fan – for instance to Harrison Ford.

Guinness built a bar in George Clooney's house, after he admitted to being partial to a drop of the black stuff in a magazine interview. Goods worth tens of thousands of pounds are given away in each Oscar goodie bag, in the hope that some A-listers will be seen (i.e. photographed) using this product at a later date.

The Toyota Prius is the best example of a green product built on adoption by Hollywood celebrities. Famous Prius drivers include Cameron Diaz, Brad Pitt, Kirsten Dunst, Will Ferrell, Tim Robbins, Billy Joel, David Duchovny and Bill Maher. Seinfeld creator Larry David has three of these cars, and, not to be outdone, Leonardo DiCaprio's family has four. Reports interviewing stars about their cars have pointed to the fact that they like the incognito, low-key appearance as well as the environmentally friendly benefits.

For others buying the Prius, the Hollywood glamour must be a factor, far more than its understated character. You can enjoy a secret glee that, for a relatively modest outlay, it is a car that *anyone could drive*, getting you out of the car status stakes. Its only serious competitor is the Honda Civic hybrid. Very similar cars, but the Prius was the one adopted by the A-list tribe, and so they could hardly be more different as brands. You can also go one further if you have a garage with electricity and get a G-Wiz. The drivers of these in London include a newspaper editor, high-ranking government officials, big names in fields like film, PR and IT. There are only 850 in London and, for those in the know, they may make you look like a 'someone' (almost like a Rolls Royce!) Beyond using celebrities as an adoptive tribe, this is establishing the idea of inverted status; that small is the new big.

It's entirely possible that this agenda could take hold. Imagine that driving a 4×4, taking five holidays a year, spending thousands at Christmas (on things like energy inefficient flat screen TVs) and so on . . . suddenly all go massively out of fashion; being seen as bloated, crass and low-class. A new Puritanism emerges, based upon aesthetics of a beautiful life; one of order and simplicity and focus. It would be a return to the enjoyment of refinement, as seen in ancient Chinese (and later Japanese) ritual, and in the good life pursued in ancient Greece. The pursuit of pleasure in Western hedonism is (quite wrongly) traced back to the Greek philosopher Epicurus. An *epicure* is someone who enjoys food, drink, sex and other pleasures. Epicurus did equate pleasure with good in a moral, or philosophical sense. But his philosophy of living (as opposed to his abstract moral and religious philosophy) was anti-excess, encouraging a simple, communal and secluded life where friendship and tranquillity are valued rather than possessions and self-indulgence. There have been occasional glimpses of this style of life and way of thinking in modern self-help publishing trends, such as downshifting, simplifying and 'a few good things'. You can see this atmosphere emerging in the popular luxury spa resorts and in the warm but minimalist designs of recent leading-edge architecture. If you ask people what's wrong with the lives we live today and distil what they say to an essence, my guess is that *chaos* would feature highly in the list. It bears thinking about.

Commentators like Bruce Sterling and Sut Jhally have been saying we need to make sustainable lifestyles 'sexy' for nearly a decade. But there is an interesting and quite literal variant that keeps cropping up, which is making sexiness green.

Babeland, a funky women's sex shop founded by Claire Cavanah and Rachel Venning in 1993, is a values-led company responding (in the early 1990s) to the lack of women-friendly sex shops. One of their items that caused quite a stir on the green blogs is their *Eco-Sexy* kit, featuring a *Laya Spot* vibrator made of *Elastomer* (a latex and phthalate free material), massage candle made of soy oil and other thoughtful products.[51] There are also numerous sexy lingerie ranges, which use environmentally conscious design and materials. These aren't just leading edge in terms of ecology but also fashion; for instance, Enamore's range working with recent fashion graduate Ayton Gasson has been a major success, earning plaudits at London Fashion Week and commercial success in boutiques across the UK.

One now longstanding example of this coupling of two vibrant cultural trends – green and women's sex retailing – which I covered as a case study in my last book is *Coco De Mer*; the erotic emporium founded by Sam Roddick, Anita Roddick's daughter. Founded in 2001, this store (and web store) combines a Victorian boudoir aesthetic with eco-conscious products. The creative execution of store and web design is sumptuous. A very cool brand, for sure. It's the meeting of two current cultural ideas: a new confident take on female sexuality and a newfound interest in things natural, sustainable and green. And it just kind of works as a cultural mythos.

There's a general principle here for green brand development: find something that's 'cool' and then give it a green twist. There's then a compound effect, it creates a double demand (it's already desirable and it has a green twist, which makes it contemporary and different) and also these brands start to change the image of green overall. Other examples include;

ECO SPORT (mountain biking);
ECO SKATEWEAR (Howies);
ECO FESTIVAL (Live Earth);
ECO WEB (green blogging, Hugg);
ECO TOURISM (responsible travel, e.g. overland);
ECO FASHION (organic cotton);
ECO GOURMET (Green & Black's).

With web 2.0 you can go further with the *iconic brand as tribe* insight; you can build your brand around a community. One recently launched example is *Global Cool* (http://www.global-cool.com). Its objective – very laudable – is to take a billion citizens carbon neutral. The scheme is a social network; something you join. This also involves making pledges, but a mass team effort rather than just solitary 'new year's resolutions' – a joint endeavour rather like the writing of Wikipedia.

This touches on what has become almost a standard of collaborative green marketing; getting customers to make pledges and take actions and tracking the collective effect, often with a counter on a website saying 'tonnes of carbon saved so far'.

A new initiative from the Climate Group (*We're In This Together*) in the UK is tracking the net effect of a list of household name companies introducing a green innovation each:

- B&Q home insulation price cuts/support;
- Barclaycard *Breathe* – 50% of profits to carbon reduction projects;
- British Gas free home energy audits;
- M&S encouraging customers to wash their clothes at 30;
- O2 offering £100 credit if you keep the old handset when renewing a contract;
- More Th > n offering eco-insurance and discounts for eco-friendly cars;
- Sky announcing (its long-awaited) no power standby feature;
- Tesco offering half price energy efficient bulbs.

There's also a site where individuals join up and track the effect of their shopping, individually by logging those 'solutions' from this list which they have bought, and collectively by tracking the carbon impact of the total sales of these offers.

There are a number of these corporate 'join our pledges' sites (Honda and Yahoo! are other examples), but they don't seem to be successful in signing up masses of volunteers. Would you join a corporate pledge site? Much more successful has been introducing an *OurPlanet* channel in MySpace. In its first couple of weeks it attracted 62000 friends to sign up. If you want to build a community, ask a community!

Global Cool's core idea is to use A-list celebrities to make factual content, for instance TV programmes, about climate change issues. Alongside this, they are also running a programme of pledges and offer 'carbon coaches' to help people on their carbon reduction journeys. The home of the initiative is their website: http://www.global-cool.com. The uniting of brands directly with entertainment properties (rather than hiring them as advertising 'personalities') is a hot topic in branding in general; in my world it's known as 'Madison and Vine', after a famous speech by the then Coca-Cola COO, Steve Heyer, calling for co-operation between showbusiness and brand marketing. Global Cool is an example of a green brand jumping straight in with the tactics of the U2 iPod (and skipping fifty years of advertising, which assumed that if a star appeared in an ad for a bank, phone or car, then their personality might rub off; as if they were recommending this product or used it themselves). *Madison and Vine* is all about partnerships; buy the U2 iPod and get the album six weeks early, get a special edition signed by the band and so on. They certainly got good content for their site as a result; personal green video messages from hot stars (Lily Allen's was the one that caught my attention).

The latest in a series of consciousness raising initiatives from Bono, rock star turned philanthropist, is *Edun* – nude spelled backwards – launched together with his wife Ali Hewson and fashion designer Rogan Gregory. The range is stocked in upmarket department and fashion stores. It is a Fairtrade fashion model; creating trade not aid. Fabrics are (where possible) organic and sourced from Africa too. There were several things I really liked about Bono's statements during the launch publicity – one being the description of a different ('end of bling') lifestyle and the other being that it wanted to succeed as fashion, not just as worthy fashion: 'We do not want you to buy these jeans because of poor Africans. We do not want you to buy this shirt for any reason other than you think it's the most beautiful shirt on the rack.'

I would say this is part of an urban ecologist trend; dressing like a hippy or 'Boho' certainly, but hardly 'down on the farm'. *Wired* magazine described this fusion of fashion, lifestyle and identity as the *Ecosexual* trend (the new *Metrosexual*). But the opposition to bling – excessive conspicuous consumption – is an interesting angle. And even within 'bling', the *conflict diamonds* issue (as raised up the Hollywood agenda by *Blood Diamonds* starring Leonardo DiCaprio) has brought sustainability at least into consideration in the pampered elite world of the A-listers we are all supposed to envy.

The 'envy' insight is much broader than celebrity glamour though. Envy is a primal emotion. Anthropologist and philosopher Rene Girard described a similar pattern in social apes, the so-called *mimetic rivalry*. It is observed even in ape societies that two chimpanzees will often quarrel over the same piece of fruit, even if plenty of others are available. Girard wrote that as 'two hands reach for the same object simultaneously, conflict cannot fail to result.' And that in the same way, 'humans learn what to desire by taking other people as models to imitate.' We want a car, or other lifestyle accessory simply because we see others enjoying it. Which links identity (literally identifying yourself by taking others as a model) with desire: 'aware of a lack within ourselves, we look to others to teach us what to value and who to be,'[52] and imitation. The application of this psychology to brands – that you want things because others have them – is not limited to luxury goods. For instance, the brilliant launch of Gmail traded on this feeling. The world did not need 'another hotmail'. Until, that is, Gmail restricted its supply, by making it invite-only. Google bloggers (at Blogger. com) were given six invites to share. Suddenly they were hot property. People bid upwards of $100 for them on eBay. There was a site where people made offers of swaps for Gmail invites; one woman baked a cake in return for hers.

The Anya Hindmarch 'I'm not a plastic bag' was also made hot property by restricting supply, first giving it only to celebrities at *London Fashion Week*, then in very small numbers through Hindmarch's boutique in London, Collette in Paris and Villa Moda Kuwait; and a similarly restricted supply on the *WeAreWhatWeDo* website. The result was huge pent up demand. Stars like Keira Knightly began to turn up in paparazzi photographs carrying this £5 'must have' item. Only recently were they sold to the general public through mass retail outlets like Sainsbury's, and still in restricted numbers. There were several unfortunate postscripts. One is that the scheme was criticised when it reached the public phase, because the bag is not organic cotton, nor Fairtrade. The scheme was also criticised by all the people who queued up overnight, were handed raffle tickets and in many cases still failed to get a bag. And that's something you have to figure if you use envy to build a green brand; you are dealing in negative emotions.

Startling marketing initiatives behind green agendas could emerge from similar insights. Imagine if certain less environmentally friendly products and lifestyles were promoted *back* into a position of extreme scarcity and luxury. The motor car and holiday (originally the millionaire's chauffeur-driven carriage and villa by the sea) were invented for the very rich and never intended to be mass consumer luxuries; they were the private jets of their day. A simple way to achieve this is taxation. If *any* flight cost £3000, some of this amount to be used to undo historical aviation related damage, then it would become an elite thing again. Even business travel would only be done when absolutely necessary. You might only ever fly on your honeymoon. A deepening oil and climate crisis could have such drastic effects; although a much better state of affairs would be a world in which people didn't need or want to travel so much. Scarcity is a viable means to justify a price premium in a world where everything has become a commodity. It is the 'limited edition'. But ultimately anything that excites this sort of desire and associates it with consuming products is open to question. Isn't it party to the same decadence it is trying to dismantle? Shouldn't we be getting off this merry-go-round, rather than spinning it faster using green power?

The Empathy (Inclusive) Iconic Approach

Instead of helping some people feel they are better than other people, why not just make everyone feel good? Is that a utopian view? Surely people are competitive? We are told we even have selfish genes. But in fact that is only half the story.

A distinction was drawn by Marcel Mauss in anthropology between the *gift economy* and the *commodity economy*. The gift economy covers all those exchanges in society where something is given to another. The gift must appear generous and gracious. But it is only apparently a free and spontaneous gesture. The gift economy has strong rules of its own:

- Reciprocity. The person given to is under obligation to reciprocate. People on your Christmas card list are supposed to have you on theirs. In some cases you're meant to give back the same object; the so-called 'indian giving' which settlers found unsettling. In one famous case, the Governor of New England had already sent the peace pipe gift in question to the British Museum!
- Building relationships. The underlying point of gifting is to build interpersonal relationships, not just between individuals but also in a closely knit network. You could say it is our equivalent of grooming in apes.
- Enduring attribution. A gift always remains 'that teddy auntie Claire gave me'. The giver remains associated with the gift. Whereas something I pay for becomes 'mine'. Property does not just divide, it depersonalises.

The gift economy has to be contrasted with the commodity economy to understand it fully. The idea of a commodity is that it separates you from others. It is yours alone. It is the economic basis of envy and a uniquely human invention. The gift economy exists to create social cohesion. With just a commodity economy there would be little social capital or community.

The gift economy is an interesting framework within which to examine the social production and volunteering models of web 2.0, and also the workings of values-led companies. The new stars of sustainable business are often a bit of a paradox:

- creative, playful, often slightly childlike, generous and inclusive
- but disciplined in their sustainability behind the scenes.

There is no conflict though. Nice people tend to be freer and more human in their dealings with others, at the same time as being careful ethically.

innocent's marketing (if you can call it that, it doesn't feel like being 'sold to') includes a massive free festival event, knitted hats on bottles (for Age Concern) and naïve TV ads featuring animated fruit (straight out of a 1970s children's programme). Their website is full of nice touches, like inviting anybody who is in the area to pop in at *Fruit Towers*. Their office is full of astroturf, park benches and people who are so friendly you vaguely wonder if there is something in the water (or the smoothies). I love the way that they use language too – for empathy rather than envy:

> Hello, we make lovely natural fruit drinks like pure fruit smoothies and fresh yoghurt thickies. Everything we produce tastes good and does you good. (www.innocentdrinks.co.uk)

It's a soft approach to brand marketing. But it's not a soft business. What this hippy way of relating belies is the discipline of an operation which doubles in profit every year, currently turning over around £100 million, and is the 62nd biggest brand in the UK (from a standing start only nine years ago).

And there is nothing naïve about their approach to sustainability either.

- The product: all natural, healthy and delicious.
- Responsible procurement: they investigate every piece of fruit they use; buying accredited where available (for instance under

the Rainforest Alliance) and auditing and improving where it's
not.

- Sustainable packaging: the company uses PLA, a new nonpetro-
chemical plastic that's 100% compostible, requiring much less
energy in manufacture too.
- Emissions: the car fleet is hybrid and their vans run on LPG/
biodiesel. The company is carbon negative, supporting forest and
energy projects.
- Operations: the company aims to be zero waste and is hot on
issues like recycling. It pays fairly, shares profits and has nice perks
like a bonus if you have a baby.
- Charity foundation: 10% of profits go to projects in countries
where they source the fruit.

Far from greenwashing, the company is modest about its ethics:
'In a nutshell – innocent is a company that wants to leave things a
little bit better than it finds them and still have some fun along the
way' according to Richard Reed, co-founder.

Another company with many of the same characteristics is
method. (Notice, a defining characteristic of empathy brands is they
don't use capital letters in their names!) This is a company in the
much less dynamic or sexy category of household cleaning products.
Nonetheless it has just been named America's 7th fastest growing
company by *Inc* magazine, with 3-year growth of 3390% (and no it
wasn't founded three years ago, but in 2001). Meanwhile, a few
months earlier, PETA (People for the Ethical Treatment of Animals)
recognised method's founders for 'creating a trailblazing line of
surface cleaners, soaps, home fragrances, and more that make it easy
for caring consumers to choose products that haven't been tested by
blinding rabbits and poisoning mice.'

method's brand idea is *people against dirty*; clean products from
an environmental point of view, with beautiful design, which keep
your house and body clean too. The thing about method's products
is that they are soooo beautiful. I particularly like the ones with what

I would call 'jellybean' design. They look fantastic. Like something from Apple's design studio. The original insight for the company – apart from environmentally conscious products at parity prices – was that there had been little innovation in packaging within this industry for 50 years. They have nice fragrances and thoughtful features like selling concentrates (a first in the USA), saving packaging and transport costs. The marketing is very playful. In my last book I covered a 'confessional' site where people could post anonymous confessions – which other visitors could browse through – of anything bad they had done in the past, and then 'wash away their guilt'.

There are lots of other companies with friendly, naïve hippy values and clever business models and product designs. Companies like Love Tea and Howies for instance. The next wave of empathic, inclusive brands with a conscience will probably grow out of communities. Because where the 'tribal thing' has gone in web 2.0 is self-organising, fluid, co-created.

How will this work? Launch an internet magazine that defines a tribe. Then market products to that tribe, born out of the unique philosophy. A company that has done just that and which is – tangentially – green is *Real Simple*. It's tangentially green because it is about simplifying your life and also often calls for the reuse of discarded products and packaging. *Real Simple* is the magazine for the new domestic goddess; what we in the UK call the *yummy mummy*. Bake offs with friends, walking the labrador, studying for a PhD in your spare time . . . somehow, the 'housewife' identity seems to have come back in. What *Real Simple* does is share the folklore. For instance, my IKEA client who met them on a trip to the States has started carrying a rubber glove in his car. Why? Because one wipe along the back seat and the static electricity has enabled it to pick up all the dog hair! From a funky housework magazine, and then a PBS TV show, *Real Simple* has now launched a range of products, sold at Target.

This is 'where to go next' with the superabundance of pledge sites I suspect. Make ingenious products that do it for you. Like the toilet hippo from Thames Water (you put it in the cistern and it saves about 1/3 of the water every flush). Perhaps it would be possible to launch a service that chipped cars to improve their fuel use; e.g. a maximum speed of 71 miles an hour, and perhaps setting maximum revs too, unless you floored the accelerator to get some emergency acceleration. There are many such control devices that could be built in to make doing the right thing an automatic choice; for instance, with thermostats, lights that switch themselves off, circuit breakers with timers that you plug 'standby' type devices into and so on.

Speaking of toilet hippos, *AntiApathy* has a mini-site dedicated to their promotion. This is a small, creative community in London which organises events and online campaigns. Their new community website, currently in beta, is TheNag.net, a site which not only records your pledges and commitments but offers to nag you until you have done them. I think it might just be a hit, but in general their actions are small but beautifully formed. As I write they are about to host an event in east London called *Sex and Climate Change*, featuring Sam Roddick (founder of *Coco de Mer*), a tantric sex teacher, comedy acts, DJs and 'world-saving disco moves'. A much larger event last year I went along to was their ethical fashion show, with about a thousand people from ecology and fashion, which got widespread PR coverage. The thing about AntiApathy is that they represent a new idea about communities and network businesses, which is that small, local and sociable (really meeting in real life) is better. The AntiApathy events are places where you meet what seems like everyone in the hardcore of the green scene in London. You could say they are like the coffee houses where bankers met 400 years ago. I am seriously tempted to talk to them about the launch of this book too, because they do throw extraordinarily good parties, and I am due to meet them on something next month!

The most impressive UK social network brand for climate change so far though has been *iCount*. This has 65000 members and counting and seems to be reaching critical mass. It offers an interesting mix of actions, some personal (wear a jumper and turn down your thermostat, cut a foreign holiday plane trip a year), and many political (there are four petitions on various new white papers, G8 meetings, etc.) The community part of the site is under construction, but I can imagine this being successful; a MySpace for the concerned, which today means getting on for half of all young adults. They also produced an excellent little book called *Your Step-By-Step Guide To Climate Bliss*. *iCount* is supported by some of the biggest names in more traditional membership organisations such as Greenpeace, the WWF and Unison (a trade union). *iCount* launched with a 25000-person rally in Trafalgar Square in late 2006. It is linking up with the Live Earth concerts in the summer, which could give it a huge further boost in awareness and membership. When you join, one of the first things it prompts you to do is to sign up other friends. As with most ideas that spread, their creative quality is, in my view, a big factor. They have a way of talking with people, using phrases such as 'you are irresistible', which is inclusive, clever and empowering. I love their graphic design too.

By this time next year someone will be *the YouTube of green*. MySpace has its eco channel, Yahoo! a green portal and so on. But history suggests that a new entrant with the right provenance and sharper, more innovative ideas will do better than incumbents straying in from neighbouring fields. My friend Naresh (along with Andy Hobsbawm) is just about to launch a major content site and community called *Green Thing*, which I suspect could be a contender. They will work through the medium of uploaded video content about lifestyle change; for instance, the pilot film they are shooting is about people walking more. Their idea is that creative ingenuity is what is needed and that the process of making, sharing and rating films about this will stimulate big new ideas that take hold. Like some of the examples I quote earlier, it is a hybrid; the best of web 2.0 meets green. By the time you read this, the site should be live, so do check it out.

Compare and Contrast

This is a really interesting fork in the green marketing road. Should you make green options glamorous, enviable, elite and work *with* consumerism? Or should you make them funky, inclusive, almost childlike and work *against* it?

My problem with glamorous, elitist, Viridian consumerism is that it leaves the decadent, excessive American dream lifestyle intact. In a world with such a wealth gap, is 'flaunt it' really such a great sustainability strategy? Yes, it can popularise products and services, but it leaves the cultural assumptions intact. One recent example, which made me feel a bit queasy, was a recent Marriott hotel (on YouTube) video promotion. I liked all the ingredients; joining Environmental Awareness Month, submitting YouTube videos demonstrating what your family is doing for the environment, winning an eco-vacation, doing conservation and clean-up work, partnering with a charity, planting trees. I know Costa Rica is a world leader in reforestation too. I think it's just the idea of their actual hotel: 'The Los Suenos Marriott Ocean and Golf Resort sits on an 1100 acre rainforest'. A rainforest with en-suite luxury hotel and golf resort? Is it just me that finds that obscene?

My money is on the 'nice' brands and the inclusive communities, which may represent the next wave. If all other things were equal, they have the potential to change the culture. They are just as 'sexy' in the broadest sense of currency and style, in many ways 'cooler' than the celebrity-endorsed, elitist route. The key to these sorts of companies is their creativity (that's even what lies behind their being a bit childish in tone). And more than anything, what we need to be going for is creative ideas about how to live better.

A key dilemma is what happens when a nice company 'sells up'. Being part of a multinational holding group can undermine your special relationship with customers, who felt like part of the family precisely because the deal was that this was a tribal brand. Plus, it is also significantly likely to cut across the practices that made the company great; doing things for values and never just for profit. The sense of selling out relates to the true ownership of the brand and company by its audience. 'We made this' can turn to betrayal when it is sold up. There are many who have decided they can't actually reach a scale to achieve world-changing status without teaming up with a bigger venture. In commercial terms that may of course be right. In cultural terms it can be tricky. One key 'reprieve' factor is that you can show radical independence from the parent.

With iconic brand building, the vitality of the brand comes from adoption by a tribe or community. It is *their* brand and they manufacture much of the meaning and folklore. This means that mass marketing is seldom appropriate, at least until the community has had a chance to adopt and incubate the brand. It can feel like you are looking over their shoulders at a party otherwise. Even in mature phases, it can be better to recruit and work with new communities than lapse into classic mass media selling; it sends the wrong signals, and word of mouth or imitation is much more credible and compelling (and much cheaper) anyway. The internet has made what used to be one of marketing's cultural rarities – the iconic brand which was driven by a style tribe or clique – into perhaps the central approach in building 21st century brands.

B3: Change Usage

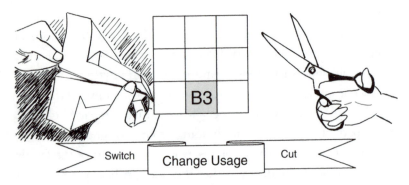

Figure 19 Grid B3

This section is about asking your customers to do their bit once they have bought your product. In this way, a company can have a much greater impact; it's all very well making hybrid cars, but when and how people drive has a huge impact too. In addition, there are cultural benefits to involving people in this way; making green living normal, a willingness to do your bit, spilling over from one activity to the next. Most green marketers thus far seemed to intuitively know that greenwashing wasn't the right way to go. A very common way out of this bind is to ask customers to do their bit too. People will see you are a green-minded company, but you can hardly be attacked for boasting about virtues when you talk about responsible usage. Hence the near ubiquitous pledge: you do your bit as we do ours. One example being Ariel's 'Turn to 30' campaign.

The thing is, that to engage with these issues, companies have to get deep into what really makes a difference. Sometimes there are lifestyle changes, which do fit brands really well. But as I said in an earlier chapter, sustainability is a complex moving target. It seems worthwhile to start by exploring some of the difficulties that lie ahead with this mode of marketing.

One immediate issue is the dearth of clever ideas about what people *can* do, which are brand relevant. It's something of a shortage. M&S has followed Ariel's lead and is now asking its customers to *turn to 30* too. That's great for the temperature that washes are done at, but with each new brand in the same sector, there is less ownership and involvement being created. It would have been nice if M&S, to reinforce its position as a trailblazing leader, had found a more original angle.

If M&S really wanted to go after domestic laundry, there were other angles. For instance, hanging washing out to dry (as everyone used to) instead of tumble drying saves about three times as much carbon as washing in cold water (not 30 degrees, but cold). It would also save you about £75 on your annual electricity bill. However, unfortunately for M&S, a much bigger impact comes from eating local food at least once a week, not something that's as easy for them to get behind:

Annual estimated carbon saving:[53]
Local grown, unprocessed food just once a week   2268kg
Hang clothes out to dry   .   635kg
Wash your clothes in cold water   228kg

You can see from these figures what an interesting couple of years ahead supermarkets face over the *eat local* issue. It's one of the key things (along with cycling not driving) dark greens typically do with rigour. The thing about supermarkets, even putting aside the ridiculous strawberries in December, is that they are too big to source and handle local foods with their current supply chains. Even a fairly local UK item would have to travel through 800 miles of supply chain, via warehousing, to arrive in your store.

Historian De Toqueville said it is never so dangerous for incumbent regimes as when they start to reform. You have to wonder if the supermarkets can remain the darlings of sustainability, as the market hardens in its views on issues like local sourcing. Of course an Ocado (or indeed an M&S) may be needed to make mass delivery of local goods efficient (I doubt farmers' markets are going to work for 60% of the population). But this could still be the biggest thing to hit retail since the supermarket came on the scene in the 1950s. Overall, it should be a great saving. Instead of goods making multiple trips (from farm to processing to warehousing to regional distribution centres to store to home by car) they could pretty much go from farm to local warehouse to customer (by electric van). That means fewer vehicles on the road and many fewer food miles, and hence reduced costs. The internet should make matching my need for tomatoes to a local grower simple too. The tricky bit is how we get from here to there, given the amount invested in existing infrastructure.

Cars are another big resource intensive market. And they are a prime example of the manufacturers actually playing a small role in the emissions caused by people using their product. Volvo estimates that the manufacture of the car is roughly equivalent to a journey of 1500km in carbon emission terms; i.e. probably only about 1/100th of the impact the car will have in use. Buying an energy-efficient new car will hence quickly outstrip continuing to keep an old gas-guzzler on the road. If car manufacturers want to significantly address how much impact their product has, it's about how and when they are used, as well as producing step changes in fuel efficiency (which most are working on; both Toyota and VW have said they will have 100mpg cars quite soon).

Honda is one of the leaders in developing cleaner, more efficient engine technologies. But it made a slightly strange choice of platform for its climate change marketing effort. It is not just a corporate ad campaign; it is a vehicle (literally) to sign people and brands up to do their bit for climate change. It's all based on Honda's F1 racing team. The cars feature, instead of traditional advertising signage, a painting of the earth. The website to accompany this campaign, www.myearthdream.com, allows people to make a donation to an environmental charity, choose a pledge of a lifestyle change which will reduce their carbon footprint and in return buy pixels on the (digital version of the car), which, when clicked on, features their name.

Here is the list of potential pledges people can choose (from the Honda website):

- share my car
- cut unnecessary flights
- fit at least three energy-efficient light bulbs
- take the bus or train
- cycle or walk to the shops or work
- turn my thermostat down by 1°C
- give up ironing
- no unnecessary standby/phone on charge
- turn off the tap while I clean my teeth

- recycle all my paper
- switch to a renewable power supplier

I really love the idea of sharing my car. We do about 3000 miles a year, and actually that will probably fall this year as we are using it less and less. But just occasionally it's a real boon to have a car. But how could we share it with others? I don't know of any friends offhand who are up for this, and actually if I did I'm not sure how they'd feel about buying a part share in the car or paying per use. This is a prime example of the utility of a scheme I am developing, in conversation with a bank (it's all about insurance), to enable people to loan each other under-utilised goods. I'd be happy for people to borrow my car, if I got credits I could spend on other things like borrowing holiday homes around the UK. Meanwhile, I would guess the number sharing their cars, as opposed to what they probably really mean (which is giving lifts to colleagues and so on), would be low.

Back at Honda, once you've made your pledge, you get a pixel with your details on the digital version of the car. I was disappointed to find you can only select from their official list of pledges. I guess they might have been concerned about getting a few activist entries, like the famous 'SWEATSHOP' branded trainers entered into an online Adidas design competition. But limiting people's participation to a pull-down menu is not very '2.0'.

Ostensibly this whole F1 thing looks naïve – almost asking for trouble. Honda says it is aimed at F1 fans, but surely they must have realised it would be visible to a much wider public audience, including those who think F1 driving with its 4mpg cars and its fleets of trucks and equipment are part of the problem, not part of the solution. Shell was slammed for trumpeting its green credentials while also supporting F1 (which NGOs said encouraged the whole culture of motoring and driving fast). It's a bit like using livestock for a vegetarian campaign. But maybe it was also a smart move; allying green with technology? An awkward fit at first, for sure. But apparently Honda is planning to introduce new technology into the car too. Honda's explanation, according to its F1 team boss Nick Fry, is that 'F1, with its huge global profile and cutting edge technology, can play an important role in not only highlighting the issues but also playing our part in developing solutions.' For example, by 2009, 'devices for energy recovery' will be in place on their racing cars. Rather like the trickledown from space race technology, Honda is saying that practical solutions for all of its cars can be developed by engineers working on its F1 programme.

I can certainly see what Honda is trying to do here. They do make cars. At least they aren't dodging that (compared with BP ads featuring wind turbines). Rather, they are pushing a different argument from the classical green view; that technology may be part of the solution too. They are trying to make this a showcase for green innovation. If they do indeed unveil radically carbon-efficient F1 cars in future years, with technologies that trickle down to their consumer vehicles, there could hardly be a more visible platform. The 'eco-friendly racing car' is a story waiting to be written. They might just be warming that story in this first year's painting and pledging guise. It's hard to read. Green commentators seem slightly baffled, most seem to have given Honda the benefit of the doubt, recognising that, overall, they seem to be one of the good guys.

The list of ten pledges (like ten commandments?) seems to be becoming a standard format, although the details vary slightly depending on context and the relative strictness of the regime proposed. Here is *Glamour* magazine's fairly mild version (they had some advice for this from Greenpeace USA):

1. Change a bulb.
2. Drive a fuel-efficient car.
3. Even better: bike or take public transportation.
4. One word: recycle.
5. Clean green (household cleaners).

6. Eat local or organic.
7. Buy energy-saving things.
8. Conserve water.
9. Adjust your thermostat.
10. Speak up/spread the word.

It would be fantastic of course if everyone did do all of these things. This and Honda's ten pledges look quite similar, and indeed a number of the items are the same. But the Honda list feels stronger and I suspect there are two reasons for that: first, it urges bigger actions (e.g. three light-efficient bulbs rather than one); but secondly, and perhaps more importantly, it contains a greater number of things to *cut* (or share), rather than simply *switching* to near-identical greener alternatives.

CUTS

Glamour: less car journeys, save water, turn down thermostat
Honda: less car journeys, save water, turn down thermostat, less flights, stop ironing, unplug standby/charger, share your car

Psychologically that's a big difference. And it represents something of a split in opinion about how we should tackle green issues. Some think it should just be better products (i.e. greener) but no sacrifice. Others say the notion of sharing responsibility means that consumers having to cut back or make an effort is actually more involving and satisfying. I don't think anyone knows the definitive answer (if there is one), but it is a key debate.

The weakness of these ten commandment lists from a brand point of view is that they don't feel very ownable. Especially now that they have become such a publishing standard. It is brilliant for the environment that the same simple actions keep getting reinforced and endorsed. But I doubt there is much benefit to Honda or *Glamour* magazine, you probably wouldn't even remember that you got 'stop ironing' from them rather than a green consumer guide or news article. Also, one of the lessons from classical marketing is to focus on one thing you want to communicate rather than a list. If I tested you on the Honda list, right at this moment, how many would you remember? (Try it and see!) And finally, I am not entirely sure it is Honda's place. Increasingly there are independent 'what can I do?' brands, like the excellent *Change The World For A Fiver*. I do believe that brands can play a huge role in educating people – but I'm not sure these lists are a brand's bag. Let's look at the Cut vs Switch approaches in more branded, ownable formats.

The Switch Approach

At the inaugural *Green Awards* event in 2006, which recognises 'creative work that illustrates and communicates the importance of corporate social responsibility, sustainable development and ethical best practice', Tony Juniper from Friends of the Earth gave a keynote speech about how great it was that green marketing was overcoming the negative perceptions of ecological lifestyles; the idea that 'they involve compromise and sacrifice'.

This is the core idea behind the *Switch* strategy. Making sure that changing to a better behaviour involves a minimum of cost, effort or sacrifice. The Toyota Prius, for instance, is deliberately designed to be 'without compromise' – with higher quality features in comfort, audio, air conditioning and electric window than you'd expect in a standard family hatchback. It's also actually one of the safest cars of its size. Although that's a direct conflict with the fuel economy, since it involved making the car heavier. But it's a key criterion for family buyers. The money saved on fuel and road tax and similar probably more or less balances out the fact that the car is quite pricey to buy. The argument for products like the Prius is that in the mainstream, people will be willing to switch to a nice green alternative, all other things being equal. The Prius brand has established quite an image too, based on its 'tribe' of celebrity adopters, which helps (see B2).

Switching relies on offering a greener, but otherwise near-identical, alternative in return for the same price or a small price premium. A premium actually counters the feeling that you haven't done anything; it feels quite satisfying to 'do your bit'. Many ethical and environmental groceries fall into this bracket. You aren't stopping eating bananas. You are just switching to Fairtrade or organic bananas. Whereas the darker green approach would be to *Cut* down on tropical fruit and eat local and seasonal types instead.

These sorts of alternatives can also be used to differentiate a service, making it attractive to those with ethical and environmental motivations. For instance, Hertz offers a *Green Collection* of more fuel-efficient family saloon cars. These all do 28 mpg and over. This has to be seen in a US context, where the mpg on offer can be much lower. In the US rental fleets, it at least picks out some cars which are better than others on offer. Launched in late 2006, this collection has over 50000 cars, ensuring that anyone who wants to book one at an airport location will be able to get one.

There are also a number of *Eco Limo* services, including the famous one by that name in Los Angeles, which ferries the A-list stars to high profile events in a Prius or biodiesel car. In London, the *Green Tomato* cab company is a popular pick with corporations such as Sky, who have pledged to go carbon neutral. *Green Tomatoes* are cleverly branded with a distinctive (green tomato) graphic over the classic silver Toyota Prius; giving them high on-street visibility. As well as using the greenest car available, which is suitable for private hire, they also offset their emissions by investing in tree planting. Which brings us onto the most topical and controversial switching strategy of all – genius really (although now quite controversial) – the ultimate like-for-like switch, which is to make no switch at all, but rather buy the same product or service with a built-in *carbon offset*.

The offset payment is used to fund alternative energy development, tree planting and so on. Suddenly you could jump into a Computer Cabs black cab (one of the first firms in London to offset), knowing that your journey would be carbon neutral on average. This approach is very appealing to marketers, as it can be built into the value proposition. Others who rushed into carbon offset schemes include online travel companies, like Expedia.com, Travelocity.com and SkiGreen.org. Dell offers to plant trees to offset computer purchases, charging an additional £2 per notebook and £6 per tower for this as an additional service. Another computer company, VIA, is offering offsets for free.

This offsetting craze is, as critics have pointed out, basically a cause-related marketing scheme. There are charities (or in a few cases like Terra, for-profits) doing work with donations, which undoes some of the harm. Quite a few concerns have been raised about offsetting recently; that it is an inefficient approach compared to reducing emissions at source, that trees only absorb carbon temporarily (while alive) whereas fossil fuels release it permanently, that it doesn't reduce other environmental impacts, that it encourages ongoing or even increased guilt-free consumption. There have been questions asked about the reliability of the offsetting companies, which are not regulated. It has got to the point where protesters occupied a carbon management company's building. Clearly it raises concerns in some quarters, as much I suspect for its over-ready acceptance as a panacea as any of these detailed objections. The balanced view among green commentators seems to be that offsetting should be used within a system of measures to reduce emission – known as 'carbon management' – rather than just carbon offsetting as a quick fix. It's not clear where this issue will net out in public perceptions. But offsetting is increasingly offered as an option, for instance with M&S deliveries. In some ways it is a microcosm of the whole *Switch vs Cut* debate.

One company that has gone beyond offsetting is Eurostar. It has recently announced its carbon plan, to the usual fanfare. What supporters like Tony Juniper from Friends of the Earth pointed to as the good example set by this scheme was the company's effort to reduce carbon emissions by 25%, making difficult reductions rather than going straight to offsetting. Even before these changes, Eurostar is ten times better than flying in carbon emission terms. Yet it barely takes any longer, from central London to central Paris, door to door. And it is that factor which makes this a switch strategy; highly competitive in marketing terms, beyond setting a good example. Eurostar runs the only train from London to Paris/Brussels. Its direct competitor is all the airlines. A recent survey by BBC World[54] found that 28% said they were changing travel plans because of concerns for the environment. I am one of them. I have a conference in France in the summer that I would have had to say no to (with my new foreign conference cutting footprint reduction strategy!). But now I am going by train. I leave first thing in the morning and will make it to Provence in time for dinner. That's a long day, but actually faffing around getting to and from airports, allowing time to check in, etc. would have taken half a day, even though the flight itself is quite short. And I will get so much reading and work done. That may sound like an isolated example, but think of all the corporate travel done by companies committed to reducing their footprint. Companies like Sky already use green taxi services, couriers and so on. The choice of Eurostar for travel by these corporate clients over flying is a no-brainer.

The Cut Approach

With *Switch* strategies, the collaboration with customers only extends to their buying choices. *Cutting* implies reducing your purchasing or reducing use once the goods are bought. That may, at first sight, seem a strange thing to be discussing in a marketing book. So we need to look at some examples to see how they are working with brand agendas.

A recent *Cut* initiative, which I absolutely loved, was the latest in a series of attempts by Sainsbury's to wean its shoppers off the disposable plastic shopping bag. Shopping bags – reducing the impact thereof – are suddenly at the leading edge of creative marketing. And so they should be; we get through 10 billion of them a year in the UK. Shopping bags are not only made in China but many are shipped back there from the UK for recycling. It's crazy – a good example of the inefficiency of a world which never counted the external cost of carbon – and we need to change our habits. First, Sainsbury's reduced the plastic content of its distinctive new orange bag by 43%, it contains 33% recycled plastic and this proportion is being increased. Still not great for the environment they'd be the first to admit, but better. They've also been offering nice(r) 100% recycled reusable 'bags for life' for a long while. Then, the Anya Hindmarch 'I'm not a plastic bag', covered in the last section, was a more attention-getting move; 20000 of these went on sale in selected Sainsbury's stores on the 25th April 2007. But given the objective of getting a large part of the population to reconsider and reduce their throwaway supermarket bag use, I suspect what they did next was more effective: on 27th April there were NO BAGS (i.e. none of the usual disposable ones) in any Sainsbury's store. Instead, they gave out around 7 million of those 10p *Bags For Life* for free. 'We want to make it as simple as possible for our millions of customers and thousands of colleagues to take action now' said their Customer Director, Gwyn Burr. I hope they keep it up, maybe do it once a month. There's nothing like habits being jolted; an enforced *cut*. We turned off email for a week at St Luke's once and it was really interesting what it taught us about how we usually communicate. There's nothing like changing behaviour to change your thinking. The Hindmarch bag was a big idea, certainly it got people talking about the issue and coverage in the media, but it was subsequently criticised, partly because it was so ostentatious (I doubt the *Bags For Life* are Fairtrade either, but they didn't set themselves up as the ethical *must have* of the year). And it even goes rather well with their 'try something new today' campaign. I was in a Sainsbury's this weekend and there is very prominent messaging around all the checkouts about reusing plastic bags or obviating the need for them. And from what I saw, the message is getting through. My impression was that nearly half of the shoppers (small sample and this is middle class liberal north London) were doing something other than loading up with fresh disposable plastic bags.

The simplest *Cut* collaboration strategy is to ask people to use your product less, once they have bought it. A classic German Mercedes TV commercial encouraged owners to leave the car in the garage for short trips and use a bicycle instead. It's a really arresting idea; you think 'how can that be in their interests?' But actually why not? They already sold you the car. Why not help you feel good about it and encourage you to reduce the problems, which we all face together? Some would, of course, not feel it is a car manufacturer's place to talk to you about this (that was the reaction in the early 1990s when I suggested and researched a potential VW car-sharing scheme in focus groups).

Another example is the Ariel 'Turn to 30' campaign, in association with the Energy Savings Trust. P&G have also been blazing a trail in marketing innovation, being one of the leading companies in digital media, buzz marketing and social marketing programmes. You probably think of them as associated with crass TV commercials for low interest products (broadly true, but their ads are getting better). But this is also the company that started a women's empowerment web 2.0 social network (www.capessa.com), has been coaching parents in Mexico on telling better bedtime stories (for Pampers), created a hit viral film on YouTube (for Folgers coffee) and ran a popular brand ambassador programme in the gay community (for Crest Whitestrips – sending a *Smile Team* of hunky men with beautiful smiles into gay venues, events and festivals). So you shouldn't be surprised that they have done some pioneering green marketing too. 'Turn to 30' was an integrated campaign using TV commercials and an informative website along with point of sale and packaging. The message was very simple; turn to 30 and you will save 40% of the energy used by your washing machine. That will save you money and save the environment. And because Ariel is such an effective cleaning product, it will work very well, even at these lower temperatures, with just about anything you throw at it.

It's not just me that thought this was ahead of its time. Ariel *Turn to 30* won a 2006 *Green Award* for the best large integrated campaign. It was beaten to the *Grand Prix* award though by another very ingenious *Cut* strategy, this time from O2. For owners of Nokia phones who were getting a new Nokia model, O2 encouraged them to keep the same charger. If they did so, their new phone would come in a special smaller pack, which would fit through the letter-box, saving them a trip to the local O2 store. They could then freepost back their old phone for recycling in a handy postal return pack included. A customer could also opt to have a (ubiquitous carbon-offsetting) tree planted in their name. It's a very engaging process, but one which is low on hassle. It had numerous benefits in the supply chain too, from manufacturing less phone chargers, to being able to transport more phones per vehicle. O2 also communicates with customers around the use of phone chargers: pointing out that 95% of the energy drawn by phone chargers is wasted. Only 5% actually is used to charge the phones. The other 95% is used while the charger is plugged into the wall but not switched off (O2 website[55]). O2 also offers a special tariff to encourage people to keep their old phone when they renew their contract. Its latest announcement is a £100 incentive to customers who keep their old phone handset when they renew a contract. The rate of significant innovation in phones seems to be slowing anyway and the savings it passes on could make this a real win:win.

Contrast the vague long list of pledges on the Honda site with what they could have done as their version of a *Cut* strategy: a brilliant idea from one of my favourite green consultancies live|work – the *70Max* campaign:

If everyone in the UK drove at 70mph max, we would reduce CO_2 emissions by 1 million tonnes a year. Sign Up. Display a sticker. Stay below 70mph (www.70max.com)

The site goes on to point out it is also cheaper and safer. This is the sort of idea that Honda could have integrated with its marketing, its cars and its dealerships. It would make great messaging on the actual cars. It's about time we had a range of bumper stickers to rival the 'Nuclear Power, No Thanks' of the 1970s. Media planners take note. Bumper stickers; it's the next wall charts!

Compare and Contrast

I think it's probably fairly obvious that I am more of a fan of *Cut* than *Switch*. But there are advocates on both sides. It depends where you see things going. If you think we can meet our carbon emission targets through great CSR work and getting consumers to buy the resulting responsible products (or offsets) then it's fine. But if you believe we need to build the audience of people living more sustainable lifestyles, then *Cut* is the only way to go. This, in turn, rather depends on your reading of human nature. My view is that, given a reasonable opportunity, most people will want to do the right thing (e.g. recycling). I don't think we are (only) a selfish species, we are also a social one. And when faced with guilty or shameful feelings, it feels good to actually do something to put things right; to feel that you have made a difference. One good behaviour can pave the way for another. You get into the habit of doing the right thing.

An analogy is this. If people could take a magic pill and lose weight, would you promote that as the government? Or would you still try to get people to exercise?

On the other hand, there is definitely an argument that green lifestyles need to lose the hair shirt image. Organic food is tastier, healthier and increasingly easy to get hold of. It's a real no-brainer, and it also has environmental benefits (especially if it's local and in-season).

It's probably not an either/or. More of a case of working out what is best for your business and what you can contribute on the green front too.

With both tactics we are probably past the point where simply adding any sort of pledge list or carbon balancing offer or eco-label is enough. We need breakthrough ideas, ones which are compelling, relevant, integral – like some of the examples in this chapter. Pushing well-known lifestyle change ideas will hit diminishing returns. Introducing new ones, like *70Max*, can add fresh impetus. It's about taking the creative skills from advertising and design and applying them to lifestyle change formats. Diet and self-help gurus have been doing this successfully for years, after all.

I had an idea the other day, which, by the time you read this, I may have persuaded a (re)mortgage company to help on. The idea is this:

FROM HOUSING BOOM TO HOUSING BLOOM: JOIN THE 1% CLUB

We have seen, on average, 140% growth in housing prices in the last ten years.

Why not reinvest just 1% of the profit you have made? (an average of £1100).

Putting that in home efficiency improvements like insulation (there are grants available to part-fund this) will save you money on your bills, will increase the value of your home* and will also make a big impact on your carbon footprint.

*Energy Savings Trust research shows that: 'many buyers are prepared to pay up to £10000 more for an environmentally friendly home.' This will be brought into focus when homes for sale get energy ratings soon. Trials show that in an energy-banded market, people do try to get their house into the top two bands, to increase its marketability.

C: Supporting Innovation (Greenest)

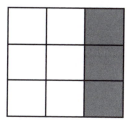

Figure 20 Column C

We consumerised our way into this mess and I think there are grounds for doubt that we can entirely consumerise our way out of it. We need to change what people consume and how they consume it too, substantially. To come anywhere near the targets of – for instance – a 70% decrease in carbon footprints, without a cata-strophic decline in economies or (real) quality of life, there are going to have to be some cultural breakthroughs. And with big changes come big entrepreneurial opportunities. The capitalist system means there are fortunes to be made by pioneering green alternatives. For instance, according to a report in the FT, the solar energy sector will grow from $20B in 2006 to $90B in 2010. That's 145% a year. To put that in context, eBay's been growing at roughly 60% a year. In fact, in *Fortune*'s list of fastest growing companies in 2006, the fastest revenue growth recorded (annual average of last three years) was 126%.

But that doesn't mean we can introduce functional solutions and hope they gain mass acceptance. Products are just the starting point. What will replace 20th century consumerism has to feel just as human, intuitive, desirable and imaginative. The cultural world can change beyond recognition, as historical upheavals have shown. And the crisis conditions for that to take place, I will argue, were already here, even without looming ecological catastrophes. We need to build a culture of everyday life where green is second nature. Changing culture is a big topic, many attempts by well-meaning governments, philanthropic causes and so on have failed. To be effective in this means grasping how culture change works. Anthropology is the obvious place to look for this theoretical structure; what can we learn from the hundreds of examples in anthropological fieldwork where a society has managed to go through deep cultural change? Anthropologist A.F.C. Wallace developed such a theory of what he called *cultural revitalisation movements*, based upon studies of hundreds of records of wholesale changes in line with new external demands and conditions. Typically, these changes had arrived at the same time as anthropologists; with modern colonial powers interrupting traditional modes of life. Cultural revitalisation is an adaptive social response (presumably innate, given the widespread spontaneous recurrence which Wallace uncovered) whereby the present values, customs and beliefs – which are dissonant and incompatible with the new circumstances – are analysed and recombined into a new synthesis or gestalt. Wallace defined revitalisation movements as 'deliberate, organised, conscious attempts by some or all of the members of a society to construct for themselves a more satisfying culture.' He observed that they were more likely to occur in societies undergoing rapid and/or devastating social change.

There is every sign that our own society is in a destructive phase. If you look at the incidence of diagnosed mental illness it is pretty shocking. Here are the figures from USA psychiatric survey data:

Anxiety disorders: 16.4% of adults (USSG)
Depressive disorders: 9.5% of adult Americans (NIMH)
Bipolar disorder: 1.2% of the population (NIMH)
Schizophrenia: 1.3% of adults (USSG)[56]

1 in 6 suffering from anxiety disorders (note this doesn't mean 'feeling anxious' – it means major symptoms such as obsessive–compulsive disorders, agoraphobia, post traumatic stress syndrome and so on) kind of makes the point on its own. You could also point to rates of poverty, loneliness, obesity, social exclusion, relationship failure, splits in communities, crime, decline of trust in authorities and so on. There have been other very troubled times, notably the Dickensian cities of the early Industrial Revolution. But those statistics at least make the point that current levels of stress and poor mental health are very high; far too high to argue on utilitarian grounds that we have got things about right for general happiness in the population.

Wallace found that the way out of the personal and social disintegration was often a very dramatic reformulation of the culture; a movement he found taking similar lines in hundreds of unconnected cases. He called this *Mazeway Resynthesis*:

> . . . each one of (us) must form a mental image of the culture in which he or she lives. It is this image Wallace calls 'the mazeway'. He coined this term because it best summed up for him the highly complex model formulated by each individual of himself or herself living in the context of society as a whole. 'The mazeway is nature, culture, personality and body image as seen by one person' he wrote. (Stephens and Price, 2000)[57]

What I think is so powerful about this is *the role of ideas* – individual flashes of creative brilliance – in synthesising new cultural gestalts; ideas about a more 'livable world'. I don't think it's at all surprising that one of the leading lights in current thinking about a new way of life – combining economic, social and environmental progress – happens to be an award winning science fiction writer (Bruce Sterling).

Bruce Sterling's *Viridian Manifesto* predicted the end of 'cut-and-paste, appropriation, detournement and neo-retro ahistoricality, postmodernity'.[58] Postmodernism, as its own proponents recognise, is a phase. Something quite similar happened in the *Fin de Siecle* period at the end of the 19th century. And whilst it has its liberating aspects, it is as much a symptom of a general disorder as a bold new cultural era to be celebrated. A lot of that stress and mental illness can be related to a prevailing uncertainty and chaos; a loss of structure, order, meaning, continuity, control, inclusion and so on. Postmodernism could be described as a society-wide breakdown.

In Sterling's view you could divide recent Western history into three broad stages:

1. Modernist, PROGRESS, industrial age.
2. Postmodernist, CHAOTIC, information age.
3. (insert name here), SETTLING, sustainability age.

This last stage, yet to be named, is when we build new institutions and ways of life, which are sustainable in every sense. Anthony Giddens's image of late modernity (he buys many of the features of postmodernity, but argues it is just a radicalised version of modernity) is that of the *juggernaut*; hurtling, always out of control, on the edge of risk.

We may already be well on the way to a new SETTLING. You can see this in little glimpses, like the attitudes and lifestyles of young people who are stereotypically understood as rebellious and antisocial; whereas research finds them to be mostly ambitious, sensible, hard working and holding quite traditional views (e.g. approving of marriage). We've been through a cultural explosion:

divorced parents, the end of jobs for life, lifelong education, new lifestyles, a housing boom, mobility, the ascendancy of women, new styles of child rearing, changed diets, lack of exercise and obesity, food scares, potential pandemics; but also new wealth and access to further education, travel, IT . . . – and we now face further – likely dramatic – changes in response to a climate crisis.

SETTLING is the response to a period that has been unbearably UNSETTLING.

Where I don't entirely agree with Sterling is that his combination of technology, business, green and everyday life(style) is, in any way, easy or obvious. For a sci-fi writer it's an intuitive mix, but not for the culture at large. I see all four areas as being separated by fault lines. These are the very splits which a mazeway resynthesis would tackle. But they need to find new intuitive, holistic, livable forms. It's not only a technological or even a design issue. It's a cultural issue, and I think the important role that marketing (or at least people with marketing skills) can play is in *synthesising ideas* which allow conflicting elements to be reframed and to form a greater whole.

What are the modern fault lines? There are many. But the main ones I want to explore are between:

- technology;
- business;
- ecology;
- everyday life.

Fault line one is between green and tech. Traditionally (i.e. back in the 1970s), greens rejected technology, business and modern lifestyles. This is an awkward impasse given technology holds some of the keys to sustainable development. One commentator who thinks that technology is a big part of the answer and that traditional green views get in the way, is the eminent sociologist

Anthony Giddens. He has described the current situation as an acute crisis, and one in which human ingenuity and specifically new technologies (such as new energy sources) will play a key role. 'Environmental technologies are likely to be for the next 20 years what information technology has been for the last 20 – a driving force of wider economic and social change.' (*Guardian*, 1/11/06[59]) Giddens has suggested that the Green Movement (the group of people who pushed green issues historically) is now in danger of holding us back, as it is hostile to modern industry and technology as well as being conservative. The new green entrepreneurial sector in the US is calling itself *Clean Tech*, perhaps for similar reasons – calling itself *Green Tech* could pigeonhole it in an unhelpful way. You could counter that actually Giddens is the one behind the times here, and that many modern greens are quite excited about technology; certainly those that blog are always on about solar power, new materials, home efficiency and so on. But in the popular understanding of going green, this is still a cultural block.

The second fault line is between green and business mindsets. Sustainability remains an uneasy truce between a commitment to both economic growth *and* a greener, cleaner world. The militant anti-corporate wing of the Green Movement is far from being pro-business, seeing even CSR as a sham, a way of avoiding regulation. And conversely many of the business people who have advanced CSR policies, base them solely upon 'the business case' – i.e. reassurance that it is all ultimately in the service of growth, revenue and profit.

The interesting point for our discussion is whether such conflicts can find breakthrough new resolutions – both in products and also in lifestyle or cultural norms. The answer lies with ideas. Only ideas can reconcile the previously irreconcilable. We need lots of breakthrough new ideas. That, in practice, is what mazeway resynthesis consists of.

A third conflict we come back to later is *greenophobia*: a conflict between green and the norms of everyday life. But there is more conflict to be resolved than just that between green and the other elements. There are also fault lines between disruptive technology and business – imagine being a telco when Skype launched! And between technology and everyday life. For instance, imagine having been a bank branch clerk at the time of the introduction of the call centre and cashpoint machine. (Fortunately for bank clerks though, banks have recently discovered that the most effective sales channel is face-to-face. Now banks can't open branches again fast enough).

There are anomalies – legacy issues – even in new 'green' behaviours. Take recycling. This takes a huge amount of energy, as well as effort, manpower and expenditure. We should really live in a much less 'throwaway world' in the first place, with minimal packaging waste, durable products and so on. There are similar inefficiencies in concepts like ownership (vs sharing of many large and/or occasionally used items). And there are many unexploited opportunities as a result of IT. There's no real reason in future not to buy goods direct from farms or producers, with internet efficient markets making the middle men (Tesco) look vulnerable.

It's that sort of dramatic restructuring which this section will look at. Disruptive innovation is needed to move towards a climate-neutral human society. And it really is an emergency. James Lovelock, a pioneering eco-scientist (author of *The Revenge of Gaia*) speculates that only 20% of the human race will make it to the end of this century, largely because populous regions (the USA, continental Europe, China) will become uninhabitable and this may trigger not only mass migration of refugees, but wars over the territory which is inhabitable. Let's hope it isn't going to be as serious as that, especially if we do manage to make sweeping reforms and changes. Cultural resynthesis will be needed to get these big changes adopted fast. The net result *should* be a more satisfying way of life, beyond the fault lines and corresponding anxiety and suffering of today.

Victor Papanek saw much of this coming decades ago. He called the challenge *Design for the Real World*.[60] One of my favourite

Papanek stories is his dispute with a congressional hearing on car safety. The industry said it would cost millions and take years to develop the car safety bumpers that campaigners were calling for (now standard of course, but this was many years ago). Papanek made an impromptu bumper out of beer cans, a plank and some string. He then crashed his car at high speed into the outside wall of the building where the hearing was taking place. His point was that you could do it today, if you didn't start with expectations led by appearance. Muji is a beautiful design brand, but its design aesthetic is deliberately 'raw', basically the product of spending the least amount possible and using the most environmentally conscious materials and processes. Muji represents a very exciting tendency, one of revaluing the aesthetics of greenness.

Objective-led design is where marketing can make an immediate difference, not only to the impact, but also the culture of consumerism. Let's get rid of all unnecessary elements concerned with appearance and develop a new aesthetic out of the result. But what has to give is consumerised design; we need to live in a world in some ways where the bumper made with cans, string and a plank is preferred. Actually, I'd argue we are already well on the way. Lo-Fi, retro, homebrew, distressed graphics, industrial (i.e. unprettified), user generated, reality TV . . . these are all pulling in the right direction. The web has got us used to thrilling functionality in drab graphic settings. The overall shift is to a culture which is folksier; more like YouTube or eBay, less like a glossy advert.

The culture of excessive consumption is largely a product of advertising and design. Post-advertising brands, like eBay, Amazon, Skype, Wikipedia and Linux, did not craft images, nor did they attempt to convey consumerist values of aspiration, individualism and so on. They just work great. But reform within marketing creativity is not enough. We need to invent some new ways of life. Everyone has been saying that culture change is key. But it won't come about without some radically new cultural ideas. This section addresses the triple objectives I described at the start of the book:

commercial, green and culture change. It's only if you start with objectives beyond profit that you get to such radical, yet (in retrospect) common sense ideas as the ones we will be exploring. An absolutely key point is that many of these ideas won't *look* green. Rather they will *do* green. Existing green cultural codes are inadequate; too implicated in consumerism – i.e. luxury – or too associated with puritan fringes – i.e. niche. These are not vehicles for cultural resynthesis. We need to reach outside the field.

Some innovations will be low tech, for instance electricity for devices from cranks, pumps and other mechanical means. One idea I would love to explore with an industrial designer is whether the actual energy used in striking the keyboard could be used to (at least partly) power a very simple word processing device (beyond the typewriter function, having simple editing and storage). I'm sure the physical force expended in typing this book could have charged a few batteries!

But other innovations will be very strange indeed, involving not just new technology, but new types of technology like biotech, nanotech and so on. Anthony Dunne and Fiona Raby made a fascinating exhibition at the Science Museum to encourage children to think differently about energy by positing three scenarios: one was where children would have to produce hydrogen to get their pocket money; one was about using human poo as an energy source; and one was about using blood as an alternative (with microbial fuel cells) to batteries. Interviewed about this exhibition, Dunne commented that new technologies of this sort are going to have a big impact on our lives and perhaps sooner than we think. 'I think it's important that designers start thinking about how to get involved. It's not just about new skills or a new medium, but very different ways of thinking. What does it mean to design living or semi-living materials and products?'[61] What Dunne was describing – and exploring in exhibits – was resynthesis; how to make disruptive new ideas intuitive and non-scary. That's one example of how marketing has a big part to play.

The theory may sound abstract but the challenges are very concrete. We need to create demand for products like composting toilets (to name one current example). These are great products. They use almost no water, don't smell and are generally not a problem grow. But how to sell these? How to even broach it? Yet we have only a short time to accustomise people to thousands of such ideas. There are two steps:

- invent a different, radically greener product, service and/or lifestyle idea;
- graft on a 'chunk' of existing culture from an unrelated sphere which acts as a kind of 'Trojan horse' in building acceptability, making it feel normal.

We do have a good precedent to study and learn from; how modern culture succeeded in humanising technology; first the telephone and car, later the domestic appliances, recently the computer and now even the robot (e.g. Sony Aibo).

Much of the art of the last two hundred years could be described as an attempt to assimilate this, through a fusing of the technological and the human. An early myth – one expressing a rejection of this development – was Mary Shelley's Frankenstein. The same idea was present in the epic 2001, the story of an inhuman computer with a human voice. It was the mythologising of technophobia, a fear of the inhuman and prosthetic. But over the last 30 years something has shifted. Computers have become 'friendly' (despite the occasional re-emergence of the older view, for instance in the Y2K bug). How has this transformation been accomplished? How did we go from technophobia to internet enthusiasm within the lifetime of one generation? One factor was the grafting of computing technology onto existing cultural forms:

- The hand-held tool. The computer mouse. The iPod. The mobile phone. We are defined as a unique species by our relationship with hand-held tools. We tend to think with our hands, for instance gesturing to feel the meaning of our words.

- The desktop/graphical interface. A familiar office environment reproduced on a familiar (TV) screen. Plus a typewriter keyboard. Whereas previous computers (when I was learning computer science at school) used punched card readers.
- The laptop. Which is also called a notebook, because of what it resembles.
- The mind as computer/computer as mind. One of the greatest ever pieces of corporate myth making was *Deep Blue*, the chess match between Kasparov and an IBM computer. But the computer theory of mind was already all the rage, pioneered by cognitive scientists such as Marvin Minsky. Not to mention sci-fi.
- The computer for the *me generation*. The discourse of the 1960s rebel is very important to understanding today's computer culture. Apple, with its *1984* vision of the personal Macintosh, was intended as a response to IBM. But it proved to be a much broader cultural innovation. The connection was already there in the Californian IT industry (why do you think we 'surf' the web?).
- Computers as fashion; notably the Apple computers and accessories. iPod being the latest in this (a wearable hard drive).
- Computers as companions; the *Tamagochi* and *Nintendogs* games, breakthroughs in their industry because they attracted women to take to computer gaming and gadgets – they also took the idea of a relationship with a machine to new levels.
- The computer as a mind gym. The latest, most intimate or prosthetic development, exemplified by the Nintendo DS and *Dr Kawashima's Brain Training*, which would have looked like science fiction only a few years ago.
- Interpersonal computing; social communities, blogging, SMS, file sharing. We have almost forgotten by now that these have anything even to do with computing. They're just everyday devices, like the TV or a microwave oven.

In archetypal terms, the computer has gone from a monster (like HAL in *2001*), to a magical implement; like a wand (pointing the mouse), crystal ball (gaining knowledge simply by gazing through the screen) or a portal into another world. *Second Life* and *World of Warcraft* are only literal expressions of this imaginary (virtual) universe. It gets even more interesting where you get closer to specific myth-making. Steve Jobs's brief to the designers of the iMac was to make a computer that was 'like a sunflower'. On a less fanciful level, isn't it interesting how the iPod (taking its lead from Mp3 players like the Zen) was effectively a remake of the good old Walkman? A Trojan horse indeed.

What we have seen in mainstream culture up until now is *greenophobia* (by analogy with technophobia). Greenophobia consists of a number of ideas about green lifestyle products:

- they are primitive, dirty, rough, smelly, unpleasant;
- they are a step back from modern living standards;
- they are inconvenient, time-consuming;
- they represent a sacrifice, the loss of benefits and satisfactions;
- they can be uncomfortable, 'a hair shirt' (e.g. cycling in the rain);
- with no compensating positive benefits other than 'virtue';
- they are weird, for weird people, hippy;
- they are part of a fixed lifestyle, you'd have to conform;
- they are more expensive and less effective.

It's not entirely unfounded. There are plenty of green innovations which may take longer to find mainstream acceptance, such as those (odour-free and incredibly water-efficient) composting toilets. Modern versions of these are often self-contained and yield a dry organic compost some decades later, which is a tiny fraction of the solid waste they capture. It's arguably a symptom of modern life, alienated from nature, our bodies and so on that we would struggle with this idea. They are already finding acceptance in public facilities and in pioneering developments such as the carbon neutral *BedZED* in south London. But it's not where the mainstream is going to start, just as Linux was never going to be the entry point for computer virgins.

People need a cultural Trojan horse. This kind of acceptance of radical product concepts is the ultimate example of making green stuff seem normal. And the thing is, with great green design it's actually going to be much better when you get used to it. Our role as marketers is to work with the development of these products from the early stages, to ensure they are built around acceptability and accessibility. Which usually means adding *an organising idea*, which makes it feel intuitive and familiar. Just like the Trojan horse, which looked exactly like a gift (as it was traditional for a defeated army to give the gift of the general's horse to the victors, out of respect). We have to turn technologies into humanly graspable utilities. And we have to add fun, style and forms of enjoyment.

The organising idea is there to perform a number of roles:

- make it feel familiar, safe, accessible;
- synthesise it so people can grasp it as a whole;
- communicate positive benefits, functional and emotional;
- provide a platform for marketing and a basis for word of mouth.

Let's explore greenophobia a bit further; what exactly are we up against? A joint piece of UK research in mid 2006 by the National Consumer Council and the Sustainable Development Commission with 100 (very) mainstream consumers who attended a one and a half day workshop explored this issue.[62]

The research found, in spontaneous discussion, that the environment in the broadest sense was on most people's agenda. People could also imagine in the long term that changes in lifestyle that looked unacceptable now were possible; pointing, for instance, to the smoking bans and wearing of seatbelts. However, there was a tendency to shift the blame to others. Why bother when other countries are worse than the UK they asked? Or, what difference could one individual make? And there was an evident outright rejection of anything involving (perceived) sacrifice of modern life-style enjoyment, convenience or status. People said that once you have had things it is hard to manage without; that they didn't want to sacrifice when others around them might not be sacrificing too; that the habits of buying whatever is cheapest and most convenient would be hard to break; that steps like going back to public transport instead of private cars would be particularly difficult.

When specific product service innovations like a car club were introduced, the rejection was quite vehement (evidencing what I call *greenophobia*). They painted a very negative picture of how this might work, seeing sharing cars as a kind of invasion of their personal space; only to then claim that (on the basis of this negative construction) it would never work. They imagined, for instance, that it would be a nightmare to organise how to share the cars and hence that it would be like not having access to a car when you needed it.

Similarly, none could imagine flying less. The ability to go abroad on holiday was a major aspiration. Many took frequent low cost flights into Europe. The thought of going back to substitutes – to holidays in the UK or using the train – was rejected quite strongly. They'd tried that before, didn't like it and didn't want to 'go back'. These findings have to be tempered with the realisation that attitudes are moving incredibly fast. A survey by BBC Worldwide in 2007 among 14000 adults in 21 countries across the world found that '20% have bought or plan to buy a smaller car and 28% have changed their travel plans as a result of concerns about climate change'.[63] A spokesman from Virgin Atlantic, commenting on aviation and climate change in the FT, said, 'Where there is a train alternative, customers are taking it. On long haul, customers want to know about offsetting their flights and how we can contribute in other ways' (14/5/07[64]). Research just published by YouGov about how Britons intend to travel on holiday this summer showed that one fifth intended to drive. *The Independent* newspaper commented: 'British families have traditionally flooded airport departure lounges every summer in an attempt to escape to sunnier climes. But research published yesterday suggests the trend has taken a downturn as holidaymakers prepare to take their holidays by car, motivated by the environmental impact of flying' (20/5/07[65]). That statement would be more convincing if they had data for the previous year, showing the scale of this 'downturn'. But there is clearly a growing concern, and the situation is quite fluid. My suspicion is that the attitude will move faster than the behaviour though. People will reduce flying, but I doubt they are ready to give up their foreign holidays en masse quite yet.

In many cases, people are locked into a set of habits and assumptions, which make them assume that alternatives aren't possible. For instance, people hate grocery shopping. It's crowded, kids get grumpy, it's a drag. You can't wait to get it over with and get on with your life. You therefore can't imagine taking much longer over shopping, traipsing from local butchers, to bakers to greengrocers and so on. People therefore can't imagine living without modern supermarkets. But why not embrace shopping the continental way; enjoy it, try the cheeses or breads, chat to the shopkeepers or stallholders, treat it as a pleasurable way to spend a Saturday, not a Tuesday night chore. Of course it helps if you are lucky to live in a 'village-y' community with nice local shops. Or a short drive from a farmers' market (of which there are over 500 in the UK, listed at http://www.farmersmarkets.net/). It's all about your mental model approaching household shopping. Do you see it as a chore or an enjoyable way to spend time? The knock-on effect of shopping for food like this, is you start to think more about what you eat too. Or if you really do not have time, have other commitments 24/7 like volunteering, then delivery is a great way to go and (whilst greenest when ordering local seasonal food direct from farmers) even on the Ocado or Tesco.com level is much greener than driving to a store.

There are several possible responses to greenophobia. One is to build sustainability in, both into taxation and regulation and also into goods and services. It is hard to imagine going very far with either without consumer support; an unpopular tax (for instance effectively pricing out flying) or an unpopular price point or policy (for instance delisting out of season foods) would be difficult. But you can make hundreds of invisible changes, which do improve matters. That's what CSR is all about in the first place. There are amazing energy efficient products in development. Like the hyper-car, which, through a combination of streamlining, weight reduction and engine design, should achieve a fuel efficiency five or six times that achieved today. Hydrogen fuel cells, if we can develop a mass hydrogen production technology that isn't based on fossil fuels (for instance using bacterial biomass), could take these measures even further. Electric cars, if charged from renewable sources, are already a very green alternative. These don't have to involve major compromise; there is an electric sports car (the Tesla) in development. That's all product innovation; a new level of environmental performance within the existing product format. And the marketing of such substitutes is covered earlier in the book; e.g. functional benefits (save money) or cultural ones (celebs drive the Prius).

The classical marketing approach is to 'fish where the fish are' – avoid areas where people have greenophobia about the substitutes and work in areas where people are willing to change – as there are easy and attractive ways to do so. But that's not going to get us to a 70% reduction in footprint with this late mainstream audience. In fact, just the projected increases in flying in the UK could wipe out all other gains.

That's why I believe we must change the culture, reframe the choices and build some Trojan horses. This will involve product and service redesign and/or changing habits. A key approach to doing this is what is known as *product–service systems*. These are about developing new alternatives which meet the same needs better. This manoeuvre has long been recognised in sustainability circles. For instance, in a classic *Harvard Business Review* paper (a forerunner of their book *Natural Capitalism*), Lovins, Lovins and Hawken pointed to a move from manufactured goods to 'a solutions-based business model' where 'value is instead delivered as a flow of services – providing illumination for instance rather than selling the light bulbs.'[66] Another example is, if you focus on the ultimate need for 'warm homes', then insulating each home well looks a much better solution than building a (very expensive, unpopular and potentially dangerous) nuclear power station. Only if 'energy supply' were your frame of enquiry would you go for the nuclear option. I'm aware that this is a contentious statement to make, although I am only repeating a view that's been put forward since the 1970s. I'm not anti-science by any means, but I am swayed by the arguments put forward by the likes of *The Ecologist*, one of their key points being the unacceptable risk; for instance, they discovered that no insurance company in the world will cover a nuclear power station. But all of that is a distraction from my main point; a shift to focusing on the ultimate need met, not the current industrial set-up designed to meet it. A much tamer version of the same idea is encouraging people to buy a service rather than a product; Friends of the Earth suggested this in their *Green Christmas* campaign: 'Treat people to a special experience instead of an item – such as theatre tokens, annual membership of a gallery or a weekend at a spa.'[67]

Green development doesn't necessarily look 'green'; in fact it can be quite counterintuitive. Studies have shown that if you double population density, use of the car falls by 40%. The design of mixed-use areas, where people simply don't need cars, is a better solution than any form of car technology. Living in the centre of London, I managed without a car for eight years (and living in a slightly less convenient location now, I still use the current car less than once a week). It's a surprising reframe if you think about it; concentrated service provision means the greenest way forward is living in much more crowded cities, rather than in rural idylls. We have only been thinking about organising society along more sustainable lines for such a short time; there are lots of discoveries being made, and still to be made.

One pioneering line in *product–service systems* is looking at ways to redesign urban systems of living, away from individual ownership and use. City car clubs (with computerised membership and booking, guaranteed car parking spaces, flexible car use for an hour or for several days) are proving successful with constituencies such as US university students, who can't afford to own and run a car and only need them occasionally. These ways of living are readily adopted by greener fringes, but the very same ideas of 'car sharing' – as we saw in the recent UK government-funded research – can meet very high resistance in the mainstream, albeit admittedly based upon a limited understanding. It's not just sharing cars and cutting flights that have been rejected. Joel Makower reported on an innovative Electrolux pilot scheme in Sweden to give people free washing machines and then charge them per use.[68] Consumers were offered a machine on a pay-per-use basis (10 Swedish Kronor per wash). This meant that Electrolux could take full responsibility for the product throughout its life, ensuring that it was well maintained and replaced at the best point for a more efficient model, also being able to reuse parts and handle the recycling and disposal. Unfortunately, and executives admitted that it might just have been the way the scheme was presented, there was little public enthusiasm for this scheme. People pay per use in lots of markets, for instance in renting DVD films and pay as you go mobiles. Many would be familiar with launderettes (also pay per use) and perhaps that is a drawback? If you did three or four washes per week, this system would cost you about £100 per year, which sounds pretty good value for a state-of-the-art appliance.

I wonder if it is the concept of paying to use something in your home that is culturally dissonant? Like if they had put a coin slot in the machine to reinforce the point; it's not yours. The central myth of the modern household is self-sufficient 'nuclear families'. Increasingly, in fact, the typical situation is a single person household. The number of kettles owned keeps rising as a result. The pre-industrial mode of life where an extended family or village community shared many resources and activity is far greener. It's also more 'human' (the situation we evolved to be born to expect). Currently our communal instincts are satisfied by a mix of workplace community and watching soap operas. I know this is a very North European perspective, when I have visited places like Madrid, I am aware how much more social and communal daily life tends to be. But perhaps this is the opportunity in our current housing crisis; the government is predicting the number of households in the UK will grow by 3.5 million in the next 20 years. Maybe it shouldn't. Maybe we should live in more communal, and hence less wasteful, arrangements. The scourge of our modern cities isn't crime or work related stress (in my view), it is loneliness. So many problems of modern life would be solved if we lived in a more integrated way. The 'dream' of individualism has proved to have a heavy price tag.

My view is that with sufficient ingenuity and marketing insight into what people really want (including status, independence, new experiences), we can find a way to reframe and resynthesise many components of modern life. At various points in history, human sacrifice, shamanism and stockbroking have all looked normal! So long as a green innovation doesn't involve incest (the only known human cultural norm with a genetic basis) and you can imagine it as a workable way of life, then it is a cultural possibility; but in its raw functional form it can appear a cultural cul de sac. Marketing (or however you want to describe cultural concept engineering) can be a vital missing link. Calling something 'organic' is light years from calling it 'chemical-free horticulture'!

The framing idea doesn't have to look green. In fact it may be an advantage to make green a background consideration, or even keep it out of view. There are examples of mainstream product–service systems which achieve major green objectives without even appearing green. eBay is a prime example.

In some ways we need unrealistic solutions, i.e. ones that are BIG enough to make a difference fast enough. Ones which even prepare the ground for other changes (once you have given up your car, changing to local shops is secondary and actually a logical expedient). One person who's not been afraid to propose bold changes in the way we live is George Monbiot, who suggested a 10-step practical programme, including a carbon cap for individual consumer spending on energy, transport and so on, new building regulations and energy efficiency standards for developers and landlords, banning the sale of the most inefficient and wasteful products, the development of much better public transport infrastructure, freezing road and airport expansion and, most interestingly given the dominant place of supermarket retailing in consumer behaviour:

10. Legislate for the closure of all out-of-town superstores, and their replacement with a warehouse and delivery system. Warehouses use roughly 5% of the energy. Out-of-town shops (. . .)(also involve) the car – delivery vehicles use 70% less fuel.[69]

Many such government and society-wide initiatives are possible. The congestion charge in London is one successful example, and marketing (for instance, its branding and communication) played a role in accelerating motorist awareness, understanding, registration and compliance. Flying could be a key target for similar measures. But the fascinating thing is that few of the other ideas on Monbiot's list are necessarily government initiatives. Governments tend to be slow and inefficient. The Labour Party touted carbon rationing last year, but there is little evidence it was entirely serious. Why don't private companies introduce green delivery services, offer leasable car batteries, encourage greater renewable energy use, ban bad products or mark them up with a hefty premium to more than reflect their environmental impact?

In many ways these are marketing solutions (involving new consumer behaviour) rather than regulatory issues. Certainly companies have the opportunity to pioneer on these issues and demonstrate public support. That's what has really happened with the M&S, HSBC, Sky and other carbon neutral announcements. At some point quite soon, all companies will be subject to such stringent carbon taxation that it will be in their economic interests to go carbon neutral. These pioneering companies saw the advantage of bowing to the inevitable and introducing choice immediately. The notion of free choice (rather than compulsion) is a huge subject in green marketing, both for the companies and their consumers; the psychology of choosing (rather than compliance) is very different. Wherever possible, governments must give us the opportunity (on both sides) to choose to do the right thing; our wellbeing depends on this, it is the wellspring of motivation and morale. If we simply experience a series of restrictions being imposed on us, the future looks grim. If we can choose to live (simpler but) better, we may well be happier for it. It's also far more likely to work if you build things from the ground up, with companies and communities involved. It's more organic, there is more opportunity to experiment and indeed to fail. Sweeping top-down reforms nearly always fall down on some incidental or unintended consequence. Regulation should – in my view – consolidate and reinforce and generally take its lead from such changes – except in contexts where there is a clear case of market failure (e.g. overfishing).

There are many types of bottom-up innovation that could work to achieve climate harm reduction. It's sometimes useful when you are brainstorming for a new idea in your sector to look at a list of abstract types of idea. So here are some of the many possible headings:

- Substitute products which are much less damaging or resource depleting yet also have economic (e.g. cheaper) and/or cultural advantages (better once got used to).
- New systems, cutting out parts of a process (e.g. distribution) which are wasteful, or using new efficiencies, such as those enabled by network technologies.

- Ideas which extend the usage or lifetime of existing products, or reduce waste in similar ways (e.g. refills, durable or repairable products).
- Ideas which do less damage when their time is up (e.g. recyclable, reusable).
- Ideas which involve customers sharing, pooling, swapping or otherwise co-operating to reduce their collective impact.
- Ideas which promote cultural realisations (such as 'less is more') which are environmentally beneficial beyond that specific product category.
- Ideas where the company takes more total responsibility for the product lifecycle; renting or leasing rather than selling, and reusing or recycling for zero waste.
- Ideas which establish consumer precedents (habits or affiliations) which other environmentally friendly businesses can build upon.
- Ideas which promote regulatory change in a whole industry or on a whole issue.
- Ideas which satisfy psychological needs without physical products being produced.
- Ideas which damage the prospects of 'bad' companies, for instance by finding a clever way to legitimately offer a substitute or copy, for free.
- Ideas which undermine consumerism, individualism, selfishness, false image.
- Ideas which promote better living, collective values, real happiness.
- Ideas which are so innovative they may be ahead of their time, but which spawn imitators which do break through in the mainstream.
- Ideas establishing new business models, or even new forms of capitalism.
- Any type of idea I have missed, which achieves both commercial and green goals(!)

In summary, we have a dual challenge: innovation, to create something radically different and better, and then making it feel intuitive, familiar and easy to adopt. The means to do this are simple to describe but difficult to execute – we need lots of brilliant ideas.

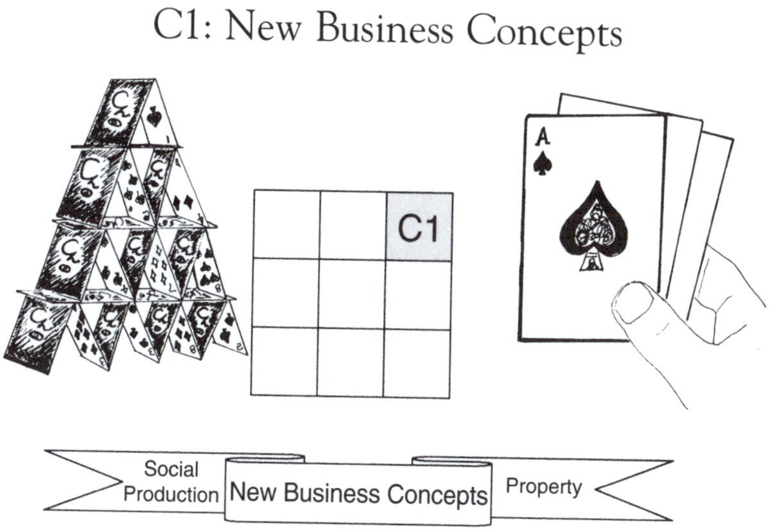
C1: New Business Concepts
C1
A
Social Production
New Business Concepts
Property

Figure 21 Grid C1

How will the sustainability age economy work? What will the companies that drive it forward be like? The hope is that they will simply be more 'human-friendly'. The era of industrialisation could then be seen as like teeth braces – uncomfortable but only transitory – prior to a return to an improved fit with human nature. Some features of this changed configuration seem here to stay, like large-scale cities. But many do not, like *work as battery farming*, which is now being displaced by *free range* knowledge and service work, where initiative and freedom is integral. Overall, life (in our populous future super-cities) may become more village-like again; pedestrianised, localised, with more rich social contact with and reliance upon other people, and hence less alienating. It took the invention of *meetup.com* (and countless other social networks) to counter the *bowling alone* trend, mass loneliness being the inevitable conclusion of individualism and industrialisation.

In the web 2.0 culture, person-to-person connection is the key. This may be achieved through a noticeboard type function – one person posts a thought, another reads it and adds to it, some people vote on it, a moderator improves or approves it – for instance as in Wikipedia, Amazon reviews, threaded discussion forums. It may also be achieved through clever modelling and matching; for instance, recommendation engines based upon other people who made similar choices to yours. Or it may be a direct P2P interaction, which includes file-sharing, friends listings and all sorts of P2P connections, as well as direct human communication through IM, twitter and so on. From a human point of view, in other words, it's not just information technology, it's *Belonging Technology* (I should trademark this idea and sell it to British Telecom). Virtual community and identity construction has stepped in to make life more human again, as the old social categories broke down. We are constructing our identities actively. We have lost some of our sense of being a 'type' related to role models and scripts (underpinned by age, class, gender, religion, region and so on) and our bearings. But we are refinding ourselves in this criss-cross world of six degrees of separation. The traditional pre-industrial culture was very localised. You grew up in a small community and knew your place within it. Modern life became disembedded and you then only knew your place through images of status and aspiration in adverts, sitcoms, films, fashion magazines and so on. The media offered to be your window on the world. But what it showed you was a world of goods, which once bought, would secure you an identity. The same images conspired to make people feel poor (relative to the lifestyles portrayed) in the midst of unprecedented (and quite possibly unrepeatable) levels of human affluence. Through the internet, people are getting back to that 'village' identity; social networks where you can get ideas about how to live and who to be from peers.

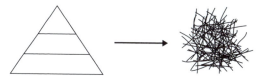

Figure 22 Hierarchy to network

Many of the new ideas, such as product–service systems and new collaborative design, production, retail and delivery models, are only possible on any scale because of the internet. It is all part of the pattern I suggested earlier, of shifting from hierarchy to network (Figure 22).

Here are just a few examples of this same 'shape' of shift:

- From corporate hierarchy to 'the individualised corporation'.
- From bureaucracy to 'adhocracy' (Toffler).
- From broadcast to peer-to-peer (and other network distribution models).
- From schooling to lifelong learning.
- From trusting expert authorities to self-reliant research, e.g. in health matters.
- From demographic destiny (e.g. class) to self-made identity.
- From aspiration to folksy (e.g. YouTube) cultural ideals.
- From audience to community.

A particularly deep and thorough analysis of these developments is provided by Benkler's *Wealth of Networks* – a book based upon a ten-year study of phenomena such as Napster and Wikipedia – which charts the rise of what the author calls *Social Production*.[70] This is where amateur collective labour (but working to professional standards) builds viable products and content. Demos, in a recent report by Charlie Leadbeater and Paul Miller, called this the *Pro–Am* revolution:

> Enthusiastic amateurs pursuing activities to professional stan-
> dards will have an increasingly important role in our society
> and economy. From astronomy to activism, from surfing to saving
> lives, Pro–Ams – people pursuing amateur activities to professional
> standards – are an increasingly important part of our society and
> economy.[71]

Where Benkler's study differs from this individualised definition is that he is most interested in the public implications, exploring the new creative commons, their legal and economic implications (Benkler being a Yale law professor). But it's the same trend.

The current interest in this model is based on the outstanding success of internet-enabled social productions; including Linux, Wikipedia, Digg, YouTube, Flickr, Del.icio.us, OhMy! News, MySpace and blogging networks. The economics of these are, depending on your point of view, either futuristic or pre-industrial (or both). Interestingly, science had been developed in this way for centuries; and in fact the open source movement referenced science as a role model, and perhaps more significantly this was its origin; university geeks like Linus Torsvalds (Linux founder) swapping code. What the internet allowed was for the science model of co-operation, peer review, publishing and so on to be extended into commercial software, retailing and entertainment businesses.

What the same connective and collaborative software platforms have done to traditional brands (and some new ones) is build customer involvement into the 'production' process: for example with Amazon *reader reviews*, Lego *Factory* (user-designed kits), Gmail invites, the eBay community and feedback system.

This is not an entirely new idea for business though. Customer involvement (for instance collecting and assembling your own flat-pack furniture) is a core principle of the IKEA model. But the ability to have such rich customer dialogue, unrestrained by the alienating filter of market research reporting is new, outside small or local businesses. And the internet makes collaboration with customers efficient. Indeed, customers are collaborating with each other whether you like it or not. My music engineering and equipment forum spends a great deal of time debating the best thing to buy, on behalf of its individual members. I also get great support and education there, with access to *Grammy Award* winning experts. All out of a new (or old) spirit of self-help community and co-operation.

The Victorian institutions – such as retailer co-operatives supplying factory workers with affordable basic goods – were born out of the newly industrialised cities. And like industrial cities, they were imposed from the top down. Today the most promising basis for new institutions is web 2.0. This gives us access to new bottom-up ways of organising, involving people en masse, educating, sharing, joining communities and much besides. Web 2.0 has a peculiar characteristic, which is vital to get. It has reinjected 'free' (i.e. common property, as well as, e.g., *advertising free*) back into the commercial space. The Victorians left us our shared services and institutions such as roads, waterworks, railways, public libraries, schools and hospitals. But these were not common properties, even if the use of some was later made 'free' (paid for by taxes rather than directly). The commons of old England were all owned by private individuals, but were places where others had rights: the right to graze, fish, take turf or firewood. Just as Linux today is owned and can be bought in a serviced version but can also be used freely.

Alvin Toffler's idea of the *Prosumer* (producer–consumer) from his book *The Third Wave* in 1979 has proved prescient; he basically foresaw (at least in outline) much of what I covered in section B (i.e. participative marketing and business, co-creating and sharing responsibility). Where does Toffler think things are heading now? In his recent writings he has returned to this concept and explored the extent to which the economy is being driven by such efforts and yet they are often *nonmoney* enthusiasms. He makes the point that disparate activities are lumped together under the term 'economy', the only thing they have in common is that they are monetised. Toffler's *Prosumer* category simply looks at similar activities, which are not monetised (yet). Toffler describes this as having 'a powerful aggregate impact on the money economy'. Warning economists not to discount or ignore this informal side to the economy, Toffler pointed to the example of Napster paving the way for the phenomenal global success of the *iTunes* music store. But it is not as neat a distinction as that, as I'm sure Toffler would recognise. There are also examples of prosumerism (a labour of shared enthusiasm) *embedded within* major money-making business sites. Conversely, you could describe this as money-making businesses being embedded within a broader society, and specifically a network of non-paid activities and relationships. For instance, over ten million Amazon reviews have been provided for free by readers, out of enthusiasm for books, and now provide a valuable part of the service.

The *social production* revolution has a formula which I think developers of new green businesses, particularly internet-enabled ones, would do well to learn from:

1. A tightly defined killer app. The thing about big web 2.0 hits is how singular they are. The narrower and deeper the application, the better. Of course they have secondary features and utilities; these tend to be used to differentiate alternatives once the first-mover advantage is gone. But the 'hook' is simply something 'you always knew you wanted' in retrospect. It wasn't possible to share pictures, bookmarks and video with large parts of the population unless you owned a national medium. It wasn't possible to Wiki, to Digg, or to blog or to Google (a sure sign of something useful and unique in life is that it becomes a verb).

2. Shared enthusiasm. It's not just about the content; it's the shared interest and energy. People aren't visiting YouTube for passive TV-like entertainment; it's a place for hobbyist auteurs and critics. The hits on YouTube happen not because of official

charts but because people share the juiciest videos they come across. That enthusiasm can be political (the so-called blawgs), lifestyle or interest-based (e.g. scrapbookers or snowboarders), about identity (e.g. feminist), family, work-related or similarly defined by many sorts of social grouping or interest.

3. Utilities and platforms. Web 2.0 is 'stuff we couldn't do before the internet'; in contrast to web 1.0, which was, for instance, putting your newspaper articles and archive online. The crucial role of web 2.0 developers is turning possibility into easy and intuitive capability: Wiki, Blogger, YouTube, Flickr, MySpace, Netvibes, Stumble Upon, Pandora, Twitter . . . There are also interesting support utilities like S3 (Amazon's unlimited virtual storage service), Technorati (a blog search and analysis tool) and so on. In most 2.0 situations, someone has created a very simple format for users to author (or similar) within.

4. The creativity of crowds. The only way to get a great idea is to have a lot of ideas. The number of contributors in a large 2.0 community ensures that the quality is high. Either because the best contributions are of very high creative quality and these get highlighted by decisions to view and word of mouth, or because of collective effort in improving each other's work – for instance with Linux or Wiki entries, or because good decisions are being made by large averaging effects. The original 'wisdom of crowds' thesis (by Surowiecki[73]) was about factual issues, but many have argued that it also applies to value judgements.

5. User production (including, but not limited to, creative ideas). In 2.0 sites, the distinction between producer/consumer is blurred. On a blog, not only does one person write their own journal, but others can comment. So even when it's a professional journalist writing, there is an audience contribution. The content can be text, videos, podcasts, photos or designs, gps data, a survey or screen capture. But it could also be computer code. Or meta-data such as tagging or voting on a news

story (*Digg it*) . . . This makes the content like a living system; developing both due to internal planned changes and environmental influence.

6. Community and advocacy. All web 2.0 hits seem to involve community. Some are literally social communities where individuals meet, draw up friends lists, twitter and so on. Others have embedded community, for instance the lattice of blog links and blog rolls that ensure people find each other in relevant clusters. Others still just have the community at work behind them, like Wikipedia. All have a basic public community currency; being known to be *the way that things are done these days*, based on news reports, word of mouth and so on. And many are built and also operate through advocacy, such as the ability of blogs to embed YouTube videos of interest.

7. Outside effects. The superficial view of web 2.0 is one of a disappearing act of all social life into the computer screen. But my theory is that all notable web 2.0 applications have an impact beyond the internet. Meetup.com is a literal example (it allows its groups to organise real life meetings). But all of the relationships, exchanges and learning are real even if the shared space is virtual (we don't think of telephone conversations as less real just because they took place through an electronic medium). And the effects of those exchanges often spill into the real world, such as with couples that first met on the net.

Most web 2.0 applications grew out of geek lifestyles and hobbies. Applications like freecycle.org (where people pass on goods they'd have otherwise thrown out – see below) show how these seven points can be reapplied to green lifestyles.

All of which is an introduction to the idea of *green alternatives that tinker with the configuration of the company, business model and customer relationship*. In the following section we will first look at *nonmoney* (social production) models. And then consider various ways to monetise the same sorts of new models behind green agendas.

The Social Production Approach

Web 2.0 phenomena often start as nonmoney enterprises. Many of the great internet hits started as a bunch of code someone 'wrote over a thanksgiving weekend' (this has become the software founding myth equivalent to the 'two guys in a garage' of hardware start-ups). Some had a business in mind, but many did it as an experiment or as something they needed or wanted themselves, which wasn't available (these coding pioneers being the original user–consumers). The worldwide web itself was produced in this spirit by Tim Berners Lee; as a way for a global community of scientists to share a directory of scientific papers, cross-referenced using hyperlinks.

We are going to consider how to integrate these with business later. So for now you need to suspend belief and consider how something quite alien to modern economies – social production, web 2.0 – is driving progress. It's alien because it doesn't obey normal rules of ownership and exchange; but also because it requires little or no investment and has no 'friction' – a little app can turn into a worldwide phenomenon within months.

We are seeing myriad green initiatives and projects being put up online every week. For instance, *Lime* (a green blog) is trying to get people to walk the equivalent of the circumference of the world (22000 miles) by swapping car journeys for walking. It's a very simple thing; you join their community and register miles walked. They then count miles and also kilograms of carbon saved. It's an accumulator; a bit like the ones that children's show *Blue Peter* uses in its charity appeals. The bigger it gets, the more compelling.

There is potential for brands to be dabbling with such schemes too. If Nike can do *Run London*, why can't Clarks shoes (the leading children's school brand) do the walk to school? As a result of my research for the book, and also being confronted with the problem of school-run traffic on a daily basis, this is one of my pledges going forward; I am organising a meeting next month of various nice brands, a London council and several media publications, to see if we can't do a little campaign to make it more popular.

There are some very useful green information resources that are built out of web-enabled communities and volunteers, such as:

- Grist;
- Treehugger;
- WorldChanging;
- Hugg.

These are simply brilliant for people – like me – who need a wide selection of everything that's going on in the sustainability and green innovation space. They are mostly professional and activist resources in other words, more than consumer interventions.

Blogs are a great source of information that's close to the ground elsewhere in the world. One site I particularly like is www.globalvoicesonline.org. Volunteer bloggers across the world round up and link to key English language blog stories. It's an amazing source of topical round-up reports, even for your own country. It was here that I read about a blogger being sent to jail in Egypt for criticising their prime minister online, about a Chinese group of PhD students' proposal to reject Christmas and return to local ways, about Bush's visit to Brazil and the protests against ethanol crops taking over food land.

A new site that caught my eye, using the Digg engine to evaluate stories, is www.dotherightthing.com. This site takes things a bit further than just accessing the story, it is a citizen rating of companies. It uses the familiar Digg engine to rate the importance and +/− evaluation impact of stories on the rating of companies. They open the books on a company and anyone can post stories during a time limit, after which an official rating and ranking is published. It's very new and so quite random – e.g. a heavy negative Google digg concerned an April Fool's joke (where Google offered to send your emails printed out on paper). There are about 2000 people enrolled. This is actually bigger than the core of volunteers working with Wikipedia and would be a huge quantitative sample. Their conclusions make interesting reading. Because what it assesses is not only people's perceptions of different stories but also how many people really feel moved by them (to rate them important). It can be rather 'internet-biased' though. Yahoo!, for instance, got a highly negative rating for its involvement in a dissident in China being imprisoned and a highly positive rating for announcing it is going carbon neutral, but what really screwed its profile (after 236 people rated it important, leaving Yahoo! 5th from the bottom of the league, below even Exxon Mobil) was this story:

> ... a recent upgrade to Yahoo Messenger includes an innocuous 'auto-update' option. When the user gives Yahoo! permission to 'update' – what they think is just Yahoo Messenger – the up-dater ... then proceeds to hijack many browser preferences – including search engine settings.[74]

The most successful of the web 2.0 green sites so far is freecycle. org, with 3.5 million members and counting (it actually grew by 150000 members during the time it took to write this book). Free-cycle was started in 2003 in Tucson to help reduce waste and save the desert from landfills. Its mission statement is as follows:

> To build a worldwide gifting movement that reduces waste, saves precious resources and eases the burden on our landfills while enabling our members to benefit from the strength of a larger community.[75]

The idea is simple. Instead of throwing something away which still has some use in it, why not give it to others?

Freecycle works through an email list and the only rule is to keep it 'free, legal and appropriate for all ages' ('free' includes no trading – the site is only for giving away). There are now over 4000 Free-cycle local communities, each run by a volunteer. The amazing thing about Freecycle is that it has 'a staff of one'. The local

Freecycle groups are built on the *Yahoo! Groups* platform. It is a lesson to anyone considering a one million pound web build; if your idea is strong, you can often use existing web resources. The media have nicknamed the site *FreeBay*, although Freecycle give advice to media not to describe it as 'a great source of freebies' but in a more rounded way, as they have found that how it works depends critically on how it is portrayed and who joins.

Pledge Bank is a great British site. The idea is that you make a written commitment in the form 'I will do X if Y other people do it'. The pledge listing then shows how many signatures are still required and how many days are left. It's another very utilitarian site design, built and run by volunteers. But, like Freecycle, it's not about website design, it's about the content. Pledge Bank is thrilling to read – every pledge has a story. Typical pledges, which happen to have green themes, include a pledge to no longer fly between points in the UK linked by the rail network, one to collect and recycle plastic bags which are littering public areas, and one about switching to a renewable energy supplier, a pledge proposed by the founder of the site, Tom Steinberg. I signed up to that last pledge. I was thinking of doing it anyway, but it's nice to feel that I am doing it in a community of fellow pledgers.

Those all sound quite sensible. There is also something of the 'dare' about some of the pledges on the site (such as citizen arrests of police lawyers and dressing up as a lion). This presumably drives the word of mouth and enjoyment of regular browsing here. The people – all unpaid *Pro–Ams* – who built this site are also responsible for *Neighbourhood Fix It* (helping people report things that need fixing to local councils) and a number of other great ideas, all having something to do with encouraging citizenship.

The Money Approach

Volunteers can achieve a lot. They built Linux for a start. Freecycle has a staff of one, but a whole network of volunteers running local groups. And actually the true cost of the scheme is carried by the Yahoo! free groups service. It's explicitly a noncommercial service; it's about giving stuff away. So any commercial development would be difficult. The Freecycle brand is another matter. The name and the membership and communication channel could be a fascinating basis for green innovations, for instance (taking a rather literal lead from the name) a bike-sharing scheme. But it's probably happy as it is, and likely to remain so, especially if it grows to 10 or even 100 million.

But when things scale they usually need money, because they start to cost a lot to run. Wikipedia does this through donations amounting to $1.5m. Craigslist, which is the number 7 website in the USA, has 24 mouths to feed (and with five billion page views per month, the hosting and ISP charges must be a bitch too). Craigslist is still growing too; in fact it seems, according to recent data, to be accelerating. Craig Newmark could have sold the business to Google or Murdoch for zillions. But he didn't want to. His stated reasons include not wanting to have to worry about personal security. So instead he invented a little business model on the side; they make a small amount of income from job classified ads in selected US cities, charging just enough ($75 per ad) to cover their costs. They don't allow any banner advertising – being FREE in the full commercial-free sense – except once on April Fool's day when they pretended to have caved in on this! They are said to turn over $10 million, which is a lot of money for 24 people, but tiny compared to their scale of operation.

Linux reached the point when, if it was going to compete with Microsoft, it would need support companies – like the mighty Red Hat, whose IPO announced the end of the *nonmoney* days with Linux. You can still use Linux for free if you know what you are doing, but Linux had needed to enter a market (e.g. small businesses) that didn't.

Those are retrofit business models, but it is a key message of this book that good business in the sustainable sense and good business in the commercial sense are not necessarily incompatible. You can start with a green vision and business model. If you just want people to make pledges or give away old goods, then charging something for this is questionable of course; businesses are supposed to supply goods and services. But as Amazon has shown, there still can be some fascinating hybrids.

The key dimension nonmoney models bring to money sites is the *first-person* factor. Amazon offers ten million *first-hand* reviews from other readers. eBay listings are *first-hand accounts* – often second-hand goods in the sense of being used of course, but 'first-hand' in another way:

- you buy from an individual with a trust rating;
- they create an original advertisement for each item;
- each object is unique; only new goods are identical; used ones have some history, they may have a story and definitely have a condition;
- you *deal with an individual* through a formatted system of rules and steps.

What eBay has done is introduce advantages over buying from other sources – price, efficiency, reassurance . . . But more than that, eBay has a game mechanic – it is like a sport or pastime. Some people say it is addictive. That's a key lesson for product–service systems – develop something *more compelling than shopping*.

I've argued that there is a sort of hybrid vigour in green and commercial agendas mixing. Here are some other reasons why green marketing might also aim to achieve ambitious commercial objectives, through breakthrough innovation:

- Winning the resources to scale up any business, product, service or technology that brings more dramatic, effective change.

- Establishing a successful model that will be copied, both in some of the precise details and also as a general type of entrepreneurial or innovative venture.
- Winning the support of investors and other stakeholders to innovate further against green and cultural agendas, and the resources to invest in R&D.
- Attracting the most talented workers, especially those who can invent and execute.
- Generating substantial profits, some of which can be donated to charities and causes pursuing green and cultural agendas that are not as commercial.
- Proving to the world media that there is substance behind the green hype.
- Generating the *right sort* of bandwagon, a commercial success story (like the iPod) which itself reflexively extends this success.
- Generating profits which go to the right people, for instance that stay in developing world communities where goods are produced.

I am not just talking about creating wealth for capitalist investors. If that is the sole focus of a business (for instance in a private equity-backed phase) all ethical considerations can go by the wayside. But I do tend to think *the business* must be commercially successful, for the reasons I have stated. It's about being 'for success', rather than just 'for profit'. Pioneers are never usually in it primarily for the money. If they are, they will often make bad decisions, for instance in terms of planning a business strategy around 'an exit'.

A common development path is launching commercial ventures from successful green content businesses or publishing ventures. You already have a brand and a following, why not extend it into new offerings? If Freecycle made a bicycle-sharing scheme, it would have a huge audience of enthusiastic potential members on tap. Its marketing costs would be almost zero.

However, you need to be careful in a case of charging for something that used to be free. Meetup.com went through a painful transition (losing a lot of members) when it started charging subscriptions. It now has 16000 groups, compared with the 194000 it had when it was a free service.[76] There's an argument that using something ancillary to the actual meet ups which made money would have been better. For instance, they could have launched a killer research business by polling the very richly diverse groups on their beliefs, attitudes and behaviours. But I hear they are back in a growth mode, and Doug Atkin (author of *The Culting of Brands*) now works there, so watch this space anyway.

With money businesses launching a social venture, you *must* keep them clearly separated financially *because* they are related. Think of it as a sort of incest taboo. Starbucks did a great café-based community charity project with Timebank and the RSA called PerkUpYourLife. It is like a cross between meetup.com and Pledge Bank. Local groups can organise meetings and apply for grants of up to £1000 to do something for the area. It has its own name, its own website and is a more credible presence in store for being like an NGO which has been allowed space in today's quintessential meeting space. They kept a good separation between the two. The Starbucks *Evergreen* educational online game I mentioned before is also built in partnership with Global Green, an independent charity. Starbucks is clearly paying for the thing, and no one is making any money.

It's vital that things are always not just transparent, but clean and logical. People make those sorts of assessments in moments; they are snap judgements. When a carbon-balancing group is *for profit* (when it's effectively a cause-related donation to good deeds) it raises concerns, for instance. Your profit comes from my donation.

The real opportunity to fuse business and nonmoney models comes when you invent a business from scratch, especially if it is very new. Here's a business I am in serious discussion with a certain global bank about launching together. The details may change (including the bit about actually launching it!) but it makes the point.

Bank of Barta: Outline

Everyone's talking about sustainability. Brands are queuing up to announce how green their existing or slowly improving operations are. But the really exciting potential is in g-commerce; radical new business and service models that provide a step change in both environmental and commercial terms.

Bank of Barta, from a consumer perspective, is a breakthrough service, the eBay of sharing. Many consumer goods are bought by individuals and hardly used. Power tools, for instance, are used for less than ten minutes a year on average. A huge step-change in our carbon footprints could be achieved if we loaned products to others and borrowed theirs. We would feel good about the community aspects. It gives us something more tangible and extensive to do than carbon slimming and recycling. We would also save money. A lot of money. The 'bank' bit of Bank of Barta would record credits for items shared out, which you could then spend. By loaning out everything from a drill, a car to a wedding hat, you could get a free holiday home. People love this sort of sharing community, it's the heart of web 2.0, not only in media (YouTube, Flickr, eBay) but in green areas too (e.g. Freecycle – saving the world one gift at a time – a place where you give goods you would have thrown out to others, which has nearly 4 million members).

Bank of Barta, from a business perspective, is a breakthrough new insurance model. When people lend a product to others, they need to have a safety net in case it comes back broken. Claims will likely be low, because people in this scheme are working from goodwill and will take good care of others' goods. Plus there will be an eBay-style feedback system. But still, accidents happen. The subscription people pay will cover insurance, as well as the site and service. Working with a household name bank will give people confidence in the reliability of the scheme. And this high profile start-up will also reflect well on the bank. It will be doing green rather than simply preaching it.

How would this be green? Products would live fuller lives, with much less wasteful sitting on the shelf. The assumption is that people within this scheme will buy less – and they can always save a bit more money for a very uncertain retirement.

Another typical web-enabled model is to aggregate, to tap little players into a global network or market. It's the MySpace effect for unsigned bands.

One example is to create a loyalty card for local shops. This scheme has launched successfully in several cities in the USA. In the UK, a new company founded by John Bird (the *Big Issue* magazine founder) called the *Wedge Card* launched in late 2006, focusing on London but with plans to extend to other UK and then global cities. They point to the role of local commerce, not just as a service to the community, but as a cornerstone of community; all those chats in deli counter queues, places to sip coffee with a neighbour, the local traders themselves as people who know everyone and take an interest in their lives and wellbeing. The *Wedge Card* allows you to get discounts and special offers at a whole range of local shops; competing with the big stores' 'loyalty cards' in other words. It also supports local community charities. Wedge is working with the National Council of Voluntary Organisations to sign up members to the scheme. It's a bit of a no-brainer for the charity; it gets a donation for every new member (initially two charities per area will benefit, later, users can pick).

What's interesting is that in all the press coverage, there was not one mention of whether this is a for-profit scheme or not. It easily could be. And what would it matter if it was? It's never going to take supermarket-style profits. And speaking of which, on one estimate (from The New Economic Foundation), a further one in three local businesses look set to close by 2010. It's definitely a sector that needs some help.

I think this is all just the start. I'm with Tony Giddens that the next twenty years will see as much green innovation as we saw IT innovation in the last twenty. A lot of the financial news coverage goes to new vehicles and fuel sources like (the controversial) bio-ethanol. But I bet web-enabled businesses play a major role too. For three reasons:

1. Because web 2.0 is just the visible tip of something totally revolutionary in economics. What the internet has done is take inefficiency out of markets. It has revolutionised the capital markets, in the same way that it has revolutionised dating sites. It makes matching the right parties so much more efficient, including making the search for a match so much more exten-sive. All the big internet hits – and not just eBay, which is liter-ally a market – are based upon the way that the internet makes new connections. Zopa, the bank, which lends by matching bor-rowers to savers (for a very thin processing fee) is an example of how this can be used to marketise what were formerly encapsu-lated products. And hits like *Friends Reunited* show how other needs can be electrified by making more efficient and extensive point-to-point connections.
2. Because the web is also rewiring patterns of social relationship and transaction. It gives us such flexibility to design new models such as the product–service systems.
3. Because of access. You don't need to be a global corporation to build bits of the future, in fact it almost seems to be an advantage to start with an idea and some coding skills.

All of this will bring huge changes. For instance, it is questionable whether we will need supermarkets in the future. If they still exist, they will be online and delivery-based (much greener). But they will compete with sites from pure internet players like Google that can match buyers to sellers direct in huge (economy of scale) numbers. And it won't just be on the web. Mobile is fast challenging to be the data hub of people's lives. Mobiles can do all sorts of interesting things by being in situ. Like dialling up any product or pricing detail you want (is this the greenest option, is it the best deal in my town . . .?)

Mobiles are also more democratic, being far more widespread in the world than broadband connections and computers. A new service called TradeNet in sub-Saharan Africa (one of the founders, Mark Davies, was a London dotcom entrepreneur before moving to Ghana) looks set to revolutionise the way crops and similar goods are taken to market and priced: it allows users to sign up for SMS alerts of prices for various commodities in local market centres. A farmer can then decide where to take his/her goods and even buy/sell remotely before travelling. Which goes to show that the developments won't necessarily be limited to the developed world. There is every potential to use these means to leapfrog and serve development as well as green agendas.

C2: Trojan Horse Ideas

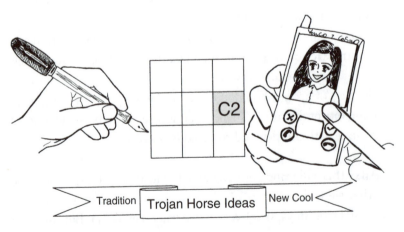

Figure 23 Grid C2

How can brands or (more broadly) social identity ideas help establish innovative new green products, services, companies, lifestyle habits and so on?

It's worth starting by recognising that there have always been three types of branding:

1. Industrial branding. Invented in the mid 19th century, this is the process by which an industrial good becomes a household name, a known quantity, associated with certain sorts of consumers, with certain values, acquires an image or personality. Some ad agencies and design agencies are used to dealing with industries (like FMCG) where this is actually about all there is to it. But this is far from being the whole story.
2. Fashion. Fashion was invented during the Renaissance. The Renaissance was built upon two key industries: banking and textiles. Fashion fused the two; you could judge someone's standing (and net worth) by their ability to keep up with fashion. Fashion today stretches well beyond clothing, into mobile phones, holiday destinations, social networks. It's all about buying 'the latest' and what this says about you.
3. Tradition. It's hard to date this, but cave drawings from 40000 years ago are one marker. Tradition is inherited culture: ideas, practices, artefacts which represent 'the way things have always been done'. Traditional brands are often rooted in specific places, connected with tightly controlled techniques, recipes or ingredients, associated with families or communities.

In my view (and not just in green terms), there is not much life left in the industrial branding model. One key reason is consumer alienation. Instead of giving a sense of how things are made, brands have hidden this from view and offered pretty lies. Stella Artois and other beers advertise a pastoral image; while the reality of big breweries is that they look a bit like nuclear power stations. The reality behind the image is not a problem with the other two models;

'the making of' is exciting for innovation (like some of the hi-tech Japanese beers) and a traditional small brewery is attractive.

Sticking with the drinks category as a source of examples, we can already see a return to traditional brewing in beer (in small batches, for local markets, with natural ingredients), the rise of craft beers and the growing success of local hero brands, in challenging the attempted 'global brands'. But I suspect the big story under the traditional banner going forward will be DRINK LOCAL. Local drinks, like local cuisines, are defining factors in your sense of home. And more to the point, how long will wine miles go unchallenged? A crisp New Zealand fizz could have travelled 12000 miles to London. Or you could buy global award-winning sparkling wine from Kent.

The fashions in drink are – if you think about it – largely concerned with physical formats and ways of serving. That's because fashions spread by (visual) imitation. The alcopop. The Sol with a lime. The Magners cider on ice. The vodka and Red Bull . . . I see these as venue brands. Associated with certain scenes. For instance, the way that Red Stripe became adopted by the punks (or recently by the snowboarders). 'You had to be there'. What is the next 'spritzer'? I suspect only a barman can tell you.

Understanding the mechanics of fashion, for instance the need for a visual signifier, could be key to getting new green brands seen to be successful. In the same way as the iPod (white headphones) took off because it was marketed as a fashion item, not just a gadget. I'm convinced that's why mountain bikes for city use have done well too.

In this section we will look at traditions (Trojan horses) and fashions (the new new thing) as ways of establishing radically new green stuff.

The Traditional Approach

Traditions re-expressed are a force to be reckoned with in today's post-traditional culture. Familiar-seeming ideas can help us adopt new patterns of living. One of the first successful social networks online was Friends Reunited. This didn't seem like joining some weird virtual community. Why? Because it was 'just like a school reunion' (only much better, you could browse what others had been up to, and so on). In the same way, a recent success was Facebook, which took the traditional campus community of the US online. MySpace became known as the place for music, music stars, fans downloading songs and so on.

Making new green stuff – products but also lifestyles – seem normal is key to radical green marketing; the more radically green the practice, the more abnormal it looks to a potential consumer. Marketing has an essential role in persuading people otherwise.

How could familiar cultural ideas be used to establish new norms? Let's start with a particularly tough example. The Mooncup is a reusable menstrual cup made from soft silicone rubber. It is worn internally like a tampon but collects menstrual fluid rather than absorbing and is not disposable, so it has major ecological advantages over tampons. The website takes a product reassurance route: it is available from Boots (therefore it's not that weird or marginal); it is better for health (no danger of toxic shock); it is more effective – being changed less often and being less leaky. It sounds like a breakthrough product, although it was actually invented in the 1930s around the same time that the tampon was invented. (Guess which one paper product manufacturers saw the opportunity to make money from!)

It also happens to be a dramatically greener alternative to the tampon (it won several awards for being the most environmentally friendly new product of 2004) and in the details of the web copy, you find that green was the motive behind launching the current company. In 2007 Su Hardy, the Mooncup founder, won a Triodos bank award (as voted by readers of *Eve* magazine) for *Women in Ethical Business.*

The Mooncup may make perfect functional sense but it's a hard cultural sell. References on the internet (e.g. Wikipedia) suggest that take-up is very low. Also, in previous generations (1930s,

1950s), attempts were made to sell this product, which failed. Here's the reaction from a journalist, who sounds generally adventurous, confident and liberated, yet freely admits struggling with the idea:

> Friends react to the Mooncup with a mixture of disgust and fascination. My sales pitch about the ecological and health benefits is drowned in a sea of urghs and pulled faces. 'Gross! You'll have to look at all that blood when you tip it out!' shrieks one. 'It'll go everywhere!', says another.[77]

Discussing the reasons for the product's rejection by previous generations, a website devoted to the history of sanitary protection products (as they are known) described how historically the marketing for such products was precisely designed to connote delicacy and 'avoidance of unseemly words, actions and things, including those related to sex and the body's secretions'.[78] Launching a product which draws attention to all of that is obviously a bit of a nightmare scenario.

But it is entirely possible. Tampons have become the norm. They are therefore not thought about in these terms. Even though in the 1930s, 'The Tampax tampon, first sold in 1936, met similar resistance from the public.'[79] It's not that this product would provoke those feelings more than tampons in principle. It's that tampons have become 'normal'. The problem is that new products bring all of this to the surface again. The feelings people have about the cup could really be the feelings they have buried about their periods. Our intrepid journalist went on to say that actually once you get used to it, there's no going back; that it really is – as the testimonials on the website say – better in use than tampons. But you've got to admit this would be a tricky marketing challenge.

One glimmer of hope is how much franker young women are today about sex, their bodies and so on. Perhaps there is something relevant about the new masculinised femininity – girl power – the girls who are *the new boys*? Not feminism (which might marginalise the product's appeal in the mainstream) but post-feminism. Certainly times have changed since the 1930s' descriptions. It has become normal to be quite frank about sex. Less so periods, admittedly. I asked some female friends and responses included 'no bloody way' (to the Mooncup) and 'women don't even talk about this stuff to each other'.

I do have an idea about how you could market this product. And whether it would actually work or not, it certainly illustrates the approach of using communities and their identity to tackle existing norms and promote new ones.

The Proposition: 'As used by women soldiers'

The Cup (I think you would consider dropping the 'moon') is more reliable, for longer, under more active conditions. Apparently, it is favoured by sportswomen for this reason. But I prefer the soldiers' route; it's more compelling. Also it sounds like something the army would actually do. Women soldiers do get education in rather frank ways on things like contraception. Why not this too? And if it is normal in the army (a highly regimented, normalised sort of place) why not elsewhere? This girl soldier thing taps into that defiant, 'getting on in a man's world' spirit. It wouldn't be for everyone, but if it could gain ground, then it could marshal greater marketing resources and credibility. The real problem is getting the first 10%; after that, straightforward marketing can do the rest. Of course you can't just make this up, you'd have to really talk to the army and persuade them to adopt the product, at least for a trial. Perhaps that conversation itself might be a valuable one to have, it really does sound like a superior product and there are getting on for 20000 women in the British armed forces.

That's an example of a product being aligned with a tradition and tribe, what about changing people's lifestyles? Greener living means restraint. Where else in culture and people's daily lives can we find a Trojan horse for this; a thriving culture of restraint?

Diets are a pretty obvious contender. Some diets work by cutting specific food types. The Atkins dieters cut carbohydrates. Vegans cut all meat and dairy products. This seems archetypal, running far deeper than modern diet fads. Look at the diets prescribed by religious traditions. And this in itself has antecedents in the occurrence of taboos in hunter–gatherer societies, often associated with food, but also with many other fields of everyday behaviour. The content of taboos is far from universal; for instance, dogs are not to be eaten in Europe, but they are in some parts of Asia. There is much disagreement about the origins of specific taboos, functional explanations vying with symbolic ones. But taboos are found in all societies, they are a human universal. Diets are not the only way to leverage taboos. The fur coat became a modern taboo, after pointed attacks by activists. But diets give a positive way for brands to approach this powerful mechanism. One very simple way to bring this idea into the green marketing field would be to invent modern lifestyle diets. You would use all the same cultural cues and media as a successful diet plan. I played around with this idea a couple of years ago with *The Ecologist* magazine. It could take on endless variants, to be proposed and selected by the readers and promoted by the magazine every month. We quite liked the idea of a month's (no) TV diet, for instance. We were aiming to break up the ground a bit, getting people to notice parts of their lifestyle, their benefits and costs (for instance, in a TV-free month, the quantity of family conversation, shared pastimes and so on might increase dramatically). But we also envisaged that some would be specific eco-friendly crash diets.

A link between carbon and diets is becoming quite common. It is literally a case of counting calories. Various people have proposed this. Lucy Siegle did a good carbon diet strand in *The Observer*. There is even a book coming out called *The Low Carbon Diet* (also the title of a *Time* magazine article back in 2006); a book of environmental lifestyle changes presented in the idiom of a diet self-help book. I think this works pretty well, although perhaps the connection is becoming overused. The notion is that of going on a diet, making cutbacks, acting with restraint across a huge range of everyday behaviours. It isn't perfect (most diets fail and are faddish). But it's a start. Whole Foods, the American retail chain, is launching a 'diet plan' this month; a marketing example, not just a content idea. The actual suggestions are pretty standard; turn off standby, recycle and so on. But there are a few nice surprises in the list, like adjusting your blinds to let more sun in the house.

Learning from holistic diet regimes (of the vegan and macrobiotic variety), systemic approaches with more education, passion and commitment would, I'd argue, be a good direction in which to take the evolution of this concept. We need good information on what is in what product, how it was made, where it was sourced from. But that's just product labelling; being a vegan is something *we* own, rather than just being a type of product. I mean creating community and identity around renouncing something, in an information and education rich way, not just about what, but why. Some fascinating regimes like this have emerged in the dark green world. One is 'the hundred mile diet' (in the US that's quite local – vs the 1500 average food miles for a typical ingredient); check the book *Plenty*, written by Smith and MacKinnon, who lived like this for a year in Vancouver.

So we've looked at communities, for instance 'as used by women soldiers', and at norms, for instance diet plans, as ways of creating pseudo traditions. What if you did both in tandem? The cultural resynthesis examples from Wallace's study were often regarded as cults. Could you launch cultish communities which are rule-based?

One idea I am hoping to launch with my friends at More Associates (we're working on a green home product launch together, and as part of the marketing intend to have a site for culture change ideas donated by creative people; and this is my starting point idea) is

The Climate Change Church of Jerusalem
(Fighting Sins of Emission!)

The idea is to tackle a different target audience from most green campaigns – employees. If employees belong to a religion, then they can legitimately ask employers to respect the observances of that religion. For instance, there was that employee at BA who won her right to be allowed to wear a crucifix to work. Our religion would have green-friendly strictures; like only eating in canteens which use local seasonal foods, never travelling by aeroplane midweek, and so on. The *Jedi Knights* succeeded in being recognised as an official religion, just by asking members to name it on their UK census forms.

Obviously this is mostly just a fun way of drawing employers' attention to the enthusiasm for green policies on the part of their employees. But it won't be as much fun as it could be if we don't take it seriously; we are planning to consult theologians, employment lawyers and of course potential acolytes too!

The New Cool Approach

Fashion is not just an industry, it's a type of marketing. The same general approach tends to apply wherever the 'latest thing' is given status, value, currency; the showroom, the designer, the models, the tastemakers, the editorial, the visual or verbal memes, diktats and so on. If you deconstruct the marketing for Apple computers, for Swatch watches, for new car models and so on, you find many of the same tropes. There are also green things which succeeded in becoming fashionable in their own right. The mountain bike is one example.

In this section I want to explore how something green (i.e. which could have been marketed and designed in a very worthy, classical green way) could instead be given the fashion treatment: how to make a green brand into a cool brand.

As a hypothetical business case, let's say the idea is to sell local foods through café style venues, with a number of sustainability agendas working together:

- all ingredients to be sourced within 100 miles, paying decent prices;

- give workers and students a healthy option, at lunchtime and for snacks;
- take on the coffee shops (too much coffee not good for you) and fast food outlets;
- normalise eating seasonal local food, teach people what can be done with it;
- zero packaging waste – no packaging, takeaways in deposit refundable boxes;
- minimal food waste – 15% of all food bought is thrown away, not eaten;
- it should be affordable and tasty – better in every sense than alternatives;
- venue used all day – for breakfast, breaks, lunch . . . then at night it will become a cookery school, plus offering home-delivered food;
- a lot of green lifestyle education included;
- the venue should be as green as possible in heating, design, kitchen, etc.

You can just imagine the result. If you followed the usual green codes it would be a whole food restaurant – sandal-wearing staff, menus on blackboards, lots of nut loaf and wholemeal bread. But that's a niche business, and it's not going to attract office workers away from McDonalds, Starbucks, or even Prêt a Manger (which is actually quite a decent halfway approximation to the sort of business I have in mind).

Instead, we are going to make it *the* coolest place to eat lunch, snack, take a break. What can we learn from the way other markets create currency and make things fashionable?

High Concept Brand

The original thought I had for the name was LoCal. It's healthy and it's local food. Which is okay, but it's a bit worthy. Fashion brands don't do worthy. They have to have a twist. The general rule in fashion creativity is one of irony, transgression, being edgy. Even The Body Shop started that way; 'body' is a confrontational word, brash, almost taboo (and doubly so if you remember that the first outlet, in Brighton, was next door to a funeral parlour).

What if we call our café chain *Mao*? That's just the name, where it gets interesting is to make the experience and service literally Maoist, a little bit of the high street which is like a communist state factory:

- Equality – everyone pays the same amount. It's £2.50 to enter at breakfast time, £5.00 at lunchtime, £1.50 at other times (for drinks and snacks). For takeaways it's the same. Once you have paid, you help yourself. Takeaway portions are limited in size by the reusable lunchboxes. Otherwise eat as much as you like.
- Education – as in a workers' cafeteria in a state factory there would be a lot of education materials, talks, even rousing music.
- Communal – it is a large self-service-style venue, with refectory tables.
- No packaging – reusable takeaway boxes are loaned out with a deposit.
- No waste – you get charged extra (a deposit that's not returned) if your tray isn't completely clean when you've finished.
- Little choice – there are brilliant fresh tasty options, but not many of them. And they depend on what was available from local suppliers.

The concept would extend to a very tight control of graphics, language, menus and so on. Maoist would be the inspiration for the style (Muji isn't far off). But we would base the design on reuse of junk, etc. too; like Victor Papanek's use of tin cans as the cases for transistor radios for the developing world. The language would be very simple. We'd also use ironic touches like marketing through brand experience events with rousing Marxist–Leninist workers' choirs, mass display teams like in North Korea, etc.

Let's apply some other standard fashion marketing tropes to this café concept.

Flagship Stores

The business model could be 'café plus'; plus local food delivery (raw or cooked), publications (e.g. cookbooks) and other secondary revenue making the profit. At night, you could come to cookery classes where you would learn how to make amazing meals from local seasonal foods. Lessons would be free, but you'd pay for the ingredients. Rather than doing lots of small venues, this concept should start with big venues in flagship locations. Places where the office worker or student traffic at lunchtime is very high. That's how fashion brands approach retailing today; and also Nike, Samsung, Apple and others take their lead from the flagship fashion stores like DKNY.

Design

More than half the value of this business in consumers' eyes would be the experience. We should create a new standard in the convenience food retail sector; the aesthetics previously associated with high-end restaurants. There are chains which have broken the mould in this way before (compared to the standards of their times): Pizza Express in the 1970s, Starbucks in the 1980s, Yo Sushi, Belgo and Wagamama in the 1990s. But this is ten years on, and all these concepts look over-designed (designer) and dated. The design challenge would be to redefine the way a convenient food venue works. One chain that did this was Nando's (they bring your food to the table, there is the whole thing with which piri-piri sauce you choose, etc.)

(Menu) Designer

All fashion brands tend to have a designer culture. Apple has been clever in making such a star out of Jonathon Ives, who has become their 'Alexander McQueen'. The key designer for our concept will be the menu designer, a culinary genius that can make creative, varied and tasty food concepts out of the very limited seasonal choices. We will need drink concepts too (tap water and fruit and veg smoothies being the main options). They will need to work to mass tastes, but educate the palate. There will be some opportunities to pickle and preserve ingredients, but mainly it will be fresh, in season. You'd either partner with a celebrity chef to take this challenge on – just look what Jamie Oliver has done for British school lunches. (If you aren't familiar with this example – i.e. are from outside the UK – do Google 'Jamie's school dinners', it's a remarkable story leading to lasting change). Or you could create a celebrity through a TV show called *Mao's Kitchen*. That would probably be a good thing to do anyway.

Seasons

Fashion has seasons. So, rather gratifyingly, does food. We would launch new ranges of recipe ideas to suit the seasons and educate a broader audience. There could be user-generated ideas too, an ongoing competition through the evening classes and online. Here's some of what you would have to work with in the UK, according to iCount (although it would vary with location too):

Jan   leeks, kale, venison
Feb   carrots, onion, rabbit
Mar   purple sprouting broccoli, scallops, spring onions
Apr   watercress, potatoes, rhubarb, pigeon, wild salmon
May   asparagus, sorrel, radishes, brown crab
June   beetroot, peas, gooseberries, lamb, mackerel

July   broad beans, cucumber, strawberries, cherries, lobster
Aug   courgettes, french beans, hazelnuts, raspberries,
        blackberries
Sept   sweetcorn, tomatoes, plums, goose
Oct   pumpkin, apples, chestnuts, eel
Nov   cauliflower, sprouts, pears, partridge, mussels
Dec   cabbage, artichoke, parsnip, pheasant[80]

It sounds tasty already doesn't it? One healthy innovation would simply be to get people to eat proper meals at lunchtime again. A light lunch and heavy dinner is the wrong way around for the body's cycle.

Opinion Formers

Most fashion brands have an established following. Which slightly disguises how fashion really works; it is a process of diffusion, from the most cool 'with it' people to the mainstream imitators. Designers only play a role in offering ideas; it is the audience – specifically the tastemakers or opinion formers – who decide what is 'in'.

Most strong fashion brands are associated with a 'scene', be it New York *Boho* or Monte Carlo *Bling*. However, fashion – the industry and media – don't have it all their own way. A good deal of fashion now comes 'from the street' through spontaneous creation, adoption or combination setting trends. This has only been expanded and accelerated by fashion blogs and similar. Often stylists will pick up on these ideas, turning something indigenous into a 'look', which gets broadcast in turn by fashion media to the mainstream, and adopted (in fast fashion cycles of only weeks) from magazine into the ranges of modern retailers such as Zara. Within this rapid cycling, some aspects are surprisingly set; for instance, dyes and materials need to be ordered quite far in advance, and here the bush telegraph within the fashion industry seems able to decide, apparently spontaneously and independently and considerably in advance, that yellow is 'this summer's key colour'.

Fashion has its own sustainability revolution underway. With organic cotton leading the way. That's testament not only to any genuine concern about the use of pesticides and GM crops detailed earlier in the book, but also fashion's shoal-like response to patterns, themes and moods in the culture; it's the same system which gave us 'combat pants' at the height of the wars in the former Yugoslavia; it is our unconscious worn on our sleeves. The thing you have to understand about fashion, within these cycles of influence, is that it is not 'dumb' – rather that it functions like a language; it makes statements and, in particular, it speaks volumes about the wearer.

How does that translate to our *Mao* café example? One implication is location. It could do worse than taking a leaf from Wagamama's book and siting early branches near to universities. Students are receptive to new trends (you arrive at college and spend three years reinventing yourself). Students are also young, funky, idealistic, communal and very prone to going for concepts which are cheap.

Another could be to offer a home-cooked meal delivery service, deliberately targeting the glitterati. You could wrap this up in a diet; for instance, tie in with a new age health guru.

But ideally you want to get to some ideas around the core fashion adoption driver . . .

Imitation

Fashion is something that people copy. It has literally no meaning as a one-off. That's like somebody inventing a new word, which no one else hears or can use.

How could our *Mao* café foster imitability? One obvious contender is the 'lunch boxes'. The concept being that reusable containers (with a deposit paid) are used to carry away food. These could be designed with handles – hence to be carried and visible on street. They could become design collectors' items in their own right; designed to be so cool that many never want to return them, some even collect them. Getting famous artists and designers to donate ideas could reinforce this. There is always a 'must-have item', be it an iPod or a Moleskine notebook.

There are many other tactics you could lift from fashion brands; the use of supermodels, the idea of a 'show', seeding diktats ('brown is the new black'), creating accessories (what if Mao had its new and unique eating utensil?) and so on.

There are already numerous such restaurants at the high end in London, serving local seasonal food; for instance, Notting Hill's *Bumpkin*. So it's not that far-fetched. But I mainly wanted to illustrate the thought process.

C3: Challenging Consuming

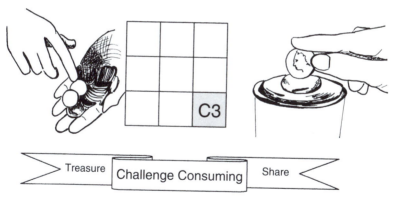

Figure 24 Grid C3

This last box of the grid takes us upriver, to the very heart of consumerism!

Society conspires to make us wasteful consumers. There's a whole system of related factors that make change difficult, from supply chains to wasteful habits. Structural, habitual consumerism is the heart of the matter. The trouble is that when you show better, but unfamiliar, everyday habits – for instance the car clubs or other sharing schemes – mainstream consumers can reject them vehemently. Status is an issue in these patterns – but it's not always about overt conspicuous consumption – rather it is embedded, for instance in the myth of personal ownership as independence. As the government research quoted earlier said, people are very resistant to the idea of 'taking a step back' on issues like seasonal food, car sharing and other such issues.

There is a need to tackle this 'locked in' habitual level of consumerism in order for us to achieve any major green goals. Two things are needed:

- a better set of everyday lifestyle habits;
- a way of making these culturally acceptable.

The key to the second of these is tackling the status issue; which is about the social 'level' attained, so it's not just about literal status-conferring items, but also your whole self-esteem linked to how you live. For instance, coin-operated electricity home meters or pay as you go phones say you are poor (even if no one ever sees them, you feel poor just having one). Adding status (or other compensating) ideas to what can initially seem a step back, and more importantly *a step down*, in the world is important. I used to have a pay-as-you-go phone which I was very proud of, because I delighted in telling everyone how much money it was saving me compared to my previous contract (roughly £600 per year). There was also an inverted snobbery about having a cheap-looking phone, in my mind.

We will be looking at two types of helpful structural change in everyday habits. One is *sharing*. This is based on the insight that while everyone with a lawn needs a lawnmower (or similar) occasionally, nobody (except perhaps a professional gardener) needs to own one all of the time. It is a waste of money and space as well as global resources. Even if you use a manual mower which you bought second-hand, you are still tying up some of the world's resources by not sharing it with another house who would have gone out and bought a new one at some point. Sharing runs directly counter to a constitutional myth of consumerism; individual identity and status being confirmed by ownership. We need quite powerful counter-myths to help sharing schemes become normal and intuitive. Most sharing schemes are a cultural idea or two short of emerging from the dark green margins. Yet such sharing is a very natural part of human societies. We just need to remythologise it.

The other sort of helpful change, which we'll consider first, as in many ways it's simpler, is *treasuring*; i.e. extending the lifetime of consumer products. The shortened product lifespan is a key driver of collective waste. We'll see that this goes to the heart of what consumerism is, and that challenges to this are at the leading edge of changing not only business and lifestyles but also the culture as a whole.

The Treasuring Approach

Before he became a leading postmodernist – and hence incompre-hensible to any but the most specialist reader! – Jean Baudrillard (the French intellectual who famously said 'the Gulf War did not happen') wrote one of the most lucid and penetrating books ever on *The Consumer Society*. In sociology, this was ahead of its time in positing a consumer society as a challenge to the Marxist orthodoxy (of a producer society). But Baudrillard's best insights, in my opinion, were those that unpacked the nature of consumerism itself:

> By their number, redundancy, superfluity, and formal extravagance, by the play of fashion and all that exceeds pure and simple function in them, objects merely simulate the social essence – status – that grace of predestination which is only ever bestowed by birth to a very few and which the majority, having opposite destinies, can never

attain. (. . .) Underlying all aspirations, there is this ideal end of status by birth, a state of grace and excellence. And status also haunts the world of objects. It is status which arouses this frenzy, this berserk world of knick-knacks, gadgets, fetishes which seek to (. . .) prove *salvation by works* since salvation by grace is unattainable.[81]

Baudrillard is effectively saying we are destined by 'lowly' birth to be *nouveaux riches*. That the locked-in habits, the 'frenzy' of consumerism and its wasteful excess is due to a doomed attempt to achieve status. He goes on to say that this has a conscious element; that we are aware in some symbolic purchases of trying to live up to the identity of our group or position in society, and also of aspiring to higher status. But that it also has an unconscious element, which is structural, in guiding the overall logic of consumption as excess; always exceeding the use function. We waste to prove we aren't poor. This leads to the otherwise inexplicable *unlimited* character of consumption; the need to have the latest gadget when the previous one performed its role just fine. Another point Baudrillard made – indicating an exception to his rule of ephemerality – could be crucial in establishing a valid cultural counterpoint to throwaway consuming-for-status:

Hence the very particular prestige of the ancient object, which is a sign of heredity, of innate value, of irreversible grace.[82]

In this statement are several potent antidotes to consumerism:

- In most phases of human history, traditional forms trumped novelties, we have a reverence for anything that predates us.
- A rediscovery of the value of objects of greater age (rather than 'the latest').
- The innate value of 'classics', iconic, definitive, exemplary; having 'grace' – and hence also retro, antiques, collecting, vintage and so on.
- The notion of heredity and other forms of grace than aristocratic birth; for instance, we also have innate status if we are born

creative or otherwise talented (nobody now judges Mozart as inferior to King Friedrich of Prussia, his patron).

The heart of the problem is the fashion cycle. We used to live in a world of objects whose authority came with age. Table linens and the furniture they rested upon were expected to last so long they would become family heirlooms. We've looked, in the last section, at how to use fashion tropes to make green goods 'cool'. But most fashion goods are not green, in fact they are almost anti-green, deliberately wasteful and building in premature redundancy to connote richness and status. Nowadays your phone is out of date within 18 months. It's a historically unique state of affairs. We're only a few generations from a situation when our objects and buildings and other cultural artefacts were expected to outlive people.

Fashion, invented in its modern form in the Renaissance, was the exception – a worn calendar of social 'up to datedness' – of being 'in' – for instance in the know, in the right circles, in touch with this season's influences and events. Above all, fashion denoted rank, as wearing this month's fashionable costume showed that you could afford an endless stream of new outfits. This was great news of course for the booming trade in luxurious fabrics. Textiles, along with banking, were at the heart of the economic miracle in Florence. This was a time, just like the 20th century, of very rapid change. The printing press had just been invented. Trade routes had been opened to the East, bringing silks as well as numerous exotic goods. The bills of exchange (prototypical paper money) had in themselves liberated trading; creating a new liquidity. Discoveries in the sciences and new styles in the arts created a kaleidoscope of change. All of which fashion could be seen as an index of. But this was limited to the wealthy minority in the 60000 person states of Florence, Venice and a few Royal courts dotted across Europe. And while there were ecological catastrophes in this time too (the felling of the forest of Europe), it wasn't the pressing issue that it is today, when billions aspire to live like these Florentine princes.

500 years later *almost everything is fashion*. It's still vaguely under-standable when new features become available; like the first mobile phone with a camera included. But mostly it is baffling. Except if understood as a system to ensure goods get replaced more quickly than they need to be, for the continuing financial growth of indus-tries whose core markets have plateaued. There's new growth in China, India, Brazil, Russia and so on (which have become these same corporations' new targets – a worry in itself), but in developed markets most of the people who will ever have a phone, car, tele-vision and so on, already have one. When did you last do something that used your computer to full processing capacity? Unless you render audio or movies, or run a payroll-sized database, probably never. And if you do those things, you tend to buy specialist com-puters or DSP cards anyway. I've written four books on three suc-cessive laptops, and if anything, the keyboard on the first was best (on the second, which was especially flimsy, I broke the keyboard twice and now I have broken the screen).

In qualitative research on mobile phones with young people, I once asked how they would feel about going down to the pub with 'a 1998 Nokia'. A significant number said they actually wouldn't go out; they'd just be too embarrassed! I probably wouldn't use my oldest laptop, which dates from 1998, to make a conference presen-tation either. It would send the wrong signals. But in functional terms it would work just as well (except that the battery is pretty shot these days). Perhaps I should, just to make the point. I could add a slogan to every chart saying 'SAVE THE PLANET: USE THE OLDEST LAPTOP YOU CAN FIND THAT WILL DO THE JOB'. Mind you, it doesn't have wi-fi.

This is the most wasteful aspect of consumerism. Getting a com-puter at home and internet connection (beyond the dial-up modem) was a big step. Wi-fi was too. Getting a faster computer, a flat screen and so on, less so. Getting a G5 because it looks more *with it* than a G4 . . . ? The iPod is honest about its position as an accessory. It is marketed on colours and its visibility. This season, iPods are being worn clipped to your jacket pocket. The iPod I use for taping research groups would hold 15000 tracks (£15000 worth of legally downloaded music). Do I need more?

It's fine for fashion to continue to thrive as a nuanced language of communication that links our identities and 'signs of the times'. There's no need – even on the greenest of views – for this to involve throwing garments away either; you can customise, alter, reuse, and these sorts of fashions are trendy now, as is retro and the 'trash' aesthetic.

But why would *all* markets behave like fashion? Even your toilet paper brand packaging gets 'refreshed' every few years. For many normal brands it's a matter of them staying current, because sporting new looks prevents then looking dated. Surely there are better ways of making money than making things to be thrown away and changing things for the sake of change? Fresh packaging design isn't itself all that wasteful (it just involves a bit of retooling at most), but it's the system it's part of which very much is. Fashion is a culturally self-replicating virus, installing a logic of its own ongoing success.

Slow is such a powerful source of value. It connotes what Baudrillard referred to as grace; born into a position you hold by right. Look at the Chanel No5 bottle over the years. It's a master-piece of restraint. The art deco design has moved from being the height of contemporary style (in 1921) to iconic. Iconic brands actually change much less. They are cultural landmarks which other brands are judged against, and usually found lacking.

There are two sorts of culture:

- that which is traditional, predates us and is 'the way things have always been' (and hence to be accepted rather than questioned);
- and that which changes within living memory and has a 'made up' character (which we can therefore decide whether to accept or revise).

The issue of short fashion cycles vs posterity was addressed by a group of designers and artists in the 1990s, the *Long Now Foundation*. They were ahead of their time in recognising the environmental implications of the accelerating throwaway culture.

> . . . the acceleration of technology, the short-horizon perspective of market-driven economics, the next-election perspective of democracies, or the distractions of personal multi-tasking. All are on the increase. Some sort of balancing corrective (. . .) is needed – some mechanism or myth which encourages the long view and the taking of long-term responsibility. (Stewart Brand)[83]

One of their many great ideas was to give a fifth digit to the years: 02008. For a generation overshadowed by the millennium, this gives us room to breathe again. It shows us a much longer horizon, because the next significant landmark in this dating scheme is not the decade (or whatever we will call 2010–19) or even century, it is the year 10000. A pessimistic view would be that we'd be lucky to make it to that date without a crisis or change of such biblical proportions that we start the calendar over again. If the sort of civilisation that dates itself makes it, at all. But for now (a long now), just adding that zero makes you see the world differently.

Long Now projects include archiving the current languages for distant future posterity (a 1000-language Rosetta stone) and a universal timeline tool for viewing human history and futures over various scales. They are aiming to use such artistic projects to create a ripple effect among other creative people. I went to one of their conferences in 2001 about extending the life of consumer products; meeting designers and ecologists from the wild fringes, alongside representatives from Philips, who were clearly ahead of the curve.

Question: How can we extend the lifetime of products?
Answer: (following Baudrillard) By endowing the objects with status, value, 'grace'.

Some objects, like artworks, already have this; it would feel 'criminal' to throw them away. Consumer goods do not have to be throwaway, just as food doesn't have to be fast food. Books are a good example of a non-throwaway good. Even in their paperback form (which was designed to be disposable) my guess is that few books get binned or sent to recycling. They hang around houses for a lifetime or get shuffled off to second-hand and charity shops. Or these days to Amazon (new and used) or eBay. Books have grace, they represent a store of ideas for posterity, that's why burning them in Nazi Germany was so symbolic as an act of aggressive destruction. Who would object if you destroyed a pile of redundant consumer gadgets? We do that every day anyway.

There are many ways to build *grace* into goods. Let's explore a selection.

Collecting

eBay has transformed consumerism. It has over 200 million registered users. It has made buying and selling second-hand goods much easier. The second-hand market in the USA was noticeable by its absence; people moving home or refurbishing would often throw out old microwaves, sofas and so on (certainly in the suburb of Washington where my parents used to live; I was quite shocked by the extent of the throwaway culture).

The key categories from a green point of view are probably the 'nearly new' (***MINT!!!!***) household goods, clothes, baby gear and so on. Things people would almost definitely have bought new only five years ago. 50000 people in the UK earned at least part of their income from eBay in 2005 according to government (i.e. tax-office declared) statistics. What eBay has done – beyond making second-hand markets more efficient and making some goods which would previously be thrown away saleable – is create thriving niches of collecting. Items like classic guitars are a booming market, people can now buy with confidence knowing they can sell on. The market sets prices, hypes the enthusiasm and creates community, at least around the buying and selling. The heart of eBay is these collectables. It's amazing what people will collect. The story that eBay tell about their first ever sale is a great example:

> . . . the site began with the listing of a single broken laser pointer (. . .) he was shocked when the item sold for $14.83. Pierre (. . .) contacted the winning bidder to ask if he understood that the pointer was broken. 'I'm a collector of broken laser pointers,' came the reply.[84]

eBay is about learning to treasure consumer objects. It associates unique objects (second-hand goods are unique, each has its own history and hence condition and value) with unique descriptions by unique people. It breaks the uniformity of consumer culture back down into something folksy; the world's biggest bring and buy sale. One caveat being the carbon footprint of eBay deliveries. A great thing for eBay to do – or some independent competitor (Craigslist?) – would be to incentivise people to bid and buy local.

One-Off

One-off goods are the ultimate refuseniks. Their singularity is stubborn. They substitute mass-produced image for an idiosyncratic, radical (in the sense of 'unrelated') position. These can help people to revert to a more fragmented individualism, picking objects which reflect stable taste groups rather than passing fads.

A popular form of one-off – much harder to throw away – is something which you have customised yourself. There are numerous products which have taken this line, a recent example being Penguin books, which released six of its classics range with a blank cover, so that the reader could design their own cover (they also have an online gallery and they describe this as 'books for the MySpace generation'). You probably wouldn't have thrown that book away anyway, but how about the piece of furniture which you painted and finished yourself, the Adicolor trainers which you coloured in or the Nike iD trainers which you designed yourself from a palette of soles, fabrics and colour schemes?

The ultimate customised good might be the pair of jeans. They go quickly from being an anonymous good from a factory to something which records your shape and also your life (those scuffs from a game of football with your child . . .). These hard-wearing garments probably on average get 50 times more wear than just about anything else in your wardrobe. The organic cotton issue aside, that would be *a great story to tell*. Jeans are potentially the greenest thing to wear. Carbon neutral firms should encourage workers to wear jeans. Ditto schools. I've been Levi's bashing for some years (because of their over-reliance on TV advertising and failure to innovate in the face of a decade of sales declines), but I think I might have finally found a positive reason to talk to them! Especially with their new Levi's Eco range coming out in November.

Niches

Fashion cycles hold in the mainstream – literally the fastest flowing middle of the river. Whereas off at the side, there are many cultural eddies where things hardly change, because they are linked to themes and affiliations that are much less ephemeral. Goths and punks today look pretty much as they did 20 years ago. I've enjoyed wearing Dr Marten's shoes and boots since I was about 13. They've just stuck with me.

If you wanted to *transform* the economics of mobile phone operators, do you know what you would do? You would come up with a reason why people would take longer contracts and replace their handsets (which are loss-making freebies) less often.

All people want to do with their phone other than talk, text and take pics (of their mates when they are drunk on Friday night) is *express their identity*. It's more a fashion accessory than a gadget in many ways. Think of it in terms of those two sides to the fashion market:

- the mainstream – a fast-flowing, swirling succession of signifiers and forms;
- the niches – stable identity niches linked to ongoing cultural affiliations.

Personalisation and niche identity brands are not new, but maybe they have a new relevance in the psychology of objects, now that extending their lifetime is a critical issue. If your phone was branded in a personal way that reflected something of your persona; be it your passion for Bingo, your love of the Zutons' first album, your work as a volunteer for Shelter . . . would you really want to give it up so readily for a few more (entirely unnecessary) mega-pixels? If you buy the latest phone, it is only 'the latest phone' for the first month of your 18 months with it. With a phone that reflects your wider cultural interests, you could have a much longer lasting relationship. This would require a change in phone design; making a customisable shell suitable for short runs of over printing in Man Utd team colours or looking like Dr Who's Tardis. The phone could then be loaded with content and would function as an extension of fan club or community membership. Imagine what a hit a MySpace phone could be (127 million members in the addressable audience). But the real potential is in cultural niches.

As content, mobile community, social apps like Twitter develop, then the ability to create meaningful and fertile niche identity and community brands increases. And if you could change the contract terms, then you could also be cheaper, since so much of the tariffs currently is taken up in paying for customer churn and the extra costs of recruitment. It's all about switching from a brand model for phones, which is like the telephone operators, to one that is more like the magazine market.

Mementos

People's lofts are full of mementos and keepsakes, things they simply cannot bear to part with because they have too much personal life history invested in them.

The more objects are associated with memory, the more feelings of attachment we have. Jeans remember our shape, and carry the marks of our lives on them. As I've already mentioned, they are kept significantly longer and worn out to a much greater extent than any other item of clothing, except perhaps a much loved and repaired old pair of shoes. It's not just a quality of the old and worn goods. I remember a woman in a mobile phones research group who said she had cried when she broke her phone, because she lost all the photos stored inside, and hence lost lots of happy memories. A green design challenge would therefore be, how to build memories into products that people currently throw away too soon. Ideally, we want them to continue in use rather than being stuffed in an attic of course (it's the replacement we have to worry about as well as the refuse). Where packaging is the issue, why not design it for secondary uses around the home? Your cheese pack might make a handy little photo frame or storage pouch.

Retro

Retro goods evoke nostalgia, or for those who were not around first time, they evoke an atmosphere of a particular era. This offers the potential to recondition and resell old goods with a fresh appeal. In London a few years ago there was a fashion for old telephone hand-sets from the 50s to 70s being adapted and used plugged into the latest mobile phones. Recently it is the Moleskin notebook which has been a key retro fashion revival.

Classic

Classics are designs that have never been bettered; almost perfect examples of form, function and materials. The best fountain pen designs hail from a century ago. The idea that design is constantly bettered is only really true in instances where a satisfactory level of performance has not been reached. Pen and paper just got there sooner. The Mont Blanc *Meisterstuck* has changed very little in design over the last century.

Lo-fi

The Lo-fi movement borrows from a very general idea that 'the old ways were the best'. The ultimate example of this is organic and other careful forms of agriculture; avoiding modern factory farming techniques, beyond just not using harmful chemicals, to animal treatment, to rotating and resting fields and so on. People don't just play old computer games because it's funny or ironic. They are actually more involving and more fun, just as a game of chess can be more interesting than a modern simulated war game.

There is great potential for revival of older designs that (were apparently superseded but) actually turned out to be better. A prime example is the carpet sweeper:

> A carpet sweeper typically consists of a small box. The base of the box has rollers and brushes, connected by a belt or gears. There is also a container for dirt. The arrangement is such that when pushed along a floor, the rollers turn and force the brushes to rotate. The brushes sweep dirt and dust from the floor into the container.[85]

Wayne Hemingway (the *Red or Dead* founder) has been working with a carpet sweeper manufacturer to develop versions with cool funky designs. As he points out, they are environmentally friendly, cheap, quiet, economical, safe, less likely to aggravate allergies . . . in other words, superior to the hoover in almost every respect.

The Definitive

When at the *Long Now* conference, I presented the idea that we would pass *Moore's Ceiling* in about 2002, when processor speeds reached about 500Mhz and hard drive memory reached 1GB. At that point you had everything you needed for most conceivable personal computing applications, even home film-making and audio. After that, if you need more speed you can buy upgradeable DSP cards. But most people don't.

What happens when you hit Moore's ceiling? The PC manufacturers keep going. The laptop I am writing on has the following spec: 2.16GHz dual processor, 1GB RAM, 80GB hard drive. And I deliberately chose the slowest, smallest current Apple option, costing half what my previous laptop (which unfortunately I had stepped on and broken the screen of) cost in 2002. I use this laptop all the time, but I doubt I have ever used above 5% of its capacity on any measure. It is the ultimate sledgehammer to crack a walnut. And I am sure it is already trailing behind the current specifications.

One indicator of where we might 'stick' is Nicholas Negroponte's (MIT media lab director) *One Laptop Per Child* project. This has culminated in a sub $100 product, being tested as I write, which is suitable for use in classrooms in about half the countries in the world. Orders have already been placed by Brazil, Argentina, Uruguay, Nigeria, Libya, Pakistan and Thailand. Here's the specification:

- 366Mhz processor;
- built-in wireless networking;
- 512MHz flash memory (no hard drive);
- two USB ports;
- Linux adapted (lite) operating system.

Negroponte says that, far from being a poor substitute, this product will be better than 'real' computers in a number of ways. One is that the files are stored in a time-based system – an electronic journal that logs everything you have done on the computer – rather than the 'desktop' paradigm. Information scientists have been arguing for years that this is the better approach. It's more intuitive, because it's how our memory works ('the documents from that class we did last Tuesday on newts'). The computer comes with a web browser, word processor and built-in RSS reader for news and other feeds. It's exactly what you need as a school student, and will need for the foreseeable future.

A significant advance from a green perspective is the zero power consumption. The lo-fi (black-and-white, low resolution) screen consumes 1 watt of power and the rest of the computer another 1 watt. The computer is charged using a foot pump, so that it does not depend on the availability of local electricity supplies. The average modern laptop consumes 25 watts and most tower computers use three times that. That suggests that green PC design has a lot to learn from this project. Compare the *Enano*, which is sold on its environmentally friendly low power consumption and yet still uses 20 watts. The 2-watt consumption also takes it within the range of the solar panel bags that are sufficient to charge media players and phones, but not conventional laptops.

The best thing of all with this computer is there would never be any incentive to switch and get the 'latest model'. It just does what you need.

Future Proofing

It's really hard work to upgrade your computer. You can buy new processor upgrades, but they are hampered by other design issues. But it doesn't have to be like this. It's because devices are built to be thrown out after 18–36 months.

IBM built the iSeries server on a very different philosophy. It spun off a 'what will computers look like in 50 years' time?' project in the 1970s. It is, as a result, the everlasting light bulb of computing. One customer (a church diocese office in New York) upgraded its iSeries server after over 20 years. They got the new box, switched it on running the same standard COBOL business programmes with the same data – and that was it. No firm-wide systems integration consultants. No downtime. No fuss. The iSeries is (and has been throughout its history) 128-bit ready (whereas Windows is just making the difficult transition to 64-bit word length). Why aren't all electronics devices built to a 'what will we need in 50 years' time?' remit, just like major pieces of furniture or architectural features? If you assume they are throwaway items, then they will be.

A truly upgradeable computer or device would be:

- future-proofed;
- modular, with swappable components;
- hardware and software would be independent (the iSeries runs a 'virtual machine' so that big changes in one don't affect the other);
- easy to maintain, with many user-serviceable parts;
- so distinctive it would become iconic, a design that never dates.

An upgradeable range could be specialised to different purposes. Built from common components and to a standard box design. The computer I no longer use as my main work computer could be pressed into service as my home media station.

DIY/FIY

The ultimate nondisposable good is something you make yourself. This has other green benefits, e.g. flat pack furniture (less volume to ship).

The funky green DIY movement members also have a *reuse* aesthetic, making jewellery out of junk and so on. DIY goods are things which you will want to keep and treasure; you 'own' things you make in a different way than merely commodities. Similarly, fix it yourself (FIY).

What I enjoy most about the DIY/FIY movements is the creativity. A great example is the *IKEA Hackers*. This started as a jokey art movement, where people would make surreal statues out of bookcase parts and so on. But now it's a serious customisation thing. One typical project posted online was about using MDF pegboard and wire to mount all your office routers, power cords and wiring off the floor, under your desk. There's no direct green benefit to that arrangement. But the site is a way of having and swapping ideas which is highly relevant, and numerous sites are setting up to capture what you might call green lifestyle hacks. The clever reuse of worn out objects is an example. At my home we have lots of cushion covers made out of old shirts, jeans and so on. It's a way to create something quite unique, retain the memories and reduce waste.

Treasuring

We live in a world with a superfluity of crap commodities. Many have argued that the way to live well is to have *a few good things*. I have only a few suits, because I hardly ever wear them. But I actually really enjoy wearing them from time to time for the novelty and because they are quite nice, not the sorts of suits you would buy for day-in-day-out practical wear perhaps. A surprising corollary of the need to extend the lifetime of consumer goods is that selling more expensive, better made, more durable and luxurious goods to a broader audience would actually be good for the green economy. Someone like LVMH should make it their mission to save us from spending on cheap disposable rubbish. If our money was tied up in a few big budget items, we would buy classics that don't go out of style, we would treasure them and take great care of them and we would derive status from their ownership. The same with holidays. If people could be persuaded that one brilliant holiday is worth ten crappy short breaks (it feels like an argument you could support), then we could cut down the airmiles considerably. It's about counteracting false economy. Let's start behaving like resources are luxuries.

The Sharing Approach

We have seen that sharing and non-ownership (rental) models can hit resistance; for instance, the reaction to the Electrolux free machine, pay-per-use scheme. How could sharing, renting or otherwise not owning be made culturally acceptable? By conferring status or by compensatory cultural benefits like belonging, perhaps?

What would it take to get people to give up owning a car and instead to share? We know from the consumer research quoted earlier that the response to this in the form of car-sharing schemes is 'absolutely no way!' That's because there is no cultural benefit unless you are the type of person who identifies themselves as a green pioneer. And if you are moving from regular use of your own car to this position, it's a stretch.

There are some really admirable and successful car-sharing schemes. These schemes involve a shared fleet of cars; in a typical scheme, you pay a deposit and monthly membership (for CityCar-Club in London it's a £100 deposit, then £5 a month) and then book a car when you need it from the internet, paying £4/hour while you use it. The cars are parked in the same location, so you can find them on an internet map, which also tells you whether they are available and allows you to make bookings. The economics are broadly comparable, for most purposes, to taking a cab. Except that you don't have that uncertainty of having to find a cab for your return journey, of grumpy drivers not liking you loading the car with your latest purchase from eBay. And unless you are a daily driver, it's masses cheaper than going out and buying a car. These schemes have proved quite popular in recent years, because of the green connotations. Schemes like these had existed for over 50 years, but only really took off in the last decade. But their appeal still seems to be at the margin; for instance, in the US, several of the most successful schemes were built from a campus base, targeting students with limited finances and car needs.

By definition, car-sharing schemes of this sort are not going to appeal to the regular drivers responsible for most emissions. But if people did share cars, it would make a huge impact – in all of the manufacturing, shipping and disposal costs even if there was no reduction in journeys. And as a pay-per-use service it would probably reduce inessential journeys too, no one would get a cab to the corner shop to buy a paper, but they do that journey in their own car without even thinking.

But those mainstream consumers in Manchester almost violently rejected this type of car-sharing club! What's to be done? We need some different framing ideas. Smaller, more efficient vehicles, ones with alternative fuels . . . of course. But what else?

Here are some made up examples.

Shareffeur

For the people who bought a 3 series BMW or C-Class Mercedes because of the snobby status, appearing to be in a wealthy elite: why not have a chauffeur instead?

A fleet of luxury (LPG converted) sedans on constant call day and night. You pay per trip. The average cost must be less than your cost of leasing and running a basic luxury marque. But that's not hard.

The total cost of ownership of a Mercedes C350 (which has good depreciation, so is a tougher example to beat than most) is roughly as follows:

New (street) price: £33730
Costs of three-year ownership:

Depreciation	£17000
Fuel	£6000
Insurance	£3000
Maintenance	£3000
Financing/lost interest	£4000
Total cost of ownership:	£33000

If you could split the costs between three or four users per vehicle, it's looking quite do-able. I posted this on my blog and one comment from a reader in the Far East pointed out it was normal to have drivers there, just as it is normal to have taxi drivers in most cities; it is partly a matter of convention whether you drive yourself.

And some people would love it. No more worrying about who is driving on a night out. Relax on your journey, or if you are so inclined, work on your phone and mobile. Giving up your car for a round-the-clock chauffeur service is a step up in the world. The drivers will ensure the cars are always clean and presentable. You never have to search for parking spaces. It's all about the cultural positioning. What is on offer is basically a private hire taxi service, but by upgrading the car/service and also upping the size of the fleet and offering it on a contracted basis, it's a product–service innovation.

I think most people would be surprised to learn that for the cost of a standard luxury saloon, they could get a nicer car with chauffeur service. That's an idea straight out of the *Viridian Manifesto*; it's making (green) car sharing popular with an elite luxury car marque buyer. It's also creating new jobs. But reducing the number of cars on the road. But it's a bit snobby. For the mainstream car owners we need a different tack . . .

Mums United

The African proverb that 'it takes a village to raise a child' is a popular standard for commentators and politicians these days; for instance, Hillary Clinton used it as the title of her booklet on American family policies (1996). It's been used as a *metaphor* for caring social services and family-friendly company policies ever since. What's often missed in these discussions is the *actual* African traditions of shared mothering:

> I grew up in the south among women, blood related and otherwise who all had a say in my daily life. I had several women to answer to. I was raised with many eyes watching me and a gathering of mother spirits who kept me in the fold when my mother was physically or emotionally absent.[86]

That's the African–American tradition, but it's also a statement of a more universal cultural form; *mothers tend to co-operate*. You can see it in the school fetes, in the networks of friends and sisters who will cover for each other. If anything, it is more prevalent in working class communities than the atomised bourgeoisie, who have child-minders, nannies and others to take on this archetypal role. I'm a very involved dad, by the way, I'm not suggesting it's 'a woman's place'. Rather, it's just that there seems to be an interesting positive cultural route into sharing in this insight . . .

Imagine a club called *Mums United*. The NCT or a similar large-scale mothers' community might launch it. Or it might be new. *Mums United* operates in little cells of local mums, with children at the same nurseries and schools, who co-operate to make everyone's lives easier and affordable. The shared second car would be a hub. Whoever had it on a particular day or week would also be ferrying the children and providing some after-school child minding and similar. Leaving the other two or three parents per car free. Weekly shopping trips could be shared. Babysitting done in rotas. In a society where over two-thirds of women never have enough time to get things done, this scheme would provide bonus time. It would also save you a third or more of your motoring costs and potentially could save some childcare costs (e.g. after school clubs or child minders) too. It would also reinforce social networks, which become support networks at times when one parent is having a hard time with a houseful of sick kids, or with a rocky relationship, or a stressful time at work and so on.

The economics of working mothering can be marginal; many complain, even in well paid jobs, that it is barely advantageous after childcare and other costs to go back to work. Cutting thousands by sharing a car *and* getting much needed support seems quite a big benefit to get in exchange for sharing a car. And I'd venture (from years of doing car research groups for VW), that many women are less status and image conscious about their car. Many tend to see it as either just a very functional A to B device, or as 'a friend' (which fits this scheme well) rather than a statement.

I don't know if these schemes are realistic. I'm just trying to illustrate the way that cultural ideas – chauffeuring, mums uniting – could create a Trojan horse to get past people's greenophobia about car sharing.

Communal Living

This is the ultimate 'hippy' lifestyle. The commune. Or is it?

Children at private schools share a dorm, patients share a ward, officers share a mess, hotel guests queue for a buffet breakfast . . . The myth that people do – and should – reside in nuclear family units is near universal. But then what about the ubiquitous young adult flatmates? Home ownership as a proportion of the population fell this year in the UK for the first time in post-war records. Both these trends are due to housing prices rising. *The Economist* has called the current housing boom, not only in the UK but also in the USA, Poland, Ireland, Spain, China . . . 'the biggest bubble in history'. In the UK market, the housing boom is rationalised as due to an increase in the demand for properties. Strangely, the population doesn't seem to be growing. And the number of young adults is down, compared to other generations. The issue is the numbers who live alone.

At the least sign of trouble, speculators exit markets. Economic history suggests that it would be a first if this bubble didn't burst. There have already been setbacks in the USA and China. The principal beneficiaries are banks, estate agents and the tax office. Ordinary people experience a notional increase in wealth (for instance, they can remortgage and take money out of their home). They feel richer; it's common to meet people who say 'I made £40000 since we bought at the start of the year'. But should they want to move to a nicer or bigger home, they will have to find an increasing differential. Plus, it is part of the overall 4×4 and foreign holiday glut culture; giving a whole generation the idea that they got rich quick. Not a good thing at first sight.

If the housing bubble did continue though, it could have very interesting green effects. One is the reduced size of affordable properties. Small is beautiful. From a green point of view, a smaller home is cheaper to heat and less resource intensive. An obvious way to 'share' without violating cultural codes about having your own space, is to carve up existing properties into smaller sub-units. Which is exactly what's been happening. Developers will turn a large Victorian house into six or eight small flats. New developments contain many 'studios'. It's the only way new buyers can afford it. The knock-on effect of small space living (as in Japan) is more minimal living, with fewer possessions.

There are historical forms that could revive the communal living approach in different forms than permanently shared living space. Such as the boarding house, which for migrant workers provides a halfway point between hotel and family. Several funky hotel concepts in recent years have been based upon this idea of community and a halfway sense of being at home for longer-term guests.

Another wildcard thought I had was building a huge chain of 'Big Brother Hotels' – linked to qualification for their next TV series –

which could provide the first decent challenge to the easyJet generation, a reason not to go abroad for your hols?

But the main potential is families sharing properties; fewer kitchens, loos and so on. It creates social tensions and pressures, but perhaps these are preferable to alienation? This is how most people have lived, as we are social animals. I think we actually 'miss' this as an unconscious, archetypal arrangement. And I think that partly explains the success of communal living reality shows such as *Big Brother*. We are pack animals in evolutionary terms. We get lonely when isolated in splinter groups. We miss the hubbub, and while employers, to some extent, have taken on this role, it is a poor substitute.

Lending Libraries

The library is an accepted format for borrowing things you don't need to own. I love to keep non-fiction books, as I can dip back in (in ten years' time maybe I will just keep the electronic copy) but there's no need to keep novels. Ten years ago I gave all my fiction away (apart from classics and a few treasured exceptions). Similarly with DVDs, library style businesses (Blockbusters) work well with any one-shot product use. Formalwear hire works for similar reasons; it's a 'once in a blue moon' need for most people.

It's an intuitive cultural form that can lend itself to surprising products and audiences. *Bag, Steal or Borrow* is a heavily funded 2006 start-up from Seattle. The idea is that for a subscription, you can borrow unaffordably expensive handbags and accessories. Not only do you get to afford the best, but you can also swap it; giving the impression that the original Renaissance fashion tilted at – of being able to afford to be up with the latest. In the highest band, subscription costs $1200 (£600) per year. For the target audience that's preferable to spending more than that amount on one bag that becomes 'so last year'. The system is identical to the popular *Netflix* idea – pay a monthly subscription and change the items – you are paying to hold a few products, but you can exchange these as often as you like. It's a different economic model (and its value for money depends how often you do exchange – it's an expensive way to rent one movie a month) but in psychological terms, it has a quasi-ownership character; you hold onto something.

The *power tool library* is a move to use literal library systems; on average, power tools are being used for under ten minutes a year, why always have them at home? And different jobs can call for specialist tools. One scheme at the Oakland public library near San Francisco holds a mind-boggling variety of professional tools, available to hire for a few dollars a day. People aren't allowed to renew on any item more than twice, ensuring that this does mainly serve the occasional user. Imagine how many other goods which we occasionally use could be loaned from libraries.

An interesting different take on the library is swapping schemes. A great one in the UK focuses on books. Here's something people buy, read once and then stick on a shelf. http://www.readitswapit. co.uk/ allows people to arrange to swap books. They list the ones they are prepared to swap. Individuals find something on each other's lists they would like to swap for. They arrange it. They each pay the postage and otherwise it is completely free. There are 110000 books listed on the service and counting. These sorts of schemes can become very popular; the community factor and search function and process can be 'addictive', as people say of eBay.

There certainly seem to be quite a few sharing and swapping schemes launching at the moment. Another one just launched from the lovely people at Futerra is *Swishing*. The idea is home parties where women friends all bring clothes and similar, then choose things from this pooled collection they'd like to take home. Home fashion-buying parties are already popular (for instance TopShop does them). With Swishing, you get clothes which are to your taste (friends tend to be quite similar), which are free, and it's green too. The website for this idea is very eye-catching and all it does is give people the idea in a formatted 'instructions for-' way. It's one of those ideas that might take off; certainly it's already been picked up by *The Times* and *Telegraph* newspapers. I also really like the way they have given the behaviour a slang name; 'swishing' = rustling like silk = like cattle rustling. Sometimes the key to establishing a new piece of behaviour is getting it into the vernacular, as with 'jogging' for instance, a term invented by one of the Nike founders.

Potlatch and Green Christmas

Potlatch is a term for a North American (Pacific coast) native ceremony, but it has become a generic term for a festivity of generosity. In the original Potlatch ceremonies, sponsors gave away various useful items such as blankets, food and tools. The more you gave, the greater the effect on your prestige. Similar rituals are observed in many other tribal societies, including our own! Think about the modern festival of Christmas. What is that other than a lavish festival of largesse? Okay, the recipients tend to be drawn from family members.

Clearly, potlatches in consumerist form are a worry from a green point of view. I know that in the US, Thanksgiving (a literal settler potlatch festival) takes some of this role; the US has its peak shopping day at Thanksgiving, whereas UK retail sales double around Christmas. The following austerity mood, when people slim and regret the excess, is met by dramatic January sales; *having spent all that money you can now save some by buying more stuff* goes the (only in consumerism!) twisted logic.

If Christmas were cancelled, we would save a big chunk of the Western footprint and glut. Christmas presents tend to be misjudged, the unwanted presents being stuffed in a drawer or returned with receipt in some more transactional families. Not only is the spending excessive and sometimes wasteful, but also the lion's share is targeted at children, teaching the next generation to expect excess.

According to research by the British Retail Consortium (2005 data):

- The average UK household spends over £900 over the Christmas fortnight.
- Presents account for more than two-thirds; £660 on gifts.
- The average child receives gifts worth more than £250.
- Britons buy an incredible 83 sq km of wrapping paper.

Technology sales have been the big story of recent retail sales at Christmas; in 2005, it was the iPod, in 2006, the 'must have' item was the (energy inefficient and arguably unnecessary given access to HD content) flat screen TV.

Yes, we do need to splurge occasionally (as evidenced by excessive festivals in all human societies). And so you could argue that the potlatch answers a deep need; it is a kind of purging as much as a splurging, upsetting the usual order and monotonous restraint.

BUT . . .

In traditional potlatch, a rich person *gives away possessions*. They may have bought them for this purpose of course. But largely, they are redistributing wealth. There are schemes where people 'give the gift of giving' – my mother gave us all charity cards showing items we had donated in third world communities and the amount spent. But that's not quite what I had in mind. With a small reframe, family giving at Christmas could extend the life of unwanted household objects (a seasonal version of the Freecycle concept), build social capital and a sense of community, cut the retail orgy and still let you have a nice time. You could just make it a swap of unwanted goods that others turn into new presents. XmasSwapFest.com, where people swap Christmas potential presents with other local people. Prime examples are kids' toys which your own have grown out of. Like Freecycle, it would be organised into local groups. Tinkering with Christmas is, of course, tricky. But our Christmas itself has been through many such reformulations. The modern family Christmas was a Victorian invention.

I'm pursuing this thought at the moment, in discussion with *The Ecologist*, who have the idea of reviving the Christmas Fayre, and some contacts in the Church of England. If we are to tackle the culture of Christmas, what better place to start?

SECTION III

Concluding Thoughts

Ideas Good, Image Bad

I think there is something in the notion we have met at various points in this book, that people will buy goods and services because of the company behind them. But I see it differently from others who have presented this as an extra image dimension. I see it instead as what is left when you strip away image branding and marketing spin. You are left with information about who made or grew a product, what others think of it, including how green or ethical it is. That doesn't exclude telling your story imaginatively, and using ideas to connect with people. It's about being true (rather than just rational).

This book is pointing towards and starting to describe the outlines of a post-brand marketing paradigm. It is not, as some greens (and Marxists) envisage, about returning to a (mythical) rationalised age of buying things only for their functional utility. It is rather about working with more authentic social meanings and ideas; ones capable of transforming lifestyles and attitudes. And this post-brand future has already arrived, when you consider internet examples like eBay. Yes, eBay has a household name, but it doesn't have a brand image. It is a marketplace; which happens to have a name, rules and a thriving local culture, even a dialect.

One distorting effect of image branding has been to overstate its own importance. Branding at its most basic offers two related things – visibility and character. And in the world of products, at first sight it's all branded. The only example Mary Goodyear could think of in unbranded products were toothpicks. But that's because she was looking at it from an FMCG perspective. We all looked at branding that way ten years ago. Now we approach it differently. Unpackaged goods, be it the fruit you pick at a country farm, the bottled milk deliveries, a handmade craft item, organic local vegetable deliveries, most furniture . . . it starts to add up doesn't it? Add services which are unbranded: financial advisors, plumbers, cleaners, after school tutors . . . Add local retail. Add tap water. Add most taxi services and public transport. Add your house (unless a new build). And so on. Much in our lives – precisely the taken for granted elements – is unbranded. Many are identified with a named provider, be they a solicitor or farmer. *Who* you buy from is the key. In fact, modern branding was invented to mimic this; giving mass-produced goods and outlets the same feelings as when you bought from someone you knew and trusted. The brand personality substituted for knowing a real person you bought from.

Now imagine a world with no brands. Many who did this in the past imagined a grey world, like the old Eastern Bloc. Today when people imagine a world without brands, it's more hopeful. Sao Paulo has banned outdoor advertising throughout the city. Auckland is thinking of doing the same. You can imagine a life in this direction that is more human, authentic, less pressured perhaps?

And it's already happening. Own label sales now account for £4 in every £10 spent on groceries in the UK. Considering they tend to be priced cheaper than named brands, that's 50% of grocery shopping baskets by volume. Of course that is not strictly 'post brand' – M&S and *Tesco Finest* are brands in their own right. But it is widely accepted as evidence of what Datamonitor call 'brand erosion'. Own-label goods are not as personality intensive; they tend to focus on intrinsic qualities of the supplying company overall. And today that includes green credentials. All retailers are making rapid changes in CSR.

There are three ways classical brand choices can be shattered:

1. Commodifying brands, by making them secondary to other criteria (with own label being only one form of this manoeuvre). If I decide to only use organic produce, then the brand is secondary to that decision, and actually brands matter less; 'organic' is the brand instead. These new 'label' decisions are creating a situation where retailers no longer need manufacturer brands at all. M&S has never sold other people's brands, and its model gets a new vitality with its leadership on green issues; you are no longer looking for your favourite brand of coffee, you 'look behind the label' as the M&S campaign put it.

2. Demystifying brands; for instance, identifying how they are made, and by whom People are sharing information and making decisions based on this information, not just appearances. Classic FMCG brands were anonymous entities, whose background was hidden, given a fictitious identity; like Mr Kipling. But it is already common practice in supermarkets, for instance, to label quality British meat with its origins, even down to the individual farm.

3. Word of mouth, advocacy, community . . . all leading to shared decision-making, based upon other people's personal experiences (rather than image). Here, the net of influence goes well beyond retailers. But they still can be involved, as with the Amazon reviews.

I reckon there could be a very interesting platform where customer comments are accessible while shopping, on or offline. It's possible that could be built by the retailers; certainly their co-operation could help. But it could be independent, if, for instance,

Wikipedia-style volunteers were willing to photograph barcodes with their phones and input their comments, Digg-style articles, research links and so on. If this happens, it will be a new social trend. It will be called something like *Smart Shopping*. You can readily see the information agent side of this becoming a hobby in its own right, people will go window shopping, scan an item, research it and then publish. Their comments could range from personal taste selections, price comparisons to ethics.

Note that the post-brand scenarios I am describing don't feel depersonalised. They are actually *repersonalised*; involving chatter in online forums or a personal connection with the maker or indeed new ideas from a blogger on what's good to buy. Branding itself is alienating; an industrial product given a false identity. Mr Kipling's cakes aren't really traditional, nor baked in a traditional manner, nor even made by an individual called Mr Kipling. Branding has got away with fictitious image and 'seeming benefits' (Kipling's cakes seem traditional). But it's a fib, basically, and deep down people have always known this; perhaps you could argue back that the cost and convenience of such mass-produced foods made it acceptable. But times are changing, and most supermarkets today are baking bread and cakes on site; it may still not be home cooked, but it's a lot closer.

I call these developments leading us beyond image branding *first handedness*. They can involve:

- *first-hand* knowledge and experience – visiting the farm you buy from;
- *first-hand* dealings with the producer – getting to know the farmer;
- *first-hand* accounts from others, recommenders, affiliates and reviews;
- *first-hand* access to people in a company – dialogue and involvement;
- *first-hand* communities, with direct access to peers;

- *first-hand* idiosyncrasy, imperfection, in a natural or raw state – customised.

First hand is meant to connote a directness, authenticity and personal relationship. It's the end of an illusion. The illusion was that mass-produced products could take on a symbolic personality, to counteract the artificial, alienating sense of industrial sameness. Image branding was a by-product of the broadcast age. The internet media revolution means new person-to-person (peer-to-peer) connections. This makes joint processes of deliberation, advocacy and adopting standards or lifestyles easy and efficient. It also allows an alternative model of matching buyers and sellers to the retailer one. The post-branding structure is first hand because the media are first hand.

Increasingly, I believe, we will buy direct from other people – not just direct from farmers and producers, but direct from individual people running intermediary sites. The affiliate sales idea has been all the rage in the last few years; the idea that a blogger writing about an area they are passionate about can link to books, resources and stores which are relevant. An eMarketer survey found that people arriving via affiliate links had a 43% higher conversion than other means of referral. It has become a fairly standard additional source of business online. What's revolutionary about this – potentially at least – is individuals marketing to individuals. In the green products and services domain, advocacy rates are unusually high, and this is a natural extension. The resulting brands could be quite low key – as 'recommended by X' would be the key hook, where X is someone you know or trust (for instance, a prominent blogger). But when I say marketing I don't mean to say you can 'hire' these enthusiasts, even if they do go as far as selling your product for a small cut. The other thing that's quite revolutionary is the scale. Over £2B in affiliate sales were made in 2006 alone according to one report.[87]

There are many other potential varieties of *first person* marketing. People remaking, adding to, redesigning your products is one thing to look for. Like Bemz. This Stockholm company offers slipcovers for many of the most popular IKEA sofas, armchairs and cushions. This allows people to personalise and also update (rather than replace) their IKEA home furnishings. The company was invented a few years ago by Lesley Pennington, while she was on maternity leave. Each slipcover is made individually to order and the whole thing has a very personal feel. The name comes from the names of her four children: Björn, Emil, Madeleine and Zoë. As they say on their site, you can give a sofa a second chance too; which makes it quite a green idea. It's a small case study, but it says a lot about the way the world is going; the repersonalisation of business, bringing individuality, choice and customisation to mass-produced goods.

An interesting economic and social development is the potential for consumers to become producers. And not just in the creative sense of YouTube and similar. It also applies in green electricity, where homes generating their own power (through solar panels) can sell their excess to a green energy supplier. It's very complicated to set up and so far in the UK only Good Energy does this. But there is an acute shortage of alternative energy (caused by a stampede of companies with carbon neutral pledges trying to switch their supplies), so the need is there. How it works is that – rather than trying to calculate the amount of excess – Good Energy pay their Homegen customers for every unit, even the ones they use on site.

With nanotech, the factory of the medium-term future will disappear; goods will become self-assembling. Which means that the location of the factory may shift to become the location of usage. But it doesn't have to be this high tech. Micro-banking is the idea of self-organised finance working in situ. It already works in the developing world, funnelling billions in funds from and through village self-help schemes. Informal (unpaid) micro producers give each other advice, support, recommendations and so on. It could work here, and Zopa was an early attempt to do something like this. And now Kiva (the case study at the end of the introduction) is linking here and there. It is a case in point; you make a $25 loan to an individual in the developing world after reading the story of what they do and what they need the money for. It is a great way to get insight into real life in other parts of the world; a gift to people here as well as over there. You also get email updates on their progress.

All of these trends have some relevance to the mainstream of marketing. They are far from marginal – including eBay, Amazon and many other large-scale developments. But they are so far an alternative sector. The question is, could it actually go much further? Could this become the new mainstream? Could *first hand* replace image?

I think it could and quite possibly *should*. The challenge posed to marketing by sustainability, the ethical consumer and better public information is one of transparency and trust. Being straight with people. Not bland and unimaginative, but nonetheless TRUE. It is possible for imaginative presentations to communicate with greater veracity, for instance, for a drama to hit home harder than a documentary. I am not saying that by dropping image we would move to a factual, rational, acultural mode.

If you examine 'green' as a brand, its cultural codes, what you find is that these are massively consumerised and pretty misleading, as well as being clichéd. What brand image does is add something exciting and desire-tickling to something's appeal. Chocolate is associated with sex, escapism, aspiration and so on.

What a green brand of chocolate did instead – *Green & Black's* – was put free samples onto the cover of leading women's magazines. That's *first-hand* marketing again. It is a brand which has done an enormous service to Fairtrade and organic foods in general, because it is just such a great product – tasting is believing. The packaging and identity design of this brand is beautiful, elegant; it successfully conveys the quality of the chocolate. But it does so in a classical way, like a nice painting or shop sign, rather than by adding a brand fantasy as so many confectionery brands did before.

The green future we need to build will not be dull, but it will be less reliant on false images. Including false green images. The cultural codes surrounding greenness – the ideas that any mediocre ad agency would apply to a 'green' brief – are pretty spent. In this I am in full agreement with the Viridian Manifesto: 'What is required is not a natural Green, or a spiritual Green, or a primitivist Green, or a blood-and-soil romantic Green. These flavours of Green have been tried, and have proven to have insufficient appeal.' But I don't agree with Sterling's conclusion that 'The world needs a new, unnatural, seductive, mediated, glamorous Green.'[88] I think we're moving beyond that, with real life, real people, real conversations overturning image marketing of this sort.

But nor do I agree with those from the other camp who believe the way forward is responsible, restrained, puritan messages. We do need to retain the imaginative exuberance of marketing. And indeed what is the current wave of ethical consumerism driven by if it is not enthusiasm? The best template for green brands in future is the digital brands; involving, person-to-person, first hand. They also involve imaginary worlds, voyeurism, flirting with identity, competition and many such human drives. It's not a less human world, it's a more first-hand, experiential, groovy world.

A good slogan for making progress would be *live local, share global*.

As we have seen, eating local seasonal produce and restricting your travel are very high on a list of things to do. But that doesn't mean a return to a pastoral village system. The cities are the place to best make use of scarce resources and also create centres of excellence in education and creativity. The difference with the world today is that we can share ideas freely, and yet not have to travel.

Local lacks one vital ingredient – scale. Internet-based models, which enable local initiatives to have a global impact (I don't necessarily mean by shipping stuff around the world, I mean by joining up the effects and efficiency of millions of 'locals'), are a significant class of future model. And non-internet networked models too, such as micro-banking, which adds up to billions, one village community at a time.

In other words, local is a potent source of future ideas. And when we crack a brilliant local idea, the internet allows us to share it with millions of other locals.

It's only when retail chains and similar exploit a 'local image' that it becomes problematic. I am not as anti-big chain as most greens; I'd rather have one giant business owning half the retail outlets in the world, if it happened to have a tiny footprint per outlet and a clean ethical bill of health. Even with local we need to be careful to think, rather than pursue the image; the idea that anything big is bad belies what we have learned about scale and efficiency.

We need to retune many of our intuitions. The old green ideas are not that much help, especially as they have been consumerised and co-opted to old-style image brands, and used to sell industrial products and lifestyles instead of sustainable ones. It seems worth deconstructing green image codes, to reinforce their dangers. The message being, when you get a green brief, do not stray into the following hackneyed territories:

1. **The Great Outdoors.** The early green movement was about conservation. It drew upon the romantic reaction to industrialisation. It became a popular political movement, for instance involving the creation of national parks in the USA. Over time this has become a fundamentally consumerised agenda. And it was already a fantasy; the dreams of factory and office workers for open wilderness spaces. People who grow up in gorgeous, unspoilt rural spaces don't even see them in this way.

   Most people can't go back to nature, most of the time, but they can buy substitutes. If you hanker for the great outdoors, you can plan and buy an exotic holiday. You can buy an outdoors-style car like a Landrover, or one of the 'Chelsea tractor' 4×4s. And in a twist of irony, the mountain bike – so fetishised by green lifestyle enthusiasts – is arguably the 4×4 car concept too; excessive in its specification for normal city use. And it is expensive, both in price and in raw material costs. Plus, many of the 'coolest' bikes are imported from America or Japan. Of course, a bike is better than a car. But I am trying to demonstrate how consumerised the green scene we have inherited already is; a product of the same culture and assumptions as the very things it attacks.

2. **Pastoral.** Consider the expensive French-style bread shops like *Paul* springing up in upscale 'villages' in London. *Paul's* prices for 'peasant-style' rustic breads are so extremely high it has become the branding equivalent of Marie Antoinette. *Paul* originated as a family bakery in Lille. But that's about as relevant today as the fact that Coco Chanel used to be a seamstress. *Paul* now offers bio breads with stringently 'authentic' ingredients like *'Unrefined Guérande sea-salt, hand-harvested in the traditional way from the Guérande salt-flats.'* This is authenticity co-opted to luxury; these breads are super-expensive. This is not a *paysan* bakery rejecting modern life; this is for the haute bourgeoisie. And successful with it; the queue at my local branch on a Saturday often goes around the block. Authenticity is always a fantasy. The real thing actually is *just reality*, but 'the real thing' is *a simulation*. And yet such authentic themes are endlessly co-opted by marketing to non-green ends. The *pure* mountain source mineral waters create huge problems for the environment, for instance.

3. **Vintage.** This ought to be really green. And it was until it got consumerised. Another example of authenticity gone wrong, thanks to marketing, is Diesel. This brand is sold on the *trash aesthetic*, i.e. the (originally environmentally friendly) fashion for retro-styled charity shop and other second-hand clothes. The trouble is that Diesel is not second hand; it only has *second-hand styling*. If it didn't exist, people who wanted this look (e.g. students) would have to buy actual second-hand clothes.

4. **Natural.** Surely 'natural' is okay? But dig deeper. Oil is a natural product. So are antibiotics. If you look at the semiotics of coffee, it is *machine made* whereas tea seems *leaf-infused*. It's a socially

constructed set, not a natural order. *Nature knows best* is the rule of thumb. But is this a reliable guide? According to a story I read yesterday, too much 'bio' yoghurt can make young women infertile. And in the green domain, an interesting case is cotton. Cotton feels like the most 'natural' fabric (other perhaps than wool). It 'lets your skin breathe'. It is suitable for sensitive skin, for instance nearly all babywear is 100% cotton. Except that actually it's not the green choice. Cotton is the single biggest pesticide-using crop in the world. Dumbing down to 'green intuitions' is a treacherous path.

5. **The Rebel.** The rebellious streak is a direct descendent of the 1960s peace movement activism. Individualism is the heart of this youth rebellion. It is the 'Me' of the 1960s *Me Generation*. 'Me' ('Look at me') is the fundamental code of consumerism. Is it, on balance, such a helpful discourse for green marketing to build upon? Given that marketing is already saturated with such themes, given that it is intrinsically a selfish and isolating perspective and given it ultimately (like all of these overarching consumerist cultural ideologies) stops people from thinking?

6. **Anti-Science.** The green movement grew out of romanticism and was, in its origins, therefore anti-science and anti-industry (although some have argued there is another longer root, into dissenting religious traditions, such as the Quakers). Anti-science is a popular cultural theme. Since Frankenstein's monster, numerous nightmares of technology have populated our fictional and artistic media. The anti-science slate underpins many green policies; against GM, against nuclear power, against vivisection. I am not saying these policies are wrong. But a blanket anti-science slate is actually about as helpful as a heedless pro-science slate would be. Citing the massive environmental problems of 'natural fabrics' like cotton, Jo Heeley, chair of the Textile Environmental Network, despairs of the simplistic turn away from man-made alternatives; 'it is both naïve and counterproductive to say one is better than

the other. Both natural and man-made fibres have a part to play in the whole of the textile industry'.[89] Quite a few of the measures in combating climate change in future will be technological innovations. New forms of energy for one thing. We can't afford to whip up a total anti-science agenda. It's lazy and thoughtless ideology.

7. **Apocalypse Now.** No survey of 'green as brand' would be complete without millennial and apocalyptic codes. I'm not sure how helpful this is in getting people to act (rather than adopt a rather fatalistic perspective). Nor to what extent the finality of it all accurately captures the long agony of an increasingly hostile climate (the IPCC report talks about 1000 years of damage, even if greenhouse gas trends were halted today). Also, Paul Ray made the point (quoting a 1500 year study by Fred Polak into various images of the future through history) that we need to take care, because pessimism has a nasty habit of proving self-fulfilling. If the only image of the future we have is gloomy, how can we build a better world?

A Fresh Start for Green Marketing

We need to get beyond image marketing to create sustainable brands. That is not to say that brands will not have social meanings. Some of the most advanced ideas in the book are forging new social meanings. The difference is between letting brands have an authentic connection and imagewashing brands. Imagewashing is making an ad campaign, design (like the BP 'green flower') that confers associations without substance. More authentic approaches include;

- partnering with a credible organisation working in this field;
- adopting a shared, independent and reputable standard such as the Soil Association 'organic' mark;
- associating with a tribe of likeminded users of the brand;

- creating new cultural codes – not dumbing down but provoking fresh perspectives.

I tend to think that to make any real and sustained progress, consumerist image-making must stop. And that affects much more than advertising. Creating new luxuries (long-haul yoga retreats and ethical safari holidays) is no way forward; it is not just advertising that is imagewashing but also the construction of products and services around similar fantasies. The 4×4 car is just a classic car ad (cornering on mountains) turned into a product design. I slightly worry about the glitzy, glossy entertainment angle on the green issue being pushed from the USA. Yes, it needs to be enjoyable and inviting, but I have so much more faith in grass roots changes than mega rock concerts.

But as we remove waste, greed and selfishness, we must add something. It is not enough to remove (needless and deceptive) aspiration. If we only take consumerism out, the danger then is that the choice will be between boring ethical products or fun, sexy, beautiful, crazy consumerist ones. I met some dock-strikers from Poland in the 1980s at a left-wing meeting in London. Someone in the audience asked 'what do you want, ultimately?' To the embarrassment of the socialist organisers of the event, the panel replied that they just wanted jeans, TVs, Coca-Cola – the Western lifestyle dream.

Green (and sustainable) products are not just responsible. They are better: more durable, cheaper, nicer, healthier, more thoughtful, offering extensions into social communities, belonging to something. The green products, services and businesses of the future are creative, in a sparky, thrilling way. They are like innocent smoothies compared to boring old Coke and Pepsi. They represent a turning away from the oppressive uniformity of mass-produced culture – a turning towards humanity in all its eccentricity and subjective diversity. No two smiles are the same. Why should two apples be?

We need to inject optimism and enthusiasm into these brands and companies.

The cultural debate about ecology has been largely concerned with the problem. Problems are messy, complicated, systemic, painful and, if you are not careful, depressing. We must not let the idea that we are all doomed create a culture of pessimism and inaction. We can't put our fellow human beings on death row for 50 years waiting for the worst. We are going to survive this. There will be suffering and struggle, but then the world will be better after than before.

Marketing is about simple – 'of course!' – solutions to complex problems. The context we have been exploring is complex. We needed to understand this to avoid greenwashing, and stuff that does more harm than good. But as we move onto marketing solutions, things get so much simpler; what is required is a series of creative breakthrough ideas, nothing more. The hope is that the 'tipping point' will draw in fresh talent from communications, design, film-making, social networks and so on – to create the same Silicon Valley effect that has driven IT over the last 20 years. We need to 'heed the call up'. We actually can't leave green to the old greens any more. They need us all to become greens, to the extent that green disappears and becomes the new normal. As we take the green agenda mainstream – it isn't green any more, it's just common sense – it will have to change. Many of the political and social codes that carried it thus far will have to go. I am betting that some of the old guard won't like it.

The same conundrum is well known in the IT industry. Geoffrey Moore's seminal book, Crossing the Chasm, argues that with a disruptive new technology, there is usually a chasm of difference between the early adopters (enthusiasts) and the early majority (pragmatists). They tend to have different cultural values and different expectations. Compare early adopters of new personal computing technologies with the mass audience. The former were the beardy homebrew geeks of the late 1970s and early 80s. We don't want geeky computers and we will probably never want dark green seeming lifestyles. Yet we will need to have much smaller carbon footprints than even most dark greens do today. But that is a different matter. It will be the way everyone lives. It won't feel like restraint, it will feel like simplicity, smart living and so on. One area that has great potential is social networks. The 20th century culture created by the consumerisation of culture (and hence politics) may be written about in future as some sort of dark age. Now we have the means to re-engage an active citizenship. The bones of this are already there in Wikipedia, Digg, YouTube and so on. You see it on the web every day, in the blogs and forums. People are starting to think things through, to understand and to share ideas and to spark off each other. And even though it is still incredibly early days, there really are signs that people are starting to change the way they eat, travel and so on quite substantially. What they need now is hundreds of ideas that consolidate this progress and take it further.

This book is hopefully a very initial survey of what is to follow. We have reached an extraordinary point in history, where the consensus is building that this is THE problem for our generation to tackle. It's a huge challenge, but actually isn't it the huge challenges which give life meaning? And we really don't have a plan B.

References

1 Homer-Dixon, T.F. (2000) *The Ingenuity Gap: How Can We Solve the Problems of the Future?* Jonathan Cape, London.
2 http://www.psfk.com/2007/04/levis_tries_to_.html
3 http://www.naturalchoices.co.uk/Marks-and-Spencers-kicks-off-2007?id_mot=7
4 Elkington, J. and Hailes, J. (1988) *The Green Consumer Guide: From Shampoo to Champagne – High-street shopping for a better environment.* Victor Gollancz, London.
5 http://www.worldchanging.com/archives//005031.html
6 http://news.bbc.co.uk/1/hi/business/1130900.stm
7 http://www.marksandspencer.com/gp/node/n/51360031/202-0585291-0092643?ie=UTF8&mnSBrand=core
8 http://assets.panda.org/downloads/living_planet_report.pdf
9 http://en.wikipedia.org/wiki/An_Inconvenient_Truth
10 http://boxofficemojo.com/genres/chart/?id=documentary.htm
11 http://environment.guardian.co.uk/climatechange/story/0,,1935624,00.html
12 http://www.co-operativebank.co.uk/servlet/Satellite?c=Page&cid=1077610044424&pagename=CoopBank%2FPage%2FtplPageStandard
13 http://ameliatorode.typepad.com/life_moves_pretty_fast/2007/05/innocent_mcdona.html
14 http://www.ethisphere.com/Ethisphere_Magazine_0207/WME-2007-Q2
15 http://www.landor.com/?do=cNews.news&storyid=507&g=1200&n=2007
16 http://answers.vizu.com/pdf/Global_Warming_Report.pdf
17 http://3mfuture.com/sustainability/articles/UK%20Government%20Sustainable%20Development.htm

18 Stern, N. (2007) *The Economics of Climate Change: The Stern Review*. Cambridge University Press, Cambridge.

19 http://www.bcccc.net/index.cfm?fuseaction=Page.viewPage&pageId=596& parentID=473

20 Mulvey, C. (2006) *The Good Shopping Guide: Your Guide to Shopping with a Clear Conscience*. Ethical Marketing Group.

21 Goodyear, M. (1996) 'Divided by a common language: diversity and deception in the world of global marketing' *Journal of the Market Research Society*, 38(2),105–122.

22 Mulvey, C. (2006) *The Good Shopping Guide: Your Guide to Shopping with a Clear Conscience*, Ethical Marketing Group.

23 Hickman, L. (2005) *A Good Life, The Guide to Ethical Living*. Eden Books, Transworld.

24 http://www.foodproductiondaily.com/news/ng.asp?n=74385-bernard-matthews-bird-flu-h-n

25 http://www.spiegel.de/international/0,1518,450254,00.html

26 Esty, D. and Winston, A. (2007) *Green to Gold: How Smart Companies Use Environmental Strategy to Innovate, Create Value, and Build a Competitive Advantage*. Yale University Press.

27 http://www.roughtype.com/archives/2006/12/avatars_consume.php

28 http://www.aworldconnected.org/debates/id.2894/debates_detail.asp

29 http://www.bbcworld.com/Pages/PressRelease.aspx?id=6

30 http://www.ft.com/cms/s/2035e78a-01b8-11dc-8b8c-000b5df10621.html

31 http://grist.org/news/maindish/2007/05/16/murdoch/

32 Lakoff, G. (2005) *Don't Think of an Elephant: Know Your Values and Frame the Debate*. Chelsea Green Publishing Co.

33 http://www.laweekly.com/general/features/frame-this/1039/?page=2

34 http://www.grist.org/news/maindish/2004/12/17/little-mackey/

35 http://www.gandalf.it/m/ogilvy2.htm

36 http://www.innocentdrinks.co.uk/supergran

37 http://www.cafonline.org/Default.aspx?page=6915

38 Reeves, R. (1961) *Reality in Advertising*. MacGibbon & Kee.

39 http://www.foodanddrinkeurope.com/news/ng.asp?id=17208-new-look-for

40 http://business.guardian.co.uk/story/0,,1880233,00.html

41 http://www.jointhebiggerpicture.co.uk/YouGovSurvey.aspx

42 http://shopping.guardian.co.uk/ethicalshopping/story/0,,1842727,00.html

43 http://www.planetark.org/dailynewsstory.cfm/newsid/12155/story.htm

44 http://news.bbc.co.uk/1/hi/education/4391695.stm

45 http://www.sutjhally.com/onlinepubs/apocalypse.html

46 http://www.viridiandesign.org/manifesto.html

47 http://www.inthenews.co.uk/news/science/schwarzenegger-pledges-make-green-movement-sexy-$1075767.htm

48 Berger, J. (1963) *Ways of Seeing*. BBC, London.

49 http://www.aynrand.org/site/News2?page=NewsArticle&id=5303

50 http://www.aynrand.org/site/News2?page=NewsArticle&id=5303

51 http://store.babeland.com/new/eco-sexy-kit

52 Girard, R. (1988) *To Double Business Bound: Essays on Literature, Mimesis and Anthropology*. Johns Hopkins University Press.
53 http://www.kyero.com/articles/lower-your-carbon-footprint.php
54 http://www.bbcworld.com/Pages/PressRelease.aspx?id=6
55 http://www.o2.com/cr/environmental_impacts.asp
56 http://www.wrongdiagnosis.com/m/mental_illness/prevalence-types.htm
57 Stevens, A. and Price, J. (2001) *Prophets, Cults and Madness*. Duckworth Publishing.
58 http://www.viridiandesign.org/manifesto.html
59 http://commentisfree.guardian.co.uk/anthony_giddens/2006/11/post_561.html
60 Papanek, V. (1985) *Design for the Real World: Human Ecology and Social Change*. Thames & Hudson.
61 http://www.worldchanging.com/archives/006284.html
62 http://www.sd-commission.org.uk/publications/downloads/Shifting_Opinions.pdf
63 http://www.bbcworld.com/Pages/PressRelease.aspx?id=6
64 http://www.ft.com/cms/s/2035e78a-01b8-11dc-8b8c-000b5df10621.html
65 http://news.independent.co.uk/environment/climate_change/article2556493.ece
66 Lovins, A.B. Lovins, L.H. and Hawken, P. (1999) 'A Roadmap for Natural Capitalism', *Harvard Business Review*.
67 http://www.foe.co.uk/resource/press_releases/dreaming_of_a_green_christ_15112005.html
68 http://www.worldchanging.com/archives//003502.html
69 http://www.guardian.co.uk/commentisfree/story/0,,1935562,00.html
70 Benkler, Y. (2006) *The Wealth of Networks: How Social Production Transforms Markets and Freedom*. Yale University Press.
71 Leadbeater C. and Miller, P. (2004) *The Pro-Am Revolution, How Enthusiasts are Changing our Economy and Society*. Demos.
72 http://www.strategy-business.com/press/freearticle/06408?pg=2&tid=230
73 Surowiecki, J. (2004) *The Wisdom of Crowds: Why the Many Are Smarter Than the Few and How Collective Wisdom Shapes Business, Economies, Societies and Nations*. Little Brown.
74 http://dotherightthing.com/entries/88-yahoo-using-dirty-tactics-to-switch-google-firefox-users
75 http://www.freecycle.org/manual/index_faq.htm
76 http://en.wikipedia.org/wiki/Meetup.com
77 http://www.ampnet.co.uk/femorabilia/mooncup.html
78 http://www.mum.org/CupPat1.htm
79 http://www.mum.org/CupPat1.htm
80 *I Count* (2006) Penguin ©Stop Climate Chaos
81 Baudrillard, J. (tr Chris Turner) (1998) *The Consumer Society*. Sage, London.
82 Baudrillard, J. (tr Chris Turner) (1998) *The Consumer Society*. Sage, London.
83 http://www.longnow.org/
84 http://ebay.about.com/od/ebaylifestyle/a/el_history.htm
85 http://en.wikipedia.org/wiki/Carpet_sweeper

86 http://www.riverwestcurrents.org/2004/October/002237.html
87 http://en.wikipedia.org/wiki/Affiliate_marketing
88 http://www.viridiandesign.org/manifesto.html
89 http://www.co-design.co.uk/jhealey.htm

Index

Index compiled by Annette Musker